INDIVIDUAL BANKRUPTCY AND RESTRUCTURING

Second Edition

by
Margaret C. Jasper

Oceana's Legal Almanac Series:
Law for the Layperson

Oceana Publications

Information contained in this work has been obtained by Oceana Publications from sources believed to be reliable. However, neither the Publisher nor its authors guarantee the accuracy or completeness of any information published herein, and neither the Publisher nor its authors shall be responsible for any errors, omissions or damages arising from the use of this information. This work is published with the understanding that the Publisher and its authors are supplying information, but are not attempting to render legal or other professional services. If such services are required, the assistance of an appropriate professional should be sought.

Library of Congress Control Number: 2006922575

ISBN 0-19-532156-1
ISBN 978-0-19-532156-2

Oceana's Legal Almanac Series: Law for the Layperson
ISSN 1075-7376

©2006 Oxford University Press, Inc.

Manufactured in the United States of America on acid-free paper.

To My Husband Chris

Your love and support
are my motivation and inspiration

-and-

In memory of my son, Jimmy

Table of Contents

CHAPTER 3:
INITIATING THE BANKRUPTCY CASE

CHAPTER 4:
THE AUTOMATIC STAY

CHAPTER 5:
THE BANKRUPTCY DISCHARGE

CHAPTER 6:
THE CHAPTER 7 BANKRUPTCY CASE: LIQUIDATION

CHAPTER 7:
THE CHAPTER 13 BANKRUPTCY CASE: INDIVIDUAL DEBT ADJUSTMENT

CHAPTER 8:
THE CHAPTER 11 BANKRUPTCY CASE: REORGANIZATION

CHAPTER 9:
THE CHAPTER 12 BANKRUPTCY CASE: ADJUSTMENT OF
DEBTS OF A FAMILY FARMER OR FISHERMAN

CHAPTER 10:
THE SERVICEMEMBER'S CIVIL RELIEF ACT (SCRA)

APPENDICES

ABOUT THE AUTHOR

MARGARET C. JASPER is an attorney engaged in the general practice of law in South Salem, New York, concentrating in the areas of personal injury and entertainment law. Ms. Jasper holds a Juris Doctor degree from Pace University School of Law, White Plains, New York, is a member of the New York and Connecticut bars, and is certified to practice before the United States District Courts for the Southern and Eastern Districts of New York, the United States Court of Appeals for the Second Circuit, and the United States Supreme Court.

Ms. Jasper has been appointed to the law guardian panel for the Family Court of the State of New York, is a member of a number of professional organizations and associations, and is a New York State licensed real estate broker operating as Jasper Real Estate, in South Salem, New York.

In 2004, Ms. Jasper successfully argued a case before the New York Court of Appeals which gives mothers of babies who are stillborn due to medical negligence the right to bring a legal action and recover emotional distress damages. This successful appeal overturned a 26-year old New York case precedent, which prevented mothers of stillborn babies suing their negligent medical providers.

Margaret Jasper maintains a website at http://www.JasperLawOffice. com.

Ms. Jasper is the author and general editor of the following legal almanacs:

AIDS Law
The Americans with Disabilities Act
Animal Rights Law
The Law of Attachment and Garnishment
Auto Leasing
Bankruptcy Law for the Individual Debtor

Individual Bankruptcy and Restructuring
Banks and their Customers
Becoming a Citizen
Buying and Selling Your Home
The Law of Buying and Selling
The Law of Capital Punishment
The Law of Child Custody
Your Rights in a Class Action Suit
Commercial Law
Consumer Rights Law
The Law of Contracts
Co-ops and Condominiums: Your Rights and Obligations As Owner
Copyright Law
Credit Cards and the Law
The Law of Debt Collection
Dictionary of Selected Legal Terms
The Law of Dispute Resolution
Drunk Driving Law
DWI, DUI and the Law
Education Law
Elder Law
Employee Rights in the Workplace
Employment Discrimination Under Title VII
Environmental Law
Estate Planning
Everyday Legal Forms
Executors and Personal Representatives: Rights and Responsibilities
Harassment in the Workplace
Health Care and Your Rights
Hiring Household Help and Contractors: Your Rights and Obligations
Under the Law
Home Mortgage Law Primer
Hospital Liability Law
How To Change Your Name
How To Protect Your Challenged Child
Identity Theft and How To Protect Yourself
Injured on the Job: Employee rights, Worker's Compensation and
Disability
Insurance Law
The Law of Immigration
International Adoption
Juvenile Justice and Children's Law
Labor Law

Landlord-Tenant Law
Lemon Laws
The Law of Libel and Slander
Living Together: Practical Legal Issues
Marriage and Divorce
The Law of Medical Malpractice
Motor Vehicle Law
The Law of No-Fault Insurance
Nursing Home Negligence
The Law of Obscenity and Pornography
Patent Law
The Law of Personal Injury
The Law of Premises Liability
Prescription Drugs
Privacy and the Internet: Your Rights and Expectations Under the Law
Probate Law
The Law of Product Liability
Real Estate Law for the Homeowner and Broker
Religion and the Law
Retirement Planning
The Right to Die
Rights of Single Parents
Law for the Small Business Owner
Small Claims Court
Social Security Law
Special Education Law
The Law of Speech and the First Amendment
Teenagers and Substance Abuse
Trademark Law
Victim's Rights Law
The Law of Violence Against Women
Welfare: Your Rights and the Law
Your Rights Under the Family and Medical Leave Act
You've Been Fired: Your Rights and Remedies
What if it Happened to You: Violent Crimes and Victims' Rights
What if the Product Doesn't Work: Warranties & Guarantees
Workers' Compensation Law
and Your Child's Legal Rights: An Overview.

INTRODUCTION

"[Bankruptcy] gives to the honest but unfortunate debtor . . . a new opportunity in life and a clear field for future effort, unhampered by the pressure and discouragement of pre-existing debt." Local Loan v. Hunt, 292 U.S. 234, 244 (1934).

This legal almanac discusses the law of bankruptcy as it relates to the individual. In 2005, individual debtors filed 2,039,214 non-business bankruptcy petitions compared to 874,642 filings ten years earlier in 1995. This figure represents 98.11% of all bankruptcy filings, business and non-business. These statistics demonstrate the growing financial problems facing many Americans today.

Bankruptcy is a legal method under federal law by which an individual may resolve or restructure their financial affairs when they are faced with debt problems. This almanac presents an overview of bankruptcy law and the bankruptcy court system, with a focus on the remedies available to the individual faced with personal indebtedness. The procedural steps the individual debtor must take in order to obtain debt relief and restructure his or her finances are also explored.

This almanac also explains the various documents which must be filed, the automatic stay protection, the exemptions available to the debtor, the difference between dischargeable and non-dischargeable debts, the bankruptcy chapters under which an individual debtor generally files his or her case, and the role of the trustee during the process.

The Appendix provides resource directories, sample forms, applicable statutes, and other pertinent information and data. The Glossary contains definitions of many of the terms used throughout the almanac.

CHAPTER 1:
OVERVIEW OF BANKRUPTCY LAW

THE ORIGINS OF BANKRUPTCY LAW

The origin of the word "bankruptcy" can be traced back to Italy during the Medieval Period. When a businessman was unable to pay his debts, the practice at that time was to destroy his trading bench. From the term "broken bench" or "banca rotta" comes the word "bankruptcy." In that period, tradesmen unable to repay their debts were dealt with harshly. Protecting the interests of the creditors was of paramount concern. The primary focus in that period was on recovering the interests of the creditors.

In England, the first official laws concerning bankruptcy were passed in 1542, under Henry VIII. A bankrupt individual was considered a criminal and was subject to criminal punishment. Penalties were severe and ranged from imprisonment to the death penalty.

In the United States, prior to the enactment of the bankruptcy laws, individuals risked being sent to a debtors' prison if they were unable to pay their debts. The focus was still on protecting the creditor and failure to pay a debt was looked upon as a very serious offense. This mindset began to change in the late 1800s when laws were enacted to assist persons who found themselves in financial trouble.

THE EMERGENCE OF BANKRUPTCY LEGISLATION

Article I, Section 8, of the United States Constitution authorizes Congress to enact "uniform Laws on the subject of Bankruptcies," however, the early federal bankruptcy laws were temporary responses to bad economic conditions. The first official bankruptcy law was enacted in 1800 in response to land speculation and was repealed in 1803.

In 1841, in response to the panic of 1837, the second bankruptcy law was passed but was soon repealed in 1843. In response to the financial crises caused by the Civil War, Congress passed another bankruptcy law in 1867, which was subsequently repealed in 1878.

The economic upheaval of the Great Depression led to the enactment of the Bankruptcy Act of 1933 and the Bankruptcy Act of 1934. This legislation culminated with the Chandler Act of 1938, which included substantial provisions for reorganization of businesses.

GOVERNING LAW

In 1978, Congress enacted the "Bankruptcy Code," which is the uniform federal law that governs all bankruptcy cases. The Bankruptcy Code is codified as Title 11 of the United States Code. The Bankruptcy Code made it easier for both businesses and individuals to file for bankruptcy protection and reorganize their debts.

The primary goal of the federal bankruptcy laws is to give debtors a fresh start by releasing the debtors from personal liability for certain debts. This release is known as a bankruptcy discharge. The discharge prohibits creditors from taking any further action against the debtor to collect on those debts.

The procedural aspects of the bankruptcy process are governed by the Federal Rules of Bankruptcy Procedure (the "Bankruptcy Rules") and local rules of each bankruptcy court. The Bankruptcy Rules contain a set of official forms for use in bankruptcy cases.

The Bankruptcy Code, Bankruptcy Rules, and local rules set forth the formal legal procedures for dealing with the debt problems of individuals and businesses. A record number of business and individual bankruptcies were filed in the 1980s and early 1990s.

Before filing for bankruptcy, one must research the law and procedure in his or her own jurisdiction. Bankruptcy law was federally enacted, and was intended to be uniform across the country. However, when conflicts arise in a particular case, a decision is made by the bankruptcy court in which the case is pending.

Unless an appeal is taken to the federal level, or the legislature intervenes to establish a uniform ruling, the various local decisions would be the law in that jurisdiction until statutorily changed or overruled at the appellate level.

Therefore, the reader is advised to check the law and practice of their own jurisdiction before filing a bankruptcy petition. Further, if the debtor's financial situation is particularly complex, it is advisable to consult a lawyer before proceeding.

The Bankruptcy Code has been amended several times since its enactment.

The Bankruptcy Reform Act of 1994

On October 22, 1994, the Bankruptcy Reform Act of 1994 was signed into law. The 1994 Act contained many provisions for both business and consumer bankruptcy, including:

(i) Provisions to expedite bankruptcy proceedings;

(ii) Provisions to encourage individual debtors to use Chapter 13 to reschedule their debts rather than use Chapter 7 to liquidate;

(iii) provisions to aid creditors in recovering claims against bankrupt estates; and

(iv) the creation of a National Bankruptcy Commission.

The Bankruptcy Abuse Prevention and Consumer Protection Act of 2005

The Bankruptcy Abuse Prevention and Consumer Protection Act of 2005 became effective on October 17, 2005. The Act contains the most comprehensive changes in bankruptcy law in over two decades. This almanac sets forth bankruptcy law and procedures under the amended Bankruptcy Act. Some of the major changes include:

(i) A provision under which the bankruptcy attorney must make a reasonable inquiry to verify that the information contained in the debtor's petition and schedules is well-grounded in fact. The attorney's signature on the petition serves as certification that the information contained in the schedules is correct;

(ii) A "means test" for Chapter 7 eligibility, under which a creditor or the trustee can bring a motion to dismiss the debtor's case if it is determined that the debtor's income is greater than the state median income. If the debtor's current monthly income exceeds a certain standard, abuse is presumed and the debtor may be placed in a 5-year repayment plan under Chapter 13.

(iii) A 5-year plan duration for a Chapter 13 debtor whose income exceeds the state median income.

(iv) A mandatory credit counseling provision under which a prospective debtor must undergo credit counseling from an approved, nonprofit credit counseling agency within the 180 day-period prior to filing. The credit counseling must be provided by a nonprofit budget and credit counseling agency approved by the U.S. trustee or bankruptcy administrator. There is an exception to this requirement in case of emergency. In addition, after filing a bankruptcy case, an individual debtor generally must complete a financial management instructional course before he or she can receive a discharge.

(v) A limitation on the automatic stay provision and, under certain circumstances involving bad faith or abusive filing, the unavailability of the automatic stay.

(vi) A provision denying a discharge to a Chapter 7 debtor if a prior discharge was received within 8 years of the new bankruptcy filing. Previously, the time between discharges was 6 years.

(vii) A provision requiring bankruptcy attorneys to make certain disclosures to prospective debtor clients, e.g., that the debtor does not need an attorney to file for bankruptcy protection. The attorney must also enter into a written contract with the debtor, and disclose all of the costs.

The Bankruptcy Chapters

The Bankruptcy Code is part of the collection of federal statutes known as the United States Code. The United States Code is broken down into sections known as "Titles." The Bankruptcy Code is Title 11 of the United States Code.

As set forth below, Title 11 is further broken down into sections known as "Chapters." The debtor generally chooses which "chapter" of the Bankruptcy Code provides the desired relief, and determines whether he or she is eligible to file under that chapter considering his or her financial circumstances.

There are four chapters of the Bankruptcy Code available to individual consumer debtors: Chapters 7, 13, 11 and 12. This almanac discusses all four chapters as they relate to the individual debtor, however, it should be noted that most individual debtors file for bankruptcy protection under chapter 7 or chapter 13 of the Bankruptcy Code.

Chapter 7: Liquidation

In 2005, individual debtors filed 1,631,011 non-business chapter 7 bankruptcy petitions. Chapter 7 is designed for debtors in financial difficulty who do not have the ability to pay their existing debts. Debtors whose debts are primarily consumer debts are subject to a "means test" designed to determine whether the case should be permitted to proceed under chapter 7. If the debtor's income is greater than the median income for the debtor's state of residence and family size, in some cases, creditors have the right to file a motion requesting that the court dismiss the case, however, it is up to the court to decide whether the case should be dismissed.

Under chapter 7, the debtor may claim certain property as exempt under governing federal and/or state law. The U.S. trustee appoints an impartial case trustee to administer the case and liquidate the debtor's nonexempt assets. The case trustee basically takes over the assets of the debtor's estate, converts those assets to cash, and distributes the proceeds to the creditors.

The purpose of filing a chapter 7 case is to obtain a discharge—i.e., a release from personal liability—of the debtor's existing debts. Certain debts are not dischargeable under the law. For example, despite receiving a general discharge, the debtor may still be responsible for most taxes and student loans; debts incurred to pay nondischargeable taxes; domestic support and property settlement obligations; most fines, penalties, forfeitures, and criminal restitution obligations; certain debts which are not properly listed in the debtor's bankruptcy papers; and debts for death or personal injury caused by operating a motor vehicle, vessel, or aircraft while intoxicated from alcohol or drugs.

Also, if a creditor can prove that a debt arose from fraud, breach of fiduciary duty, or theft, or from a willful and malicious injury, the bankruptcy court may determine that the debt is not discharged. Further, if the debtor is found to have committed certain kinds of improper conduct described in the Bankruptcy Code, the court may deny the discharge. Chapter 7 bankruptcy relief is discussed more fully in Chapter 4 of this almanac.

Chapter 13: Adjustment of Debts of an Individual With Regular Income

In 2005, individual debtors filed 407,322 non-business chapter 13 bankruptcy petitions. Chapter 13 is designed for individuals with regular income who would like to pay all or part of their debts in installments over a period of time. A debtor is not eligible for chapter 13 if his debts exceed a certain dollar amount as set forth in the Bankruptcy Code.

Under Chapter 13, an individual debtor who has a regular source of income pays his or her creditors using future earnings pursuant to a court-approved repayment plan for a certain duration, e.g., 3 to 5 years. This enables the debtor to maintain possession of certain valuable assets, such as a house or car. The amounts set forth in the plan are usually paid to the trustee, who distributes the funds for a small fee.

After completing the payments under the repayment plan, the debtor generally receives a discharge of most remaining debts. Certain debts, however, are not dischargeable, including support obligations; most student loans; certain taxes; most criminal fines and restitution obligations; certain debts which are not properly listed in your bankruptcy papers; certain debts for acts that caused death or personal injury; and certain long term secured obligations. Chapter 13 bankruptcy relief is discussed more fully in Chapter 5 of this almanac.

Chapter 11: Reorganization

Chapter 11 involves debt reorganization. Chapter 11 is designed for the reorganization of a business but is also available to consumer debtors. Its provisions are quite complicated, therefore, an individual who decides to file a chapter 11 petition is advised to consult an attorney.

Under Chapter 11, the debtor generally has the exclusive right to file a plan of reorganization for the first 120 days after the case is filed along with a disclosure statement containing information adequate to enable creditors to evaluate the plan. Chapter 11 usually involves businesses, but may also apply to certain individuals who do not qualify for Chapter 13 because their unsecured and/or secured debt exceeds the limit provided in the Bankruptcy Code. Chapter 11 bankruptcy relief is discussed more fully in Chapter 6 of this almanac.

Chapter 12: Adjustment of Debts of a Family Farmer or Fisherman with Regular Annual Income

Chapter 12 is designed to permit family farmers and fishermen to repay their debts over a period of time from future earnings. Chapter 12 is similar to chapter 13. The eligibility requirements are restrictive, limiting its use to those whose income arises primarily from a family-owned farm or commercial fishing operation.

Under Chapter 12, family farmers and fishermen with regular income propose a repayment plan over a period of time, e.g., 3 to 5 years. Chapter 12 allows a family farmer or fisherman to continue to operate their business while the plan is being carried out. Chapter 12 bankruptcy relief is discussed more fully in Chapter 7 of this almanac.

THE SERVICEMEMBERS' CIVIL RELIEF ACT (SCRA)

The Servicemembers' Civil Relief Act provides protection to members of the military against the entry of default judgments and gives the court the ability to stay proceedings against military debtors. The Servicemembers' Civil Relief Act is discussed more fully in Chapter 8 of this almanac.

THE BANKRUPTCY SYSTEM

Bankruptcy Courts

Federal courts have exclusive jurisdiction over bankruptcy cases. Although bankruptcy cases cannot be filed in state court, state laws may afford certain additional protections to debtors.

There is a bankruptcy court for each judicial district in the country, and each state has one or more districts. There are 90 bankruptcy districts across the country.

A directory of United States Bankruptcy Courts is set forth at Appendix 1.

Office of the Bankruptcy Clerk

Each bankruptcy court generally has their own bankruptcy clerk's office. The bankruptcy clerk's office provides a variety of services to the bankruptcy judges, attorneys and the public, and the staff provides clerical and administrative support to the court by filing and maintaining case-related papers, signing ministerial orders, collecting authorized fees, sending notices, entering judgments and orders, and setting hearings. The bankruptcy clerk's office also supplies the forms and local rules an individual needs to file their bankruptcy petition and related documents.

When corresponding with the bankruptcy clerk's office by mail, individuals are advised to include the case number, case name, details of the information requested, their name, address, telephone number, and a self-addressed, stamped envelope. When requesting a physical search of the court records, the individual should inquire whether there is a search fee and, if so, include it with the written inquiry.

All documents in the court's case files are public record and available to the public for inspection. Files may be reviewed at the bankruptcy clerk's office during business hours.

Each bankruptcy court also maintains a website which is accessible over the internet and provides information on bankruptcy cases for a small fee to registered users.

Bankruptcy Judges

The United States bankruptcy judge is the district court official with decision-making power over federal bankruptcy cases. A bankruptcy judge is appointed by the majority of judges of the U.S. Court of Appeals to exercise jurisdiction over bankruptcy matters. The number of bankruptcy judges is determined by Congress. Bankruptcy judges are appointed for 14-year terms.

Once a bankruptcy case is filed, it is assigned to a particular bankruptcy court judge, and usually remains with the same judge until its conclusion. The bankruptcy judge may decide any matter connected with the bankruptcy case, such as a debtor's eligibility to file or whether the debtor should receive a discharge of debts. Nevertheless, a debtor's involvement with the bankruptcy judge is usually very limited insofar as bankruptcy procedures are largely administrative, and generally carried out by a trustee who is appointed to handle the case.

The Role of the U.S. Trustee

The United States Trustee's Office is part of the U.S. Department of Justice, and is a separate agency from the U.S. Bankruptcy Court. The United States Trustee's Office is a watchdog agency, charged with monitoring all bankruptcies, appointing and supervising all trustees, and identifying fraud in bankruptcy cases. In monitoring cases, the United States Trustee reviews all bankruptcy petitions and pleadings filed in cases, and participates in many proceedings affecting the case.

A debtor may not obtain legal advice from the U.S. Trustee's Office, but may obtain information about the status of a case. The debtor can also contact the U.S. Trustee's Office if they are having a problem with a particular bankruptcy trustee.

The U.S. Trustee does not administer the bankruptcy cases, although they can bring motions in the bankruptcy court, such as motions to dismiss the case, or to deny the debtor's discharge. The U.S. Trustee is responsible for appointing and supervising the bankruptcy trustees who oversee pending bankruptcy cases. In all chapter 7, 12, 13 and in some chapter 11 cases, a bankruptcy case trustee is assigned by the United States Trustee.

Bankruptcy Case Trustees

Bankruptcy case trustees are not necessarily lawyers, and are not paid by the Bankruptcy Court or by the U.S. Trustee. Although the trustees report to the court and to the U.S. Trustee, their fees come out of the debtor's bankruptcy filing fees or as a percentage of the money distributed to creditors in the bankruptcy.

The Chapter 7 Bankruptcy Trustee

The U.S. Trustee appoints and supervises the chapter 7 bankruptcy case trustees who administer the chapter 7 bankruptcy estates. The chapter 7 case trustee is also known as a "panel trustee." The U.S. Trustee appoints each chapter 7 cases trustee to a panel for up to one year, renewable at the U.S. Trustee's discretion. These trustees are then assigned to chapter 7 cases on a blind rotation basis. The U.S. Trustee supervises the case trustees' administration of individual debtor estates; monitors the case trustees' financial record-keeping; and imposes other requirements to ensure that the chapter 7 trustees carry out their fiduciary duties.

The Chapter 13 Bankruptcy Trustee

The U.S. Trustee supervises and appoints the chapter 13 bankruptcy case trustees who administer the chapter 13 bankruptcy cases. The chapter 13 case trustee is known as a "standing trustee." The chapter 13 "standing trustees" are appointed by the U.S. Trustee to administer all cases filed in a particular geographic area. As with chapter 7 panel trustees, the U.S. Trustee supervises the chapter 13 standing trustees' administration of individual bankruptcy estates; monitors the trustees' financial record-keeping; and imposes other requirements to ensure that the chapter 13 trustees carry out their fiduciary duties.

CHAPTER 2:
ASSESSING YOUR FINANCIAL SITUATION AND EXPLORING BANKRUPTCY ALTERNATIVES

IN GENERAL

The primary purposes of the law of bankruptcy are: (1) to give an honest debtor a "fresh start" in life by relieving the debtor of most debts, and (2) to repay creditors in an orderly manner to the extent that the debtor has property available for payment. Individuals have a choice in deciding which chapter of the Bankruptcy Code best suits their needs. The serious decision of whether to file for bankruptcy, and under which chapter, depends on the financial circumstances of the particular individual.

EXPLORING THE ALTERNATIVES

It is recommended that the individual considering bankruptcy obtain competent legal advice before proceeding. All available alternatives should be explored to make certain that there are no less drastic solutions that would solve the individual's financial problems.

This is particularly so when the debtor's liabilities are primarily consumer debt, such as credit card obligations, and the individual is basically "judgment proof"—i.e., he or she has little or no income or assets from which recovery can be made—and no major changes to this scenario are anticipated.

In such a case, the individual can simply "walk away" because the creditor can't attach any property. An individual can also try to deal with the creditors directly and work out a new payment plan. As further discussed below, creditors will usually try to work out a payment arrangement rather than pursue any legal methods of recovering a debt. Often, the cooperative approach is more likely to result in payments being made.

Nevertheless, even if an individual is being harassed by collection agencies, it is still not necessary to immediately file for bankruptcy protection. The consumer is entitled to certain protection under state and federal law to stop debt collection harassment. For example, debt collectors are legally prohibited from using deceitful or threatening tactics. Further, they are legally prohibited from contacting an individual once they are given written notice that all contact should cease.

Other than telephoning and writing the debtor to request payment, a creditor has no legal right to collect on a debt unless the creditor sues the debtor and obtains a judgment. Thus, if debt collection efforts fail, a creditor has to make a decision whether it is financially wise to start a lawsuit to recover the debt.

It would be virtually impossible for creditors to sue all of the consumers who fail to pay their debts. The legal fees, costs and the time it takes to obtain a judgment would likely far outweigh any recovery the creditor could expect. Often the creditor will take the uncollected debt and write it off as a cost of doing business—known as a "charge-off"—after a period of time.

Of course, this causes considerable damage to the debtor's credit rating for approximately seven years, but collection action usually ends, and a lawsuit is not likely initiated to recover the debt. Once the applicable statute of limitations has expired, the creditor is legally prevented from filing a lawsuit against the debtor.

In considering whether to charge off the debt, or to take legal action, the creditor generally weighs a number of factors, including whether the debtor is judgment proof. If the creditor does decide to sue, and obtains a judgment against the debtor, the creditor must then attempt to collect the judgment amount from the debtor's property and/or income.

There are exemption laws, however, which protect much of the debtor's property from collection. Also, any property which is not protected must be significant for the creditor to pursue collection, because of the attendant costs of seizing and selling the property, e.g. sheriff's poundage charges.

If the creditor places a lien on the debtor's home, unless the lien is in a considerable amount, it is not likely that the creditor will foreclose on the debtor's home to collect the debt. The costs of foreclosure are substantial, and the creditor generally stands in line behind the mortgage holder, taxing authorities and any previously filed liens before getting paid, if at all. It is more likely that the creditor will wait until the debtor chooses to sell or refinance his or her home, at which time the debt must be paid at or before closing to transfer clear title to the property.

Creditors are more apt to go after a debtor's wages or other income to collect on a judgment. However, public benefits, such as unemployment, public assistance, disability, or social security benefits are generally protected. Also, if there is income—such as wages or pension and retirement benefits—eligible to satisfy a judgment, there are laws that limit the amount that can be taken at any given time.

Finally, an individual can contact one of the many debt consolidation and credit counseling services that specialize in helping consumers with credit problems to discuss other less drastic ways to resolve their debts.

Thus, consumer debt need not be the catalyst to an immediate bankruptcy filing. If the debtor doesn't have a significant source of steady income, or property which is secured by the debt—e.g. a mortgage or automobile loan—bankruptcy may not be necessary.

ADVANTAGES AND DISADVANTAGES OF FILING BANKRUPTCY

Bankruptcy is a serious step which may have certain relatively long-term consequences. One must carefully assess his or her financial situation and determine whether bankruptcy is the right course to take given all of the advantages and disadvantages.

Filing bankruptcy gives the debtor some time to rethink his or her financial situation without worrying about a foreclosure sale of his or her home due to mortgage arrears or tax debts. The automatic stay, which is further discussed in this almanac, prevents all creditors from taking any legal action against the debtor once the bankruptcy petition has been filed.

In addition, bankruptcy provides a new start to individuals who are saddled with consumer debt that they are unable to repay. Credit card debt is particularly difficult to resolve. It is not uncommon for the balance on a credit card account to actually increase despite years of payment and nonuse. This is because the monthly finance charge cancels out a significant portion of the monthly payment, and added late charges may increase the amount owed.

Bankruptcy provides the debtor a legal method to wipe out a significant amount—if not all—of his or her debts. The debtor is given the opportunity to manage his or her financial affairs without this burden. Generally, there is no minimum amount of debt necessary to file for bankruptcy.

The most apparent disadvantage of filing for bankruptcy protection is the serious damage inflicted on the debtor's credit rating. A bankruptcy filing can remain on an individual's credit report for 10 years under the provisions of the Fair Credit Reporting Act. Under the law, a credit reporting agency may not report a bankruptcy case on a person's credit report after ten years from the date the bankruptcy case is filed.

If a chapter 13 bankruptcy is successfully completed, the credit reporting agency generally retains the information for only seven years rather than the ten years allowed by law. This is a policy decision made in order to encourage individuals to opt for debt repayment under chapter 13 rather than liquidation under chapter 7.

This negative credit information generally impedes any efforts to obtain credit, e.g. for a home or automobile purchase, for a considerable period of time. However, an individual who is in debt to the degree that he or she is considering filing bankruptcy has more than likely already sustained considerable damage to his or her credit.

Nevertheless, the decision whether to grant an individual credit in the future is strictly up to the creditor and varies from creditor to creditor depending on the type of credit requested. There is no law that prevents anyone from extending credit to a debtor immediately after the filing of a bankruptcy nor will a creditor be required to extend credit.

Another disadvantage to filing bankruptcy is that the bankruptcy petition, schedules and other filings are a matter of public record. The debtor must disclose all of his or her personal financial information for at least the previous two years, and all of this information is available for public scrutiny. In chapter 13 cases, the debtor's employer may also be involved because this chapter may require deductions from the debtor's paycheck as part of the plan to repay debt.

In addition, co-signers do not benefit from the discharge obtained by a chapter 7 debtor. Therefore, if a friend or relative co-signed a loan for the debtor, they will be left wholly responsible for repayment of the debt unless they also file bankruptcy. However, in chapter 13, the co-signer cannot be pursued for the debt if the debtor agrees to pay the debt in full, remains in chapter 13, and continues to make payments to the creditor.

CHAPTER 3:
INITIATING THE BANKRUPTCY CASE

OBTAINING LEGAL REPRESENTATION

If you decide that bankruptcy is the right course of action for you, it is advisable to consult with an attorney. While there is no requirement for a debtor to be represented by an attorney in bankruptcy matters, all debtors are strongly encouraged to seek legal counsel if possible. The bankruptcy process can be very confusing and complex. An attorney can advise as to whether bankruptcy or some alternative is the best solution to financial problems. An attorney will prepare the necessary paperwork and be present during bankruptcy proceedings.

NON-ATTORNEY BANKRUPTCY PETITION PREPARERS

There are businesses who offer to prepare bankruptcy petitions for those seeking to file bankruptcy. One should be aware, however, that the services of bankruptcy petition preparers are limited to the typing of forms. They are not permitted to advise individuals on the law, and their services are subject to various statutory requirements and limitations.

Although bankruptcy petition preparers are required to sign all documents they prepare for filing, they are not authorized to sign any documents on behalf of the debtor. The bankruptcy petition includes declarations that must be signed by the debtor attesting to the accuracy of the information contained in the petition. Therefore, it is important that the information set forth in the bankruptcy petition is accurate.

If false or incorrect information is listed, it can jeopardize the debtor's case. The debtor is advised to carefully read the entire petition before signing the declarations. The debtor should also obtain copies of all documents that are prepared on their behalf by the bankruptcy petition preparer at the time they sign the documents.

Bankruptcy petition preparers are prohibited by law from collecting or receiving any of the required court fees associated with the bankruptcy case. All court fees connected with the bankruptcy case, including the filing fee and other administrative fees, must be paid directly to the court by the debtor.

The failure of any bankruptcy petition preparer to comply with the law should immediately be brought to the attention of the trustee appointed in the debtor's bankruptcy case as well as the local Office of the United States Trustee.

PREREQUISITES TO FILING A BANKRUPTCY PETITION

An individual is prohibited from filing a bankruptcy petition if, during the 180 days before filing: (i) a prior bankruptcy petition was dismissed due to (a) the debtor's willful failure to appear before the court or (b) the debtor's willful failure to comply with orders of the court; or (ii) a prior bankruptcy petition was voluntarily dismissed after creditors sought relief from the bankruptcy court to recover property upon which they hold liens; or (iii) the debtor failed to receive credit counseling from an approved credit counseling agency.

The credit counseling requirement may be waived if there is an emergency situation, or if the U.S. trustee or bankruptcy administrator determines that there are insufficient approved agencies to provide the required credit counseling. An exception is also available in case of emergency.

In addition to the pre-petition credit counseling requirement, a debtor must certify that he or she completed an instructional course in personal financial management in chapters 7 and 13 cases before a discharge is entered.

Debtor's Certification of Completion of Instructional Course Concerning Financial Management (Form B23) is set forth at Appendix 2.

FILING THE BANKRUPTCY PETITION

A bankruptcy case begins when the debtor files a petition with the bankruptcy court serving the area where the individual lives or where the business debtor is organized or has its principal place of business or principal assets. The bankruptcy petition is a document that sets forth extensive information concerning the debtor and his or her financial situation. The bankruptcy petition must set forth the debtor's name, address and social security number. If the debtor has ever obtained credit or incurred any debts under another name, that name must also be included in the petition.

If a married couple is filing a joint bankruptcy petition, information for both spouses must be set forth on the petition. Only people who are married on the date they file may file a joint petition. Unmarried persons, corporations and partnerships must each file a separate case.

A bankruptcy proceeding can either be entered into voluntarily by a debtor or initiated by creditors. If the individual who owes the money—i.e., the debtor—starts the bankruptcy, it is called a voluntary bankruptcy.

A copy of Debtor's Voluntary Petition (Official Form 1) is set forth at Appendix 3.

Creditors can petition the bankruptcy court to have an individual debtor placed into bankruptcy involuntarily under Chapter 7. Involuntary petitions are not accepted under Chapter 13. Involuntary petitions generally require a certain number of creditors to sign the bankruptcy petition depending on the total number of creditors, and the total dollar amount of the claims.

If an individual debtor is faced with an involuntary bankruptcy petition, he or she is advised to consult an attorney. In an involuntary case, the debtor gets a chance to contest the petition and contend it should not be in bankruptcy.

After the petition is filed, the bankruptcy court will send the debtor a notice which contains important information concerning the bankruptcy case. This information may include:

1. The bankruptcy case number;

2. The date the petition was accepted for filing;

3. The name of the bankruptcy judge assigned to the case;

4. The name of the bankruptcy trustee assigned to the case;

5. The date, time and place of the debtor's examination by the trustee;

6. A statement regarding the automatic stay provision;

7. Information concerning when and how creditors must file their claims;

8. The date by which objections to discharge must be filed; and

9. For Chapter 13 debtors, the details of the plan requirements to repay creditors.

After the bankruptcy petition is filed, creditors, for the most part, may not seek to collect their debts outside of the proceeding. In addition, the debtor is not allowed to transfer property that has been declared part of the estate subject to proceedings.

THE BANKRUPTCY SCHEDULES

The bankruptcy court is entitled to complete disclosure of all relevant information concerning the debtor's finances. Therefore, along with the bankruptcy petition, or shortly thereafter, the debtor is required to file their financial information on forms known as "schedules."

The schedules set forth such information as the debtor's debts and assets; income and expenses; property owned; monies owed to the debtor; monies which the debtor may inherit within six months and insurance policies which he or she holds. The debtor must also list all property owned which is considered exempt from bankruptcy proceedings under state or federal law, and any other information concerning the debtor's financial affairs.

In addition to the petition, the debtor must also file the following supporting documents with the court:

The Debtor's Assets (Schedules A and B)

The debtor must set forth all of his or her assets in the bankruptcy petition. There must be full disclosure of each item of property owned by the debtor, or in which the debtor had an interest, as of the date the bankruptcy petition is filed. These assets may include but are not limited to the following:

1. Real property, including homes, coops, condos, time-shares, gravesites and investment property;

2. Bank accounts, safe deposit boxes and cash on hand;

3. Household goods such as furniture, televisions, stereos, and computers;

4. Books, art and collectibles;

5. Jewelry, clothing and other personal possessions;

6. Motor vehicles, including cars, trucks, mobile homes, and motorcycles;

7. Boats and boating equipment;

8. Business assets such as office furniture and machinery; patents and copyrights;

9. Interests in insurance policies, wills, trusts, pensions, profit sharing, annuities, IRAS, Keogh and retirement plans;

10. Interests in legal actions the debtor has against another;

11. Tax refunds.

Schedule A—Debtor's Real Property (Form B6A) is set forth at Appendix 4; and Schedule B—Debtor's Personal Property (Form B6B) is set forth at Appendix 5.

Property Claimed As Exempt (Schedule C)

When anticipating bankruptcy, an individual is always concerned about what property he or she will be able to keep, and what property he or she will have to give up in exchange for the cancellation of debts. Many people mistakenly fear that they will be left with "nothing but the clothes on their back." This is an incorrect assumption.

As set forth below, the law permits the debtor to protect certain property from creditors even if the value of the debtor's assets is greater than his or her debts. These items are known as "exempt property" and they are not included in the debtor's assets available for distribution to creditors. An individual debtor is required to file a schedule of "exempt property" in order to protect that property from creditors.

Typically, exempt property includes but is not limited to vehicles up to a certain dollar amount, the equity in the debtor's home up to a certain amount, certain personal property and jewelry up to a certain amount, and tools of the debtor's trade. If no one objects to the exemptions listed on the debtor's schedule within the time frame specified by the bankruptcy court, these assets will not be a part of the debtor's bankruptcy estate and will not be used to pay creditors.

If the debtor does not claim an exemption to which he or she may be entitled, the property may be lost. Any property that is not protected by an exemption may be sold by the bankruptcy trustee, and the proceeds used to satisfy creditor claims. Deciding which assets are exempt and how and if one can protect these assets from their creditors is a crucial part of the bankruptcy case.

Schedule C—Property Claimed as Exempt (Form B6C) is set forth at Appendix 6.

There are exemptions available under both federal and state laws. Section 522(d) of the Bankruptcy Code specifies the items of personal and real property that a creditor cannot take to satisfy a claim. These items are known as the federal bankruptcy exemptions.

A table of federal exemptions under §522(d) of the Bankruptcy Code is set forth at Appendix 7.

The law permits each state to adopt its own exemption law in place of the federal exemptions. In some states, the debtor may choose between the federal exemptions and the exemptions allowed under the laws of his or her home state. However, the debtor cannot pick and choose exemptions from amongst the two categories.

Property generally deemed exempt under most state statutes includes but is not limited to the following:

1. A homestead exemption that exempts part of the equity the debtor has in his or her home;

2. Motor vehicles up to a certain amount;

3. Clothing and household goods and furnishings that are reasonably necessary;

4. Household appliances;

5. Jewelry up to a certain amount, and personal effects;

6. Life insurance up to a certain amount;

7. A portion of the debtor's earned but yet unpaid wages;

8. Pensions;

9. Tools of the debtor's trade or profession up to a certain amount; and

10. Public benefits such as unemployment, public assistance, disability and social security benefits.

A table of state exemptions is set forth at Appendix 8.

Objections to Exemptions

The bankruptcy case trustee and creditors are entitled to file objections to the debtor's list of exempt property. Objections must be filed within thirty days after the meeting of creditors unless the court grants an extension of time. The court will determine whether the objections have any merit.

A lawyer should be consulted if the debtor has any questions concerning available exemptions.

Debts (Schedules D, E and F)

The debtor must submit a schedule of all creditors and the nature and amount of their claims on the applicable bankruptcy schedule whether or not the underlying debt is dischargeable. This includes debts that are secured, unsecured, priority, and administrative even if the debt is disputed or the amount is uncertain. The debtor should also include any past, present or future debts as potential claims.

Secured Claims

A secured debt is a debt that is backed by property, known as collateral. A creditor whose debt is "secured" has a right to take the property to satisfy a "secured debt." For example, most people who buy new cars give the lender a "security interest" in the car. This means that the debt is a "secured debt" and that the lender can take the car if the borrower fails to make payments on the car loan. A secured claim must be paid in full if the debtor wishes to keep the secured asset.

The debtor has the option of surrendering the collateral and giving the creditor an unsecured claim for any deficiency remaining for the difference between the amount of the claim and the value of the surrendered collateral.

Under a Chapter 13 plan, a secured creditor retains their lien on the secured property, and must receive payments under the plan that equal the present value of the asset securing the claim. The secured creditor is also entitled to be compensated for depreciation. The debtor may also be able to modify the terms and interest rate of secured claims with the exception of a secured claim for the debtor's principal residence.

The most common type of secured debt is a homeowner's mortgage. If the homeowner does not pay the mortgage payments, the lender generally has the contractual right to foreclose on the property. If a Chapter 13 debtor wants to keep his or her home, the original loan must be reinstated by paying the mortgage arrears, and maintaining the payments under the original loan terms during the life of the plan and thereafter.

Schedule D—Creditors Holding Secured Claims (Form B6D) is set forth at Appendix 9.

Unsecured Claims

A debt is unsecured if the debtor simply promised to pay someone a sum of money at a particular time, and did not pledge any real or personal property as collateral for that debt. Unsecured claims represent the majority of debts listed by an individual debtor.

The most common types of unsecured claims include: (i) credit card debt; (ii) medical and hospital bills; (iii) utility bills; (iv) rent; (v) non-priority taxes; (vi) student loans; (vii) deficiency claims; and (viii) personal loans.

Under the Bankruptcy Code, unsecured claims may be classified differently according to how similar they are to each other. However, this doesn't mean that one class can be given any preferential treatment over another class in terms of payment. For example, you can't pay seventy-five percent of a credit card company's unsecured claim, but pay only fifty percent of a hospital's unsecured claim. All unsecured creditors must receive the same percentage of payment.

Further, each unsecured creditor must receive no less than what it would receive if the debtor filed under Chapter 7 and liquidated some or all of the property of the estate.

Priority Claims

A priority debt is a debt entitled to priority in payment, ahead of most other debts, in a bankruptcy case. In Chapter 7, priority claims are usually first in line to be paid if the debtor has any funds available for distribution to creditors. Full payment of such debts must be contemplated for the Chapter 13 debtor to obtain confirmation of the debtor's Chapter 13 plan.

Priority claims are generally paid in deferred cash payments at various intervals under the plan. Although the Bankruptcy Code does not require that priority claims be paid first, it is advisable to get these claims out of the way before making payments on unsecured debts. Priority debts may include certain taxes, wage claims of employees, and alimony, maintenance or support of a spouse, former spouse, or child.

Priority Tax Claims

Income taxes represent the most common type of priority debt for an individual. Taxes that are due for fewer than three years are priority debts that are not dischargeable. Further, if the taxing authority has made a new assessment within eight months of the filing, the tax debt must be listed as a priority and must be paid in full.

Priority tax claims are not allowed post-petition interest, however, interest that accrued prior to the bankruptcy filing must be paid as part of the claim. Pre-petition penalties also become part of the priority tax claim provided they are not punitive in nature. A punitive penalty becomes an unsecured claim in bankruptcy that does not have to be paid in full.

Administrative Claims

An administrative debt is also considered a priority debt, An administrative debt is one created when someone provides goods or services to the debtor's bankruptcy estate, such as the fees generated by attorneys, trustees, and other authorized professionals in representing the bankruptcy estate.

Schedule E—Creditors Holding Unsecured Priority Claims (Form B6E) is set forth at Appendix 10; and Schedule F—Creditors Holding Unsecured Nonpriority Claims (Form B6F) is set forth at Appendix 11.

Executory Contracts and Unexpired Leases (Schedule G)

Executory contracts are agreements which have not been fully completed at the time the debtor files his or her bankruptcy petition. Executory contracts may include residential leases; automobile leases; equipment leases; employment agreements; home improvement contracts; and contracts for the future delivery of goods or services.

Schedule G—Executory Contracts and Unexpired Leases (Form B6G) is set forth at Appendix 12.

Codebtors (Schedule H)

The debtor must provide information concerning any person or entity, other than a spouse in a joint case, that is also liable on any debts listed by the debtor in the schedules of creditors, including all guarantors and co-signers.

In community property states, a married debtor not filing a joint case should report the name and address of the nondebtor spouse on this schedule, and include all names used by the nondebtor spouse during the six years immediately preceding the commencement of this case.

Bankruptcy chapters 12 and 13 contain a special automatic stay provision that protects any individual who is liable along with the debtor for a "consumer debt." A "consumer debt" is one that is incurred by an individual primarily for a personal, family, or household purpose.

Schedule H—Debtor's List of Co-Debtors (Form B6H) is set forth at Appendix 13.

Current Income of Individual Debtor (Schedule I)

The debtor must set forth a detailed list of his or her current income, including the source, amount and frequency of the debtor's income. Income includes wages, commissions, business income, investment income, tax refunds, rental income, public benefits, unemployment compensation, etc. In a chapter 13 case, the debtor must also list his or her spouse's income, unless they are separated, regardless of whether the petition was filed individually or jointly.

Schedule I—Current Income of Individual Debtor (Form B6I) is set forth at Appendix 14.

Current Expenditures of Individual Debtor (Schedule J)

The debtor must set forth a detailed list of current expenditures by estimating the average monthly expenses of the debtor and the debtor's family. The expenses should be listed as they will exist after the bankruptcy petition is filed.

Current expenditures may include but are not limited to rent or home mortgage payment, real estate taxes, homeowner's insurance, utilities, home maintenance, food, clothing, laundry and dry cleaning, medical and dental expenses, transportation and/or automobile expenses, recreation and entertainment expenses, charitable contributions, health, auto and life insurance premiums, alimony and/or child support, and taxes.

Schedule J—Current Expenditures of Individual Debtor (Form B6J) is set forth at Appendix 15.

Statement of Affairs

Another important form which makes up the bankruptcy petition is the debtor's Statement of Affairs. The Statement of Affairs includes information about the debtor's financial affairs that may not be apparent in the other schedules. The Statement of Affairs includes information such as:

1. All names the debtor has used or been known by in the previous six years.

2. The debtor's current address and former addresses for the previous six years.

3. The debtor's current place of employment, occupation and income for the previous two years.

4. Names of partnerships or other businesses the debtor has engaged in within the previous six years.

5. Tax refunds due the debtor or which were received by the debtor in the previous two years.

6. Information concerning the debtor's safe deposit boxes, if any.

7. Information concerning the debtor's bank accounts, credit union accounts, brokerage accounts and/or pension funds.

8. Information concerning the debtor's financial books and records, if any.

9. Information concerning property the debtor is holding for another party and/or property being held by another party for the debtor.

10. Information concerning any prior bankruptcy filings by the debtor.

11. Information concerning any lawsuits, garnishments or property seizures pending against the debtor.

12. Information concerning all payments made to creditors within the previous year.

13. Information concerning the transfer of property or gifts from the debtor to relatives within the previous year.

14. Information concerning repossessions, casualty losses or gambling losses within the previous year.

15. Information concerning payment and/or payment agreements with attorneys and/or budget or credit counseling services.

Debtor's Statement of Financial Affairs (Form B7) is set forth at Appendix 16.

In addition to filing the above supporting documents, debtors must also provide the case trustee with a copy of their tax return for the most recent year, and continue to provide copies of tax returns filed while their bankruptcy case is pending.

An individual debtor whose debts are primarily consumer debts must also file the following:

1. A certificate of credit counseling;

2. A copy of the debt repayment plan developed with the credit counseling agency, if any;

3. Evidence of payments from employers received 60 days before filing, if any;

4. A statement of monthly net income and any anticipated increase in income or expenses after filing; and

5. A record of any interest the debtor has in federal or state qualified education or tuition accounts.

If the debtor is married, he or she must provide financial information for their spouse even if the spouse is not filing for bankruptcy relief. This is required so that the court, trustees and creditors can evaluate the financial circumstances of the household.

FILING FEES

When the bankruptcy petition is filed, the debtor is required to pay a filing fee and certain administrative fees. These fees vary depending on the bankruptcy chapter under which the petition is filed. Individual debtors who are unable to pay the filing fees all at once may request the court's permission to pay the fees in four installment payments, and the final payment must be paid no later than 120 days from the date the petition is filed.

Debtor's Application and Order to Pay Filing Fee in Installments (Form B3A) is set forth at Appendix 17.

If the debtor is able to show good cause, the court may extend the debtor's time to pay the installments, but the last installment payment in that case must be made no later than 180 days from the date the petition is filed. If the debtor fails to pay the required fees, their chapter 7 case may be dismissed.

If an individual debtor's income is less than 150% of the poverty level, and the debtor is unable to pay the filing fees even in installments, the court may waive the fee requirement.

Debtor's Application for Waiver of Chapter 7 Filing Fee (Form B3B) is set forth at Appendix 18.

THE BANKRUPTCY ESTATE

The filing of a bankruptcy petition creates what is known as a "bankruptcy estate" and the debtor's financial affairs are placed under the legal control of the trustee of the bankruptcy estate. The bankruptcy estate includes all legal or equitable interests the debtor may have in any item of property as of the date the petition is filed.

In addition, property which is obtained after the petition is filed may be included as property of the bankruptcy estate if it falls into the following categories:

1. inherited property that the debtor has a right to receive within 180 days of the bankruptcy filing;

2. divorce settlement property that the debtor has a right to receive within 180 days of the bankruptcy filing;

3. life insurance proceeds that the debtor has a right to receive within 180 days of the bankruptcy filing;

4. recoveries made by the bankruptcy trustee in avoiding fraudulent transfers and sales;

5. community property owned by a married couple which is under the sole, equal or joint control of the spouse who filed bankruptcy may be included; and

6. certain other types of property interests that the bankruptcy estate obtains after the bankruptcy filing.

The debtor is not legally permitted to sell any of the property which is deemed part of the bankruptcy estate. However, the debtor generally remains in control of his or her exempt property, and property the debtor acquires after the petition was filed.

CHAPTER 4:
THE AUTOMATIC STAY

IN GENERAL

Upon filing their bankruptcy petition, the debtor is afforded certain protections. The most significant of these protections is the automatic stay. The automatic stay prevents the debtor's creditors from taking any further action to collect debts. The purpose of the automatic stay is to take some of the pressure off of the debtor by allowing him or her to work within the bankruptcy system to manage their financial debt, without having to simultaneously deal with creditors.

In order to fully take advantage of the automatic stay, the debtor should immediately notify all of his or her creditors instead of waiting for the court to make the notification. Anyone who violates the automatic stay by continuing to pursue legal action may be held in contempt of court and suffer penalties as a result.

MAJOR PROVISIONS

Section 362 of the Bankruptcy Code details the provisions of the automatic stay. Its major provisions include the following:

Suspension of Legal Action

In general, the automatic stay suspends the following types of action:

1. wage garnishment;

2. foreclosure;

3. eviction or utility service suspension;

4. automobile repossession; and

5. lawsuits which are pending or which could have been filed prior to the bankruptcy filing, which are based upon failure to pay a debt.

Exceptions to the Automatic Stay

There are certain exceptions to the automatic stay that have been put into place by legislation and/or the judiciary. Examples of such exceptions include but are not limited to the following:

1. The commencement or continuation of criminal proceedings against the debtor are not subject to the stay. In criminal proceedings that involve both a crime and a debt, the automatic stay will only serve to suspend that portion of the proceedings that involves payment of the debt. For example, if an individual is convicted of criminal mischief for breaking a window, and is sentenced to fifteen days in jail and restitution for the cost of the window, a bankruptcy filing may stay payment of the restitution amount, but won't affect the incarceration.

2. The commencement or continuation of collection actions for alimony, maintenance or support, from property that is not property of the bankruptcy estate, is not subject to the stay. Further, paternity actions and lawsuits seeking to establish, modify or enforce child support or alimony, are not stayed by a bankruptcy filing.

3. Taxing authorities may be stayed from filing a tax lien or seizing the debtor's property, however, they may continue to conduct audits, demand tax returns, and issue tax assessments and demands for payment of the assessed tax.

4. The commencement or enforcement of any action by a governmental unit under its police powers that generally concerns public health and safety, and environmental and related matters, is not subject to the stay.

5. If a lease or other tenancy for nonresidential real estate was terminated by the landlord prior to the bankruptcy filing, the landlord may continue to enforce its rights to obtain possession despite the stay.

VIOLATING THE AUTOMATIC STAY

If a creditor continues to attempt to collect a debt after the bankruptcy petition is filed in violation of the automatic stay, the debtor should immediately notify the creditor in writing that they have filed for bankruptcy protection. The letter should include the case name, number, and filing date, or a copy of the petition that shows it was filed.

If, despite these efforts, the creditor still continues to try to collect, the debtor may be entitled to take legal action against the creditor to obtain a specific order from the court prohibiting the creditor from taking further collection action. If the creditor is willfully violating the automatic stay, the court can hold the creditor in contempt of court and punish the creditor by fine or incarceration.

Because any such legal action brought against the creditor will likely be complex, obtaining legal representation by a qualified bankruptcy attorney is advised.

OBTAINING RELIEF FROM THE AUTOMATIC STAY

A creditor may want to proceed in their collection efforts against the debtor after a bankruptcy petition has been filed. Unless the action falls under an exception as set forth above, a creditor must make a "Motion for Relief from the Automatic Stay" to the bankruptcy court to lift—i.e., remove—the stay as it pertains to that creditor. The motion generally requires a hearing before the Bankruptcy Judge at which time the creditor must demonstrate to the court that the stay is not serving its intended purpose.

For example, a debtor may file for bankruptcy protection to stop the foreclosure on his or her house. However, if it is determined that the debtor has no equity in the house—i.e., the amount of debt exceeds the fair market value of the house—and no way of repaying the arrears on the mortgage, the court may grant the mortgage holder's motion to lift the automatic stay. This enables the secured creditor to proceed with the foreclosure and sale of the property.

The creditor may also request the debtor to agree to a "Stipulation for Relief from the Automatic Stay," in order to avoid a formal hearing.

THE EFFECT OF PROPERTY ABANDONMENT ON THE AUTOMATIC STAY

If the bankruptcy trustee who is administering the bankruptcy estate believes that there is no equity in certain property of the estate, the trustee may "abandon" the property. That is because the trustee's duty is to sell assets in order to create a fund from which creditors will be repaid. A piece of property in which the debtor has no equity will add nothing to this fund.

When a particular piece of property is abandoned by the trustee it is no longer protected under the automatic stay and the creditors who hold mortgages or liens against the particular piece of property are free to proceed legally to recover the property. It is no longer protected under the automatic stay.

CHAPTER 5:
THE BANKRUPTCY DISCHARGE

IN GENERAL

A bankruptcy discharge is an order that releases the debtor from personal liability for certain types of debts. Once the debtor receives the discharge, creditors can no longer take any collection action against the debtor for those debts that are discharged. The debtor is no longer legally responsible for those debts.

Nevertheless, if there is a valid lien upon specific property that secured the debt, the secured creditor can still enforce the lien to recover the property secured by the lien unless the lien has been "avoided"—made unenforceable—in the bankruptcy case. Although a debtor is no longer personally responsible for a discharged debt, he or she may still voluntarily repay the debt. This may occur, for example, if the debtor wishes to keep the property that is subject to a lien, or when a debt is owed to a family member.

THE DEBTOR'S RIGHT TO A DISCHARGE OF DEBTS

The bankruptcy discharge given to the debtor varies depending on the bankruptcy chapter under which the debtor files his or her case, e.g., chapter 7, 11, 12 or 13.

Chapter 7 Cases

In chapter 7 cases, the debtor does not have an absolute right to a discharge. Any creditor, the U.S. trustee, or the case trustee, may file an objection to the debtor's discharge. Shortly after the case is filed, creditors receive a notice that advises them of the deadline for making an objection to the discharge. If a creditor chooses to object, he or she must file a complaint in the bankruptcy court before this deadline. The filing of the complaint starts a litigation process known as an "adversary proceeding." At trial, the objecting party has the burden of proving all of the facts essential to their objection.

The court may deny a chapter 7 discharge for any of the reasons set forth in the Bankruptcy Code (Section 727(a)), including:

1. failure to provide requested tax documents;

2. failure to complete a course on personal financial management;

3. transfer or concealment of property with intent to hinder, delay, or defraud creditors;

4. destruction or concealment of books or records;

5. perjury and other fraudulent acts;

6. failure to account for the loss of assets;

7. violation of a court order; or

8. a discharge in an earlier case commenced within certain time frames before the date the petition was filed, as discussed below.

Chapter 12 and Chapter 13 Cases.

In chapter 12 and chapter 13 cases, the debtor is usually entitled to a discharge upon completion of all payments under the plan. However, a debtor who fails to complete the required course on personal financial management may be denied a discharge. The debtor is also ineligible for a discharge in chapter 13 if he or she received a prior discharge in another case commenced within certain time frames, as discussed below.

Unlike chapter 7, however, creditors do not have standing to object to the discharge of a chapter 12 or chapter 13 debtor. Creditors are allowed to object to confirmation of the debtor's repayment plan, but once the debtor has completed making the plan payments, creditors cannot object to the discharge.

THE DEBTOR'S RIGHT TO A DISCHARGE IN A SUBSEQUENT BANKRUPTCY ACTION

As set forth above, the court will deny a discharge in a later chapter 7 case if the debtor received a discharge under chapter 7 or chapter 11 in a case filed within eight years before the second petition is filed. The court will also deny a chapter 7 discharge if the debtor previously received a discharge in a chapter 12 or chapter 13 case filed within six years before the date of the filing of the second case unless: (i) the debtor paid all "allowed unsecured" claims in the earlier case in full, or (ii) the debtor made payments under the plan in the earlier case totaling at least 70 percent of the allowed unsecured claims, and the debtor's plan was proposed in good faith and the payments represented the debtor's best effort.

A debtor is ineligible for discharge under chapter 13 if he or she received a prior discharge in a chapter 7, 11, or 12 case filed four years before the current case or in a chapter 13 case filed two years before the current case.

TIMING OF THE BANKRUPTCY DISCHARGE

The timing of the discharge also varies, depending on the chapter under which the case is filed. For example, in a chapter 7 liquidation case, the court usually grants the discharge promptly following expiration of: (i) the time fixed for filing objections to the discharge; and (ii) the time fixed for filing a motion to dismiss the case for substantial abuse, i.e. 60 days following the first date set for the meeting of creditors ("the 341 meeting"). In general, this occurs about four months after the date the debtor files his or her bankruptcy petition.

In individual chapter 11 reorganization cases involving individuals, and in cases filed under chapters 12 and 13 for adjustment of debts, the court usually grants the discharge as soon as practicable after the debtor completes all payments under their repayment plan. A chapter 12 or chapter 13 plan may provide for payments to be made over three to five years, therefore, the discharge typically occurs about four years after the date of filing.

Nevertheless, the court may deny an individual debtor's discharge in a chapter 7 or 13 case if the debtor fails to complete "an instructional course concerning financial management." There may be an exception to this requirement if the U.S. trustee or bankruptcy administrator determines that there is no adequate financial management educational course available, or if the debtor is in active military service or disabled.

In most cases, the debtor automatically receives the discharge at the appropriate time unless there are objections to the discharge that result in litigation. Under the Federal Rules of Bankruptcy, the bankruptcy clerk must mail a copy of the discharge order to all of the creditors, the U.S. trustee, the case trustee, the debtor, and the debtor's attorney. The notice informs the creditors that the debts owed to them have been discharged, that they should not attempt any further collection, and if they continue collection efforts they could be subject to punishment for contempt of a court order.

NONDISCHARGEABLE DEBTS

Certain debts cannot be discharged, and the types of debts discharged vary depending on the type of case filed, e.g., chapter 7, 11, 12 or 13. There are nineteen categories of nondischargeable debts under chapters 7, 11 and 12, and a more limited list of nondischargeable debts under chapter 13. The debtor must still pay those nondischargeable debts after bankruptcy.

The most common types of debts which are automatically deemed nondischargeable include:

1. certain types of tax claims;

2. debts not listed by the debtor on the schedules the debtor must file with the court;

3. debts for spousal or child support or alimony;

4. debts for willful and malicious injuries to person or property;

5. debts to governmental units for fines and penalties;

6. debts for most government funded or guaranteed educational loans or benefit overpayments;

7. debts for personal injury caused by the debtor's operation of a motor vehicle while intoxicated;

8. debts owed to certain tax-advantaged retirement plans; and

9. debts for certain condominium or cooperative housing fees.

Certain other types of debts, such as obligations affected by fraud or maliciousness, are not automatically deemed nondischargeable. In those cases, the creditor must ask the court to determine whether the debt is nondischargeable. However, if a creditor does not request a determination by the court, the debt will be discharged.

Under chapter 13, a debtor receives a broader discharge of debts. For example, debts dischargeable in a chapter 13, but not in a chapter 7, include:

1. debts for willful and malicious injury to property;

2. debts incurred to pay nondischargeable tax obligations; and

3. debts arising from property settlements in divorce or separation proceedings.

HARDSHIP DISCHARGE

A chapter 13 debtor generally receives a discharge only after completing all payments required by the court-approved repayment plan. However, there are some limited circumstances under which the debtor may request the court to grant a "hardship discharge" even though the debtor has failed to complete plan payments.

Under chapter 13, a hardship discharge is available only to a debtor whose failure to complete plan payments is due to circumstances beyond the debtor's control. In addition, under chapter 12, a hardship discharge is available if the debtor's failure to complete plan payments is due to "circumstances for which the debtor should not justly be held accountable."

REVOKING A BANKRUPTCY DISCHARGE

The court may revoke a discharge under certain circumstances. For example, a creditor, the U.S. trustee, or the case trustee, may request that the court revoke the debtor's discharge in a chapter 7 case based on certain allegations, including:

1. The debtor obtained the discharge fraudulently.

2. The debtor failed to disclose the fact that he or she acquired or became entitled to acquire property that would constitute property of the bankruptcy estate; committed one of several acts of impropriety described in section 727(a)(6) of the Bankruptcy Code; or failed to explain any misstatements discovered in an audit of the case or fails to provide documents or information requested in an audit of the case. Typically, a request to revoke the debtor's discharge must be filed within one year of the discharge or, in some cases, before the date that the case is closed. The court will decide whether such allegations are true and, if so, whether to revoke the discharge. In chapter 11, 12 and 13 cases, if confirmation of a plan or the discharge is obtained through fraud, the court can revoke the order of confirmation or discharge.

POST-DISCHARGE COLLECTION ATTEMPTS

As set forth above, once a debtor receives a discharge, creditors are prohibited from making any further collection attempts on the discharged debt. If a creditor continues collection efforts, the debtor can file a motion with the bankruptcy court. The bankruptcy court will generally reopen the case to handle the creditor's violation of the discharge order. The court can find the creditor in contempt of court, and assess a fine against the creditor as punishment for violating the discharge order.

CHAPTER 6:
THE CHAPTER 7 BANKRUPTCY CASE: LIQUIDATION

IN GENERAL

A chapter 7 bankruptcy case involves the "liquidation" of the debtor's assets. A chapter 7 debtor does not propose a debt repayment plan like a chapter 13 debtor. In a chapter 7 case, the case trustee gathers and sells all of the debtor's nonexempt assets and uses the proceeds to pay the creditors. Although a chapter 7 debtor is permitted to keep certain property that is deemed exempt under the law, the trustee will liquidate all of the debtor's remaining assets. Thus, if you are considering filing a chapter 7 case, you should be aware that this will likely result in the loss of your property.

ALTERNATIVES TO FILING UNDER CHAPTER 7

There are several alternatives to filing for chapter 7 bankruptcy relief. For example, you can obtain the assistance of a debt counseling service to try and work out debt reduction and repayment plans with your creditors on your behalf. You can also attempt to work out out-of-court agreements directly with your creditors.

If it is not possible to avoid bankruptcy, debtors who are engaged in business, including corporations, partnerships, and sole proprietorships, may prefer to remain in business and avoid liquidation under chapter 7. In that case, a petition can be filed under chapter 11 of the Bankruptcy Code. Under chapter 11, the debtor may seek an adjustment of debts, either by reducing the debt or by extending the time for repayment, or may seek a more comprehensive reorganization. Chapter 11 is discussed more fully in chapter 8 of this almanac.

A sole proprietorship may also be eligible for relief under chapter 13 of the Bankruptcy Code. In addition, an individual debtor who has regular income may seek an adjustment of debts under chapter 13. One advantage of filing under chapter 13 is the opportunity to prevent foreclosure of one's home by allowing the debtor to pay their past due payments under a payment plan. Chapter 13 is discussed more fully in Chapter 7 of this Almanac.

CHAPTER 7 ABUSE

The bankruptcy court may dismiss a chapter 7 case if it determines that the debtor's obligations are primarily consumer rather than business debts, and a discharge of those debts would be an abuse of chapter 7. One way a court makes this determination is by applying a "means test." If the debtor's current monthly income is more than the state median income, the Bankruptcy Code requires the application of the "means test" to determine whether the chapter 7 filing is presumptively abusive.

Under the law, abuse is presumed if the debtor's aggregate current monthly income over 5 years, net of certain statutorily allowed expenses, is more than: (i) $10,000, or (ii) 25% of the debtor's nonpriority unsecured debt, as long as that amount is at least $6,000.

The debtor may rebut this presumption of abuse by showing special circumstances that justify additional expenses or adjustments of current monthly income. Unless the debtor overcomes the presumption of abuse, the case will either be dismissed, or converted to chapter 13 with the debtor's consent.

A Statement of Current Monthly Income and Means Test Calculation - Chapter 7 Case (Form B22A) is set forth at Appendix 19.

ELIGIBILITY FOR CHAPTER 7 BANKRUPTCY RELIEF

To be eligible for relief under chapter 7, the debtor may be an individual, a partnership, a corporation, or other business entity. It doesn't matter whether the debtor is solvent or insolvent, or the amount of debt involved. An exception exists for individual debtors, who must satisfy the "means test" described above.

CHAPTER 7 FILING FEES

Effective October 17, 2005, the following fees are paid at the bankruptcy clerk's office when the chapter 7 petition is filed:

1. filing Fee–$220.00

2. administrative Fee–$39.00

3. trustee Surcharge–$15.00

THE AUTOMATIC STAY PROVISION

When a chapter 7 petition is filed, the debtor receives an "automatic stay" that stops most collection actions against the debtor or the debtor's property. The stay is "automatic" because it does not require a court order. Depending on the situation, the stay may be short-lived, however, as long as the stay is in effect, creditors are not permitted to sue the debtor, and must discontinue any existing lawsuits, wage garnishments or other types of collection actions.

The debtor should be aware, however, that there are certain types of actions set forth in the Bankruptcy Code (11 U.S.C. §362) that are not subject to the automatic stay provision.

The automatic stay, in general, is discussed more fully in Chapter 4 of this almanac.

THE CHAPTER 7 MEETING OF CREDITORS

After the bankruptcy petition and schedules are filed, the bankruptcy clerk notifies all of the creditors listed on the debtor's schedule that the debtor has filed a bankruptcy petition. Shortly thereafter, the case trustee schedules a meeting of creditors. The debtor must attend this meeting and, under oath, must answer any questions asked by the trustee and the creditors pertaining to the debtor's financial affairs. In addition, the debtor must provide any financial records or documents requested by the trustee. Based on the information gathered at the meeting, the U.S. trustee will advise the court whether the case should be presumed an abuse under the means test described above.

DISTRIBUTION OF THE CHAPTER 7 BANKRUPTCY ESTATE

Commencement of the bankruptcy case creates a "bankruptcy estate," consisting of all legal or equitable interests of the debtor in property as of the date the petition is filed. This may include property owned or held by another person if the debtor has an interest in the property. The creditors are paid from the nonexempt property of the estate, if any.

The No-Asset Case

If the debtor has no assets, or all of the debtor's assets are exempt or subject to valid liens, the trustee will file a "no-asset" report with the court, and there will be no distribution to unsecured creditors. Thus, in the typical no-asset chapter 7 case, there is no need for creditors to file proofs of claim because there will be no distribution. Most chapter 7 cases involving individual debtors are no-asset cases.

If the case trustee later recovers assets for distribution to unsecured creditors, the court will provide notice to the creditors and will allow them additional time to file proofs of claim.

A Notice of Chapter 7 Bankruptcy Case, Meeting of Creditors and Deadlines in a No-Asset Case (form B9A) is set forth at Appendix 20.

The Asset Case

In an asset case, the case trustee liquidates the debtor's nonexempt assets by selling the debtor's property provided: (i) the property is either free and clear of liens; or (ii) the property is worth more than any security interest or lien attached to it; or (iii) the property is worth more than any exempt amount the debtor holds in the property.

Proofs of Claim

A claim is any right to payment held by a person or company against the debtor and the debtor's bankruptcy estate. A claim does not have to be a past due amount, but can include an anticipated sum of money which will come due in the future.

If the case appears to be an "asset" case, in order to make a claim, unsecured creditors must file a written statement known as a "proof of claim" within 90 days after the first date set for the meeting of creditors. A governmental unit, such as a taxing authority, has 180 days from the date the case is filed to file their proof of claim. If a creditor files a claim after the specified deadline, the debtor may object to the claim as being untimely filed, and the creditor will not be paid.

The proof of claim sets forth the details of the creditor's claim and should include a copy of the obligation giving rise to the claim. If the claim is secured, the creditor should also provide evidence of the secured status.

The debtor is entitled to object to any claim filed in their bankruptcy case if they believe the debt is not owed, or if they dispute the amount or kind of debt claimed. In some circumstances, an objection to a claim can be initiated by filing a motion in the bankruptcy court. In other circumstances, the objection must be initiated by filing an adversary proceeding. The objection must be made timely, and the process can be complicated, therefore, it is advisable to consult an attorney if an objection to a claim must be filed. The bankruptcy judge presiding over the case will rule on the motion.

A sample Proof of Claim is set forth at Appendix 21.

Avoiding Powers

The trustee may also attempt to recover money or property under the trustee's "avoiding powers," which include the trustee's right to: (i) set aside preferential transfers made to creditors within 90 days before the petition is filed; (ii) undo security interests and other pre-petition transfers of property that were not properly perfected under nonbankruptcy law at the time the petition is filed; and (iii) pursue nonbankruptcy claims such as fraudulent conveyances and bulk transfer remedies available under state law.

In addition, if the debtor is a business, the bankruptcy court may authorize the trustee to operate the business for a limited period of time, if such operation will benefit creditors and enhance the liquidation of the estate.

A Notice of Chapter 7 Bankruptcy Case, Meeting of Creditors and Deadlines in an Asset Case (form B9C) is set forth at Appendix 22.

STATEMENT OF INTENTION

A Statement of Intention is a form filed in a Chapter 7 case which provides the court with information concerning the debtor's intentions relating to assets which secure debts, such as the debtor's home or car. The debtor must disclose whether he or she intends to retain the asset or surrender it.

If the debtor wishes to keep the asset, he or she must continue to pay for it. An agreement may be reached with the creditor for payment. This agreement must be in writing and may require approval by the bankruptcy judge. The debtor generally has two options for payment of the debt, as discussed below.

Reaffirmation Agreement

If a debtor wants to keep certain property that is secured by a lien, such as their car, he or she may enter into a reaffirmation agreement with the secured creditor. The reaffirmation agreement must be executed within forty-five days of filing the bankruptcy petition and prior to the granting of a discharge. The written reaffirmation agreement must be filed with the court. The debtor may rescind the reaffirmation agreement within sixty days after the agreement is filed with the court, or at any time prior to discharge, whichever occurs later. The reaffirmation agreement must be filed with the court.

Under a reaffirmation agreement, the debtor and creditor agree that the debtor will remain liable for the debt even though the debt would otherwise be discharged in bankruptcy and the debtor would no longer be personally liable. The creditor promises that it will not repossess the secured property, e.g., the car, as long as the debtor continues to pay the debt.

Under the law, a reaffirmation agreement must contain certain disclosures. For example, the agreement must advise the debtor of the following: (i) the amount of the debt being reaffirmed; (ii) how the amount was calculated; (iii) that the debtor will continue to be personally liable for the debt; and (iv) that the debt will not be discharged.

The law also requires the debtor to file a statement of his or her current income and expenses which shows that the debtor has a sufficient balance of income to pay the reaffirmed debt. If the balance is not enough to pay the debt to be reaffirmed, there is a presumption of undue hardship, in which case the court may refuse to approve the reaffirmation agreement. If the debtor does not have an attorney, the bankruptcy judge must approve the reaffirmation agreement.

If the debtor is represented by an attorney, the attorney must certify in writing that he or she advised the debtor of the legal effect and consequences of the reaffirmation agreement. The attorney must also certify that the debtor was fully informed and voluntarily made the agreement and that reaffirmation of the debt will not create an undue hardship for the debtor or the debtor's dependants

It should be noted, however, that a debtor may repay any debt voluntarily regardless of whether a reaffirmation agreement exists.

A sample Reaffirmation Agreement (Form B240) is set forth at Appendix 23.

Redemption

An alternative to reaffirmation is redemption of property. Redemption must take place within forty-five days of filing the bankruptcy petition. The debtor may redeem certain property by agreeing to pay the creditor the full current value of the property in one lump sum, even if the debt is considerably higher.

Property which may be redeemed generally includes tangible personal property intended for personal, family or household use, on which a lien has been filed. In addition, if the bankruptcy trustee abandons a piece of property from the bankruptcy estate, the debtor generally has the right to redeem that property as well.

THE BANKRUPTCY DISCHARGE UNDER CHAPTER 7

The individual debtor's primary reason for filing a chapter 7 bankruptcy case is to retain exempt property and receive a discharge that covers as many debts as possible. Under chapter 7, the discharge releases the individual debtor from personal liability for most debts and prevents the creditors owed those debts from taking any collection actions against the debtor. The chapter 7 discharge is only available to individual debtors.

Provided there are no objections to the debtor's discharge, the court will generally issue a discharge order early in the case, e.g., 60 to 90 days after the date set for the first meeting of creditors.

A Discharge Order is set forth at Appendix 24.

As set forth more fully in Chapter 3 of this almanac, the debtor's right to a discharge of debts under chapter 7 is not absolute. Some types of debts are nondischargeable. In addition, the bankruptcy discharge does not extinguish a lien on the debtor's property.

The bankruptcy discharge, in general, is discussed more fully in Chapter 5 of this Almanac.

CHAPTER 7:
THE CHAPTER 13 BANKRUPTCY CASE:
INDIVIDUAL DEBT ADJUSTMENT

IN GENERAL

A chapter 13 bankruptcy case is also referred to as a "wage earner's plan" because it enables debtors who have a regular income to develop a plan to repay all or part of their debts. The chapter 13 debtor proposes a repayment plan under which his or her creditors are paid over a period ranging from three to five years.

If the debtor's current monthly income is less than the applicable state median, the debtor's plan must extend over three years. If the debtor's current monthly income is greater than the state median, the debtor's plan must extend over five years. The proposed repayment plan cannot extend beyond five years.

As discussed below, during this repayment period, creditors are not permitted to start or continue debt collection efforts.

ADVANTAGES OF FILING UNDER CHAPTER 13

There are a number of advantages in filing a bankruptcy petition under chapter 13 instead of pursuing liquidation under chapter 7. One major reason an individual may wish to file under chapter 13 is to keep their home from being foreclosed upon by their home mortgage lender if they fall behind in their payments. Chapter 13 allows the debtor to stop foreclosure proceedings pursuant to the automatic stay provision discussed below, and pay any past due amount over an extended period of time. However, current mortgage payments must be timely made while the chapter 13 case is pending.

Another advantage to filing under chapter 13 is the ability to reschedule secured debts and extend them over the duration of the chapter 13 plan. This generally results in lower payments. A chapter 13 debtor makes his or her plan payments in a lump sum to the case trustee who then distributes the payments to the creditors pursuant to the debtor's repayment plan. The debtor no longer has contact with his or her creditors.

ELIGIBILITY

Any individual is eligible to file for chapter 13 bankruptcy relief as long as their debts do not exceed a certain monetary limit. Presently, the statutory maximum is $307,675 in unsecured debts, and $922,975 in secured debts. These limits are adjusted periodically to reflect changes in the consumer price index.

CHAPTER 13 FILING FEES

Effective October 17, 2005, the following fees are paid at the bankruptcy clerk's office when the chapter 13 petition is filed:

1. Filing Fee–$150.00

2. Administrative Fee–$39.00

THE AUTOMATIC STAY PROVISION

When a chapter 13 petition is filed, the debtor receives an "automatic stay" that stops most collection actions against the debtor or the debtor's property. The stay is "automatic" because it does not require a court order. Depending on the situation, the stay may be short-lived, however, as long as the stay is in effect, creditors are not permitted to sue the debtor, and must discontinue any existing lawsuits, wage garnishments or other types of collection actions.

The debtor should be aware, however, that there are certain types of actions set forth in the Bankruptcy Code (11 U.S.C. §362(b)) that are not subject to the automatic stay provision.

The automatic stay, in general, is discussed more fully in Chapter 4 of this almanac.

THE CHAPTER 13 MEETING OF CREDITORS

After the petition and schedules are filed, the bankruptcy clerk notifies all of the creditors listed on the debtor's schedule that the debtor has filed a bankruptcy petition. Shortly thereafter, the case trustee schedules a meeting of creditors. The debtor must attend this meeting and, under oath, must answer any questions asked by the trustee and the creditors pertaining to the debtor's financial affairs and the proposed terms of the debtor's repayment plan.

If there are any concerns about the repayment plan, the parties have an opportunity to discuss and resolve those problems at this meeting. Following the meeting of creditors, the debtor, the case trustee, and those creditors who wish to attend will appear in court for a hearing on the debtor's chapter 13 repayment plan.

A Notice of Chapter 13 Bankruptcy Case, Meeting of Creditors and Deadlines (Form B9I) is set forth at Appendix 25.

THE CHAPTER 13 REPAYMENT PLAN

The debtor must file a repayment plan along with their chapter 13 petition, or within 15 days after filing the petition. The repayment plan must be submitted for court approval, also known as "confirmation." The repayment plan must provide for payments of fixed amounts to the case trustee on a regular basis, e.g. monthly. The case trustee then distributes the payments to the creditors according to the terms of the plan. The repayment plan may offer creditors less than the full payment on their claims.

A sample Chapter 13 Repayment Plan is set forth at Appendix 26.

Classes of Claims

There are three classes of claims: (i) priority; (ii) secured; and (iii) unsecured.

Priority Claims

Priority claims are those granted special status under bankruptcy law, such as most taxes and the costs of the bankruptcy proceeding. Under the debtor's repayment plan, priority claims must be paid in full unless a particular priority creditor agrees to different treatment of their claim or, in case of a domestic support obligation, unless the debtor contributes all "disposable income" to a five-year plan.

Secured Claims

Secured claims are those for which the creditor has the right to take back certain property—i.e., the collateral—which was pledged to secure the underlying debt if the debtor fails to make the required payments. Under the repayment plan, if the debtor wants to keep the collateral that secures a particular claim, the holder of the secured claim must be paid at least the value of the collateral.

If the debt underlying the secured claim was incurred to buy the collateral, such as a car loan, and the debt was incurred within a certain time period before the bankruptcy petition was filed, the repayment plan must provide for full payment of the debt, not just the value of the collateral which may be less due to depreciation.

Payments to certain secured creditors, such as a home mortgage lender, may be made over the original loan repayment schedule, which is generally longer than the repayment plan term, provided any past due amounts are made up while the plan is in effect.

Unsecured Claims

Unsecured claims are generally those for which the creditor has no special right to collect against particular property owned by the debtor. Under the repayment plan, unsecured claims do not have to be paid in full provided that: (i) the debtor pays all of his or her "disposable income" over the "applicable commitment period" and (ii) unsecured creditors receive at least as much as they would have received if the debtor had filed under chapter 7 and liquidated his or her assets.

Under chapter 13, "disposable income" is defined as income, not including child support received by the debtor, less: (i) any amounts reasonably necessary for the maintenance or support of the debtor or the debtor's dependents; and (ii) charitable contributions up to 15% of the debtor's gross income. If the debtor operates a business, the definition of disposable income excludes those amounts that are necessary for ordinary operating expenses.

Under chapter 13, the "applicable commitment period" (e.g., 3 or 5 years) depends on the debtor's current monthly income. The applicable commitment period must be (i) three years if the debtor's current monthly income is less than the state median for a family of the same size; or (ii) five years if the current monthly income is greater than the state median for a family of the same size. The plan may be less than the applicable commitment period only if the unsecured debt is paid in full over a shorter period.

Debtor's Statement of Current Monthly Income and Calculation of Commitment Period and Disposable Income in a Chapter 13 Case (Form B22C) is set forth at Appendix 27.

Timing of Payments

Within 30 days after filing the chapter 13 petition, even if the plan has not yet been approved by the court, the debtor must start making plan payments to the trustee. In addition, if any secured loan payments or lease payments become due before the debtor's plan is confirmed—e.g., home mortgage payments or car loan payments—the debtor is required to make adequate protection payments directly to the secured lender or lessor. The debtor is entitled to deduct any amount paid directly to a lender or lessor from the amount that must be paid to the trustee.

THE CHAPTER 13 PLAN CONFIRMATION HEARING

The bankruptcy judge must hold a confirmation hearing within 45 days after the meeting of creditors. The purpose of the confirmation hearing is for the judge to decide whether the plan is feasible, and whether the plan meets the standards for confirmation set forth in the Bankruptcy Code.

Creditors are given 25 days' notice of the hearing during which time they may file any objections they have to plan confirmation. A common objection to plan confirmation is that creditors would receive more money if the debtor's chapter 13 case were converted to a chapter 7, case and the debtor's assets liquidated and distributed to the creditors. Another common objection is that the debtor's plan does not commit all of the debtor's disposable income for the three-to-five-year period of the plan.

If the court confirms the debtor's repayment plan, the debtor will start to make the required payments to the trustee, and the trustee will start making payments to the creditors according to the terms of the plan. If the court does not confirm the debtor's repayment plan, the debtor may submit a modified plan, or may convert the case to a chapter 7 liquidation case. If the court does not confirm the modified plan, and the chapter 13 case is dismissed, the trustee must return all of the funds they have been collecting to the debtor, less the trustee's costs and any funds that have already been disbursed.

If circumstances arise which negatively impact the debtor's ability to make the required plan payments, the plan may be modified either before or after confirmation. Modification may be sought by the debtor, case trustee, or an unsecured creditor.

BINDING EFFECT OF CONFIRMED CHAPTER 13 REPAYMENT PLAN

The provisions of a confirmed chapter 13 plan bind the debtor and each creditor. Once the court confirms the plan, the debtor must make every effort to see that the plan succeeds. The debtor must make regular payments to the trustee for distribution to the creditors. Thus, the debtor must learn to live within a fixed budget during the time the plan is in effect. In addition, the debtor is not allowed to incur any new debts without consulting the trustee so as not to negatively impact the debtor's ability to make the required payments under the plan.

A sample Order Confirming Chapter 13 Plan (Form B230B) is set forth at Appendix 28.

If the debtor does not make the required payments under the plan, the debtor's chapter 13 case may be dismissed by the court, or converted into a liquidation case under chapter 7 of the Bankruptcy Code, as discussed in Chapter 3 of this almanac.

THE BANKRUPTCY DISCHARGE UNDER CHAPTER 13

Upon completion of all of the payments under the confirmed repayment plan, the chapter 13 debtor is entitled to a discharge provided the debtor complies with the following:

1. The debtor must certify that all domestic support obligations that came due prior to making the certification have been paid, if any;

2. The debtor must not have received a discharge in a prior case filed within a certain time frame, i.e., two years for a prior chapter 13 case and four years for a prior chapter 7, 11 or 12 case; and

3. The debtor must have completed an approved course in financial management provided the U.S. trustee or bankruptcy administrator has determined that such a course is available.

A sample order granting a Discharge of Debtor After Completion of Chapter 13 Plan (Form B18W) is set forth at Appendix 29.

Scope of the Bankruptcy Discharge Under Chapter 13

The chapter 13 discharge releases the debtor from all debts provided for in the repayment plan, and all debts that were disallowed. Thus, creditors who have been paid, in full or in part, under the chapter 13 plan may no longer initiate or continue any legal or other action against the debtor to collect the discharged obligations.

If, however, circumstances arise after plan confirmation that prevent the debtor from completing the plan—e.g., injury or illness that prevents the debtor from working—the debtor may ask the court for a "hardship discharge." A hardship discharge may be available if:

1. the debtor's failure to complete plan payments is due to circumstances beyond the debtor's control and through no fault of the debtor;

2. the creditors have received at least as much as they would have received in a chapter 7 liquidation case; and

3. modification of the plan is not possible.

Under the law, the following debts cannot be discharged in chapter 13:

1. certain long term obligations, such as a home mortgage;

2. alimony or child support;

3. certain taxes;

4. most government funded or guaranteed educational loans or benefit overpayments;

5. debts arising from death or personal injury caused by driving while intoxicated or under the influence of drugs;

6. debts for restitution or a criminal fine included in a sentence on the debtor's conviction of a crime.

If the above debts have not been fully paid under the repayment plan, the debtor will still be responsible for these debts after the bankruptcy case has ended.

The bankruptcy discharge, in general, is discussed more fully in Chapter 5 of this Almanac.

CHAPTER 8:
THE CHAPTER 11 BANKRUPTCY CASE: REORGANIZATION

IN GENERAL

A chapter 11 bankruptcy case is also referred to as a "reorganization" bankruptcy. Chapter 11 is typically used to reorganize a business, which may be a corporation, sole proprietorship, or partnership. A corporation exists separate and apart from its owners, the stockholders. Thus, a chapter 11 bankruptcy case of a corporate debtor does not put the personal assets of the stockholders at risk, except for the value of the company stock that they may own.

In a sole proprietorship, the owner is the debtor and, therefore, does not have an identity separate and distinct from the owner. Thus, a chapter 11 bankruptcy case involving a sole proprietorship includes both the business and personal assets of the owner/debtor.

A partnership, like a corporation, exists separate and apart from its partners, however, the partners' personal assets may, in some cases, be used to pay creditors in the bankruptcy case. In addition, the partners may be forced to file for individual bankruptcy protection.

In the case of individuals, chapter 11 is similar to chapter 13. For example:

1. property of the chapter 11 estate for an individual debtor includes the debtor's earnings and property acquired by the chapter 11 debtor after filing until the case is closed, dismissed or converted;

2. funding of the plan may be from the debtor's future earnings; and

3. the plan cannot be confirmed over a creditor's objection without committing all of the debtor's disposable income over five years unless, according to the plan, the claim will be paid in full, with interest, over a shorter period of time.

The chapter 11 petition may be a voluntary petition or an involuntary petition. The voluntary petition is filed by the debtor. The involuntary petition is filed by creditors, and must meet certain requirements.

CHAPTER 11 FILING FEES

Effective October 17, 2005, the following fees are paid at the bankruptcy clerk's office when the chapter 11 petition is filed:

1. filing Fee–$1000.00

2. administrative Fee–$39.00

THE DEBTOR IN POSSESSION

Upon filing a voluntary petition for relief under chapter 11 or, in an involuntary case, upon the entry of an order for relief, the debtor is known as a "debtor in possession." This term refers to a debtor that keeps possession and control of its assets during the reorganization process under chapter 11, without the appointment of a case trustee.

The chapter 11 debtor remains a debtor in possession until one of the following events occurs:

1. the debtor's plan of reorganization is confirmed;

2. the debtor's case is dismissed;

3. the debtor's case is converted to chapter 7; or

4. a chapter 11 trustee is appointed, although this occurs only in a small number of cases.

Generally, the debtor, as "debtor in possession," acts as a fiduciary, and operates the business and performs many of the functions that a trustee performs in cases under other chapters. These duties include:

1. accounting for property;

2. examining and objecting to claims;

3. filing informational reports as required by the court and the U.S. trustee, e.g., monthly operating reports; and

4. filing tax returns.

The debtor in possession also has many of the rights of a trustee, including:

1. the right to employ attorneys, accountants, appraisers, auctioneers, or other professional persons to assist the debtor during its bankruptcy case;

2. the right to use, sell, or lease property of the estate in the ordinary course of its business, without prior approval, unless the court orders otherwise.

THE ROLE OF THE U.S. TRUSTEE IN A CHAPTER 11 CASE

The U.S. trustee plays a major role in monitoring the progress of a chapter 11 case and supervising its administration. The U.S. trustee is responsible for monitoring the debtor in possession's operation of the business and the submission of operating reports and fees. Additionally, the U.S. trustee monitors applications for compensation and reimbursement by professionals, plans and disclosure statements filed with the court, and creditors' committees.

By law, the debtor in possession must pay a quarterly fee to the U.S. trustee for each quarter of a year until the case is converted or dismissed. The amount of the fee may range from $250 to $10,000 depending on the amount of the debtor's disbursements during each quarter.

If the debtor in possession fails to comply with the reporting requirements of the U.S. trustee; fails to comply with any orders of the bankruptcy court; or fails to take the appropriate steps to bring the chapter 11 case to confirmation, the U.S. trustee may file a motion with the court to have the case converted to another chapter of the Bankruptcy Code, or to have the case dismissed.

THE CHAPTER 11 MEETING OF CREDITORS

After the petition and schedules are filed, the bankruptcy clerk notifies all of the creditors listed on the debtor's schedule that the debtor has filed a bankruptcy petition. Shortly thereafter, the U.S. trustee schedules a meeting of creditors. The U.S. trustee is responsible for conducting a meeting of the creditors, also referred to as the "section 341 meeting," in a chapter 11 case. At the meeting, the U.S. trustee and creditors question the debtor, under oath, concerning the debtor's acts, conduct, property, and the administration of the case.

A Notice of Chapter 11 Bankruptcy Case, Meeting of Creditors and Deadlines (Form B9E) is set forth at Appendix 30.

COMMITTEE OF CREDITORS

A committee of creditors is appointed by the U.S. trustee, and often plays a major role in a chapter 11 case. The committee generally consists of unsecured creditors who hold the seven largest unsecured claims against the debtor. The committee has certain responsibilities, including consulting with the debtor in possession on administration of the case; investigating the debtor's conduct and operation of the business; and participating in formulating a reorganization plan. With the court's permission, the committee may also hire an attorney or other professionals to assist in the performance of the committee's duties.

APPOINTMENT OF A CHAPTER 11 CASE TRUSTEE

As set forth above, the appointment of a case trustee is rare in a chapter 11 case, however, a party in interest or the U.S. trustee can request the appointment of a case trustee or examiner at any time prior to confirmation in a chapter 11 case under certain circumstances. If requested, the court may order the appointment of a case trustee for cause, including fraud, dishonesty, incompetence, or gross mismanagement, or if such an appointment is in the interest of creditors, any equity security holders, and other interests of the estate.

In addition, the U.S. trustee is required to request the appointment of a trustee if there are reasonable grounds to believe that any of the parties in control of the debtor participated in actual fraud, dishonesty or criminal conduct in the management of the debtor or the debtor's financial reporting.

Subject to court approval, the case trustee is appointed by the U.S. trustee, after consultation with the parties in interest. A trustee in a case may also be elected if a party in interest requests the election of a trustee within 30 days after the court orders the appointment of a trustee. In that case, the U.S. trustee convenes a meeting of creditors for the purpose of electing a person to serve as case trustee.

The case trustee is responsible for management of the property of the estate, operation of the debtor's business, and, if appropriate, the filing of a plan of reorganization. If a plan is not filed "as soon as practicable," the case trustee must file a report explaining why the plan will not be filed, or must make a recommendation that the case be converted to another bankruptcy chapter or dismissed.

Upon the request of a party in interest or the U.S. trustee, the court may terminate the trustee's appointment and restore the debtor in possession to management of bankruptcy estate at any time before confirmation.

APPOINTMENT OF AN EXAMINER

The appointment of an examiner in a chapter 11 case is also rare. The role of an examiner is generally more limited than that of a trustee.

The examiner is authorized to perform the investigatory functions of the trustee and is required to file a statement of any investigation conducted. If ordered to do so by the court, however, an examiner may carry out any other duties of a trustee that the court orders the debtor in possession not to perform.

Each court has the authority to determine the duties of an examiner in each particular case. In some cases, the examiner may file a plan of reorganization, negotiate or help the parties negotiate, or review the debtor's schedules to determine whether some of the claims are improperly categorized. Sometimes, the examiner may be directed to determine if objections to any proofs of claim should be filed or whether causes of action have sufficient merit so that further legal action should be taken. The examiner may not subsequently serve as a trustee in the case.

THE AUTOMATIC STAY

The automatic stay provides a period of time in which all judgments, collection activities, foreclosures, and repossessions of property are suspended and may not be pursued by the creditors on any debt or claim that arose before the filing of the bankruptcy petition. As with cases under other chapters of the Bankruptcy Code, a stay of creditor actions against the chapter 11 debtor automatically goes into effect when the bankruptcy petition is filed. The stay provides a respite from collection activity for the debtor, during which negotiations can take place to try to resolve the difficulties in the debtor's financial situation.

Under specific circumstances, the secured creditor can obtain an order from the court granting relief from the automatic stay. For example, when the debtor has no equity in the property and the property is not necessary for an effective reorganization, the secured creditor can seek an order of the court lifting the stay to permit the creditor to foreclose on the property, sell it, and apply the proceeds to the debt.

The automatic stay, in general, is discussed more fully in Chapter 4 of this Almanac.

AVOIDABLE TRANSFERS

The debtor in possession or the case trustee, as the case may be, has what are called "avoiding" powers." These powers may be used to undo a transfer of money or property made during a certain period of time before the filing of the bankruptcy petition. By avoiding a particular transfer of property, the debtor in possession can cancel the transaction and force the return of the payments or property, which then are available to pay all creditors.

Generally, and subject to various defenses, the power to avoid transfers is effective against transfers made by the debtor within 90 days before filing the petition. But transfers to "insiders"—i.e., relatives, general partners, and directors or officers of the debtor—made up to a year before filing may be avoided.

In addition, the trustee is authorized to avoid transfers under applicable state law, which often provides for longer time periods. Avoiding powers prevent unfair pre-petition payments to one creditor at the expense of all other creditors.

FILING A PROOF OF CLAIM

As set forth above, when the chapter 11 debtor filed the chapter 11 petition, he or she was required to submit schedules that list the debtor's creditors and their claims. Those schedules are deemed to constitute evidence of the validity and amount of those claims. Thus, if the debtor listed a creditor's claim on the schedule of creditors, and did not designate the claim as disputed, contingent or unliquidated, the creditor does not have to file a proof of claim.

If the debtor fails to list a creditor's claim on the schedule of creditors, or designates the claim as disputed, contingent or unliquidated, the creditor must file a proof of claim with the bankruptcy court in order to have the status of a creditor and the right to vote on the debtor's reorganization plan. It is the responsibility of the creditor to determine whether their claim is accurately listed on the debtor's schedules. If a scheduled creditor chooses to file a claim, a properly filed proof of claim supersedes any scheduling of that claim.

CONVERSION OR DISMISSAL PROCEEDINGS

A chapter 11 debtor has a one time absolute right to convert their chapter 11 case to a case under chapter 7 unless:

1. the debtor is not a debtor in possession;

2. the case originally was commenced as an involuntary case under chapter 11; or

3. the case was converted to a case under chapter 11 other than at the debtor's request.

A chapter 11 debtor does not, however, have an absolute right to have the case dismissed upon request. A party in interest may file a motion to dismiss or convert a chapter 11 case to a chapter 7 case "for cause." Generally, if cause is established after notice and hearing, the court must convert or dismiss the case unless it specifically finds that the requested conversion or dismissal is not in the best interest of creditors and the estate.

The Bankruptcy Code sets forth numerous examples of cause that would support dismissal or conversion. For example, the moving party may establish cause by showing:

1. a substantial or continuing loss to the estate and the absence of a reasonable likelihood of rehabilitation;

2. gross mismanagement of the estate;

3. failure to maintain insurance that poses a risk to the estate or the public;

4. unauthorized use of cash collateral that is substantially harmful to a creditor;

5. an unexcused failure to timely comply with reporting and filing requirements;

6. failure to attend the meeting of creditors;

7. failure to timely provide information to the U.S. trustee;

8. failure to timely pay post-petition taxes or timely file post-petition returns;

9. failure to file a disclosure statement;

10. failure to file and confirm a plan within the time fixed by the Bankruptcy Code or order of the court;

11. the inability to effectuate a plan;

12. denial or revocation of confirmation;

13. the inability to consummate a confirmed plan; and

14. in an individual case, failure of the debtor to pay post-petition domestic support obligations.

Nevertheless, the court is prohibited from converting a case involving a farmer or charitable institution to a liquidation case under chapter 7 unless the debtor requests the conversion.

DISCLOSURE STATEMENT AND CHAPTER 11 PLAN OF REORGANIZATION

The debtor in possession must file a written disclosure statement and a plan of reorganization with the court. The disclosure statement is a document that contains information concerning the assets, liabilities, and business affairs of the debtor. The information contained in the disclosure statement must be sufficient enough for a creditor to make an informed judgment about the debtor's plan of reorganization.

The contents of the chapter 11 reorganization plan must include a classification of claims, and must specify how each class of claims will be treated under the plan. Generally, a plan will classify claim holders as secured creditors, unsecured creditors entitled to priority, general unsecured creditors, and equity security holders.

The debtor must file and get court approval of a written disclosure statement before there can be a vote on the debtor's plan of reorganization. After the disclosure statement is filed, the court must hold a hearing to determine whether the disclosure statement should be approved. After the court approves the disclosure statement, the debtor or proponent of a plan can begin to solicit acceptances of the plan, and creditors may also solicit rejections of the plan.

An Order Approving the Disclosure Statement and Fixing Time for Filing Acceptances or Rejections of the Plan (Form B13) is set forth at Appendix 31.

The plan proponent must mail the following to the U.S. trustee and all creditors and equity security holders:

1. the debtor's plan of reorganization or a court approved summary of the plan;

2. the disclosure statement approved by the court;

3. notice of the time within which acceptances and rejections of the plan may be filed; and

4. such other information as the court may direct, including any opinion of the court approving the disclosure statement or a court-approved summary of the opinion.

In addition to the above, the debtor must mail to the creditors and equity security holders entitled to vote on the plan or plans:

1. notice of the time fixed for filing objections;

2. notice of the date and time for the hearing on confirmation of the plan; and

3. a ballot for accepting or rejecting the plan and, if appropriate, a designation on the ballot for the creditors to identify their preference among competing plans.

A sample Ballot for Accepting or Rejecting Plan (Form B14) is set forth at Appendix 32.

Exclusivity Period

The chapter 11 debtor has a 120-day period during which it has an exclusive right to file a plan. This exclusivity period may be extended or reduced by the court, but in no case can this period extend beyond 18 months. After the exclusivity period has expired, a creditor or the case trustee may file a competing plan. The creditors' right to file a competing plan provides incentive for the debtor to file a plan within the exclusivity period and acts as a check on excessive delay in the case.

In addition to the time period during which the debtor has the exclusive right to file the plan, the debtor has 180 days after the petition date, or entry of the order for relief, to obtain acceptances of its plan. The court may extend this time period up to 20 months, or reduce this acceptance exclusivity period for cause.

If the exclusivity period ends before the debtor has filed and obtained acceptance of a plan, other parties in interest in a case, such as the creditors' committee or a creditor, may file a plan. Such a plan may compete with a plan filed by another party in interest or by the debtor. If a case trustee is appointed, the trustee must file a plan, a report explaining why the trustee will not file a plan, or a recommendation for conversion or dismissal of the case.

PLAN CONFIRMATION

The Bankruptcy Code requires the court, after notice, to hold a hearing on confirmation of a plan. Any party in interest may file an objection to confirmation of a plan. If no objection to confirmation has been timely filed, the Bankruptcy Code allows the court to determine whether the plan has been proposed in good faith and in compliance with all of the requirements set forth in the Bankruptcy Code. Thus, in order to confirm the plan, the court must find, among other things, that:

1. the plan is feasible—i.e., confirmation is not likely to be followed by liquidation or further need for financial reorganization;

2. the plan is proposed in good faith; and

3. the plan and the proponent of the plan are in compliance with the Bankruptcy Code.

Because more than one plan may be submitted to the creditors for approval, every proposed plan and modification must be dated and identified with the name of the entity or entities submitting the plan or modification. When competing plans are presented that meet the requirements for confirmation, the court must consider the preferences of the creditors and equity security holders in determining which plan to confirm. The confirmed plan creates new contractual rights, replacing or superseding pre-bankruptcy contracts.

An Order Confirming the Plan (B15) is set forth at Appendix 33.

Post-Confirmation Plan Modifications

At any time after confirmation and before "substantial consummation" of a plan, the proponent of a plan may modify the plan if the modified plan would meet certain requirements. A modified postconfirmation plan does not automatically become the plan. A modified postconfirmation plan in a chapter 11 case becomes the plan only "if circumstances warrant such modification" and the court, after notice and hearing, confirms the plan as modified.

If the debtor is an individual, the plan may be modified postconfirmation upon the request of the debtor, the trustee, the U.S. trustee, or the holder of an allowed unsecured claim to make adjustments to payments due under the plan.

Revocation of the Confirmation Order

Revocation of the confirmation order is an undoing or cancellation of the confirmation of a plan. A request for revocation of confirmation, if made at all, must be made by a party in interest within 180 days of confirmation. The court, after notice and hearing, may revoke a confirmation order "if and only if the confirmation order was procured by fraud."

THE BANKRUPTCY DISCHARGE UNDER CHAPTER 11

Plan confirmation discharges a debtor from any debt that arose before the date of confirmation. After the plan is confirmed, the debtor is required to make plan payments and is bound by the provisions of the plan of reorganization. Except in limited circumstances, a discharge is not available to an individual debtor unless and until all payments have been made under the plan.

Confirmation of a plan of reorganization discharges any type of debtor—corporation, partnership, or individual—from most types of prepetition debts. It does not, however, discharge an individual debtor from any debt deemed nondischargeable under the Bankruptcy Code, including:

Certain debts are not dischargeable:

    1. debts for alimony and child support;

    2. certain taxes;

3. debts for certain educational benefit overpayments or loans made or guaranteed by a governmental unit;

4. debts for willful and malicious injury by the debtor to another entity or to the property of another entity;

5. debts for death or personal injury caused by the debtor's operation of a motor vehicle while the debtor was intoxicated from alcohol or other substances; and

6. debts for certain criminal restitution orders.

The debtor will continue to be liable for these nondischargeable types of debts to the extent that they are not paid in the chapter 11 case.

Debts for money or property obtained by false pretenses, debts for fraud or defalcation while acting in a fiduciary capacity, and debts for willful and malicious injury by the debtor to another entity or to the property of another entity will be discharged unless a creditor timely files and prevails in an action to have such debts declared nondischargeable.

Confirmation does not discharge the debtor if the plan is a liquidation plan, as opposed to one of reorganization, unless the debtor is an individual. When the debtor is an individual, confirmation of a liquidation plan will result in a discharge after all plan payments are made unless grounds would exist for denying the debtor a discharge if the case were proceeding under chapter 7 instead of chapter 11.

The bankruptcy discharge, in general, is discussed more fully in Chapter 5 of this Almanac.

CHAPTER 9:
THE CHAPTER 12 BANKRUPTCY CASE: ADJUSTMENT OF DEBTS OF A FAMILY FARMER OR FISHERMAN

IN GENERAL

A chapter 12 bankruptcy case is designed for "family farmers" or "family fishermen" with "regular annual income." It enables financially distressed family farmers and fishermen to propose and carry out a plan to repay all or part of their debts.

Chapter 12 debtors propose a repayment plan to make installments to creditors over three to five years. Generally, the plan must provide for payments over three years unless the court approves a longer period "for cause." But unless the plan proposes to pay 100% of domestic support claims—i.e., child support and alimony—if any exist, the plan must extend for five years, and must include all of the debtor's disposable income. The plan may not extend for a period of longer than five years.

Recognizing the economic realities of family farming and the family fisherman, Congress eliminated many of the barriers chapter 12 debtors would face if seeking to reorganize under either chapter 11 or 13 of the Bankruptcy Code.

For example, chapter 12 is more streamlined, less complicated, and less expensive than chapter 11, which is better suited to large corporate reorganizations. In addition, few family farmers or fishermen find chapter 13 to be advantageous because it is designed for wage earners who have smaller debts than those facing family farmers.

ELIGIBILITY

Under the law, chapter 12 is only available to a family farmer or family fisherman with "regular annual income" so that the debtor will have sufficient annual income to make payments under their chapter 12 plan. Nevertheless, chapter 12 makes allowances for family farmers or fishermen who have seasonal income.

The terms "family farmers" and "family fishermen" fall into two categories:

Individual or Individual and Spouse

Farmers or fishermen who fall into this category must meet the following four criteria as of the date the petition is filed in order to be eligible for relief under chapter 12:

1. The individual or husband and wife must be engaged in a farming operation or a commercial fishing operation.

2. The total secured and unsecured debts must not exceed $3,237,000 for farming operations, or $1,500,000 for commercial fishing operations.

3. At least 50% of a family farmer's total debts, and 80% of a family fisherman's total debts, that are fixed in amount, excluding the debtor's homes, must be related to the farming or commercial fishing operation.

4. More than 50% of the gross income of the individual or the husband and wife for the preceding tax year—or for family farmers only, each of the 2nd and 3rd prior tax years—must have come from the farming or commercial fishing operation.

Corporation or Partnership

In order for a corporation or partnership to fall within the second category of debtors eligible to file as family farmers or family fishermen, the corporation or partnership must meet each of the following criteria as of the date of the filing of the petition:

1. More than one-half the outstanding stock or equity in the corporation or partnership must be owned by one family or by one family and its relatives.

2. The family or the family and its relatives must conduct the farming or commercial fishing operation.

3. More than 80% of the value of the corporate or partnership assets must be related to the farming or fishing operation.

4. The total indebtedness of the corporation or partnership must not exceed $3,237,000 for a farming operation, or $1,500,000 for a commercial fishing operation.

5. At least 50% of the total debts for a farming operation, or 80% of the total debts for a fishing operation, which are fixed in amount, exclusive of one home occupied by a shareholder, must be related to the farming or fishing operation.

6. If the corporation issues stock, the stock cannot be publicly traded.

CHAPTER 12 FILING FEES

Effective October 17, 2005, the following fees are paid at the bankruptcy clerk's office when the chapter 12 petition is filed:

1. filing Fee–$200.00

2. administrative Fee–$39.00

THE AUTOMATIC STAY PROVISION

When a chapter 12 petition is filed, the debtor receives an "automatic stay" that stops most collection actions against the debtor or the debtor's property. The stay is "automatic" because it does not require a court order. Depending on the situation, the stay may be short-lived, however, as long as the stay is in effect, creditors are not permitted to sue the debtor, and must discontinue any existing lawsuits, wage garnishments or other types of collection actions.

The debtor should be aware, however, that there are certain types of actions set forth in the Bankruptcy Code (11 U.S.C. § 362(b)) that are not subject to the automatic stay provision.

The automatic stay, in general, is discussed more fully in Chapter 4 of this almanac.

THE CHAPTER 12 MEETING OF CREDITORS

After the petition and schedules are filed, the bankruptcy clerk notifies all of the creditors listed on the debtor's schedule that the debtor has filed a bankruptcy petition. Shortly thereafter, the case trustee schedules a meeting of creditors. The debtor must attend this meeting and, under oath, must answer any questions asked by the trustee and the creditors pertaining to the debtor's financial affairs and the proposed terms of the debtor's repayment plan.

If there are any concerns about the repayment plan, the parties have an opportunity to discuss and resolve those problems at this meeting. Following the meeting of creditors, the debtor, the case trustee, and those creditors who wish to attend will appear in court for a hearing on the debtor's chapter 12 repayment plan.

A Notice of Chapter 12 Bankruptcy Case, Meeting of Creditors and Deadlines (Form B9G) is set forth at Appendix 34.

THE CHAPTER 12 REPAYMENT PLAN

The debtor must file a repayment plan along with their chapter 12 petition, or within 90 days after filing the petition. The repayment plan must be submitted for court approval, also known as "confirmation." The repayment plan must provide for payments of fixed amounts to the case trustee on a regular basis, e.g. monthly. The case trustee then distributes the payments to the creditors according to the terms of the plan. The repayment plan may offer creditors less than the full payment on their claims.

Classes of Claims

There are three classes of claims: (i) priority; (ii) secured; and (iii) unsecured.

Priority Claims

Priority claims are those granted special status under bankruptcy law, such as most taxes and the costs of the bankruptcy proceeding. Under the debtor's repayment plan, priority claims must be paid in full unless a particular priority creditor agrees to different treatment of their claim or, in case of a domestic support obligation, unless the debtor contributes all "disposable income" to a five-year plan.

Secured Claims

Secured claims are those for which the creditor has the right to liquidate certain property if the debtor does not pay the underlying debt. Secured creditors must be paid at least as much as the value of the collateral pledged for the debt. One of the features of Chapter 12 is that payments to secured creditors can sometimes continue longer than the three to five-year period of the plan. For example, if the debtor's underlying debt obligation was scheduled to be paid over more than five years—i.e., an equipment loan or a mortgage—the debtor may be able to pay the loan off over the original loan repayment schedule as long as any arrearage is made up during the plan.

Unsecured Claims

In contrast to secured claims, unsecured claims are generally those for which the creditor has no special rights to collect against particular property owned by the debtor. The plan does not have to pay unsecured claims in full provided that: (i) the plan commits all of the debtor's projected "disposable income" to plan payments over a 3 to 5 year period; (ii) the unsecured creditors are to receive at least as much as they would receive if the debtor's nonexempt assets were liquidated under chapter 7.

Under chapter 12, "disposable income" is defined as income not reasonably necessary for the maintenance or support of the debtor or dependents, or for making payments needed to continue, preserve, and operate the debtor's business.

THE CHAPTER 12 PLAN CONFIRMATION HEARING

The bankruptcy judge must hold a confirmation hearing within 45 days after the debtor files his or her chapter 12 plan. The purpose of the confirmation hearing is to decide whether the plan is feasible, and whether the plan meets the standards for confirmation set forth in the Bankruptcy Code.

Creditors are given 20 days' notice of the hearing during which time they may file any objections they have to plan confirmation. A common objection to plan confirmation is that creditors would receive more money if the debtor's chapter 12 case were converted to a chapter 7, case and the debtor's assets liquidated and distributed to the creditors. Another common objection is that the debtor's plan does not commit all of the debtor's disposable income for the three-to-five-year period of the plan.

If the court confirms the debtor's repayment plan, the debtor will start to make the required payments to the trustee, and the trustee will start making payments to the creditors according to the terms of the plan. If the court does not confirm the debtor's repayment plan, the debtor may submit a modified plan, or may convert the case to a chapter 7 liquidation case. If the court does not confirm the modified plan, and the chapter 12 case is dismissed, the trustee must return all of the funds they have been collecting to the debtor, less the trustee's costs and any funds that have already been disbursed.

If circumstances arise which negatively impact the debtor's ability to make the required plan payments, the plan may be modified either before or after confirmation. Modification may be sought by the debtor, case trustee, or an unsecured creditor.

BINDING EFFECT OF CONFIRMED CHAPTER 12 REPAYMENT PLAN

The provisions of a confirmed chapter 12 plan bind the debtor and each creditor. Once the court confirms the plan, the debtor must make every effort to see that the plan succeeds. The debtor must make regular payments to the trustee for distribution to the creditors. Thus, the debtor must learn to live within a fixed budget during the time the plan is in effect. In addition, the debtor is not allowed to incur any new debts without consulting the trustee so as not to negatively impact the debtor's ability to make the required payments under the plan.

If the debtor does not make the required payments under the plan, the debtor's chapter 12 case may be dismissed by the court, or converted into a liquidation case under chapter 7 of the Bankruptcy Code, as discussed in Chapter 3 of this almanac.

A sample Order Confirming Chapter 12 Plan (Form B230A) is set forth at Appendix 35.

THE BANKRUPTCY DISCHARGE UNDER CHAPTER 12

Upon completion of all of the payments under the confirmed plan, the chapter 12 debtor is entitled to a discharge provided the debtor certifies that all domestic support obligations that came due prior to making the certification have been paid.

A sample order granting a Discharge of Debtor After Completion of Chapter 12 Plan (Form B18F) is set forth at Appendix 36.

Scope of the Bankruptcy Discharge Under Chapter 12

The chapter 12 discharge releases the debtor from all debts provided for in the repayment plan, and all debts that were disallowed. Thus, creditors who have been paid, in full or in part, under the chapter 12 plan may no longer initiate or continue any legal or other action against the debtor to collect the discharged obligations.

If, however, circumstances arise after plan confirmation that prevent the debtor from completing the plan—e.g., injury or illness that prevents the debtor from working—the debtor may ask the court for a "hardship discharge." A hardship discharge may be available if:

1. the debtor's failure to complete plan payments is due to circumstances beyond the debtor's control and through no fault of the debtor;

2. the creditors have received at least as much as they would have received in a chapter 7 liquidation case; and

3. modification of the plan is not possible.

Under the law, the following debts cannot be discharged in chapter 12:

1. alimony or child support;

2. money obtained through filing false financial statements;

3. debts for willful and malicious injury to person or property;

4. debts arising from death or personal injury caused by driving while intoxicated or under the influence of drugs; and

5. debts from fraud or defalcation while acting in a fiduciary capacity, embezzlement or larceny.

If the above debts have not been fully paid under the repayment plan, the debtor will still be responsible for these debts after the bankruptcy case has ended.

The bankruptcy discharge, in general, is discussed more fully in Chapter 5 of this almanac.

CHAPTER 10:
THE SERVICEMEMBER'S CIVIL RELIEF ACT (SCRA)

IN GENERAL

The Servicemembers' Civil Relief Act ("SCRA") (50 U.S.C. app. §§ 501 et seq.) was enacted in order to strengthen and expedite national defense by giving servicemembers certain protections in civil actions. The SCRA was formerly known as the Soldiers' and Sailors' Civil Relief Act of 1940.

Under the SCRA, judicial and administrative transactions that may adversely affect a servicemember during their military service are temporarily suspended so that the servicemember can focus their energy on the defense of the United States.

The SCRA provides for forbearance and reduced interest on certain obligations incurred prior to military service, and it restricts default judgments against servicemembers, and rental evictions of servicemembers and all their dependents.

The SCRA applies to all members of the United States military on active duty, and to U.S. citizens serving in the military of United States allies in the prosecution of a war or military action. Portions of the SCRA also apply to reservists and inductees who have received orders but not yet reported to active duty or induction into the military service.

The provisions of the SCRA generally end when a servicemember is discharged from active duty or within 90 days of discharge, or when the servicemember dies.

PRIMARY AREAS OF COVERAGE

There are three primary areas of coverage under the SCRA:

1. protection against the entry of default judgments;

2. stay of proceedings where the servicemember has notice of the proceeding; and

3. stay or vacation of execution of judgments, attachments and garnishments.

The language of the SCRA states that it is generally applicable in any action or proceeding commenced in any court, therefore, it is generally held that the SCRA applies to all actions or proceedings before a bankruptcy court.

Protection Against Default Judgments

Under Section 521 of the SCRA, certain procedures must be followed in all civil proceedings in order to protect servicemember defendants against the entry of default judgments, as set forth below.

If a defendant is in default for failure to appear in the action filed by the plaintiff, the plaintiff must file an affidavit with the court before a default judgment may be entered. The affidavit must state whether the defendant is in the military, or that the plaintiff was unable to determine whether the defendant is in the military.

If, based on the filed affidavits, the court cannot determine whether the defendant is in the military, it may condition entry of judgment against the defendant upon the plaintiff's filing of a bond. The bond would indemnify the defendant against any loss or damage incurred because of the judgment if the judgment is later set aside in whole or in part.

The court may not order entry of judgment against the defendant if the defendant is in the military until after the court appoints an attorney to represent the defendant.

If requested by counsel for a servicemember defendant, or upon the court's own motion, the court will grant a stay of proceedings for no less than 90 days if it determines that: (i) there may be a defense and the defense cannot be presented without the defendant's presence; or (ii) after due diligence, the defendant's attorney has not been able to contact the defendant or otherwise determine if a meritorious defense exists.

If a judgment is entered against the defendant while he or she is in military service, or within 60 days of discharge from military service, and the defendant was prejudiced in making his or her defense because of his or her military service, the judgment may, upon application by the defendant, be opened by the court and the defendant may then provide a defense. Before the judgment may be opened, however, the defendant must show that he or she has a meritorious or legal defense to some or all of the action.

The court may, in its discretion, make further orders or enter further judgments to protect the rights of the defendant servicemember under the SCRA.

Stay of Proceedings

When a servicemember has notice of a proceeding, at any time before final judgment in a civil action, he or she may ask the court to stay the proceeding. The court may also order a stay on its own motion. The court will grant the servicemember's application—i.e., request—for a stay, and will issue a stay for at least 90 days, provided the servicemember's request includes the following:

1. a letter or other communication setting forth facts demonstrating that the individual's current military duty requirements materially affect the servicemember's ability to appear along with a date when the servicemember will be able to appear; and

2. a letter or other communication from the servicemember's commanding officer stating that the servicemember's current military duty prevents his or her appearance and that military leave is not authorized for the servicemember at the time of the letter.

The court has discretion to grant additional stays upon further application by the servicemember.

Stay or Vacation of Execution of Judgments, Attachments and Garnishments

In addition to the court's ability to regulate default judgments and stay proceedings, the court may on its own motion, and must upon application:

1. stay the execution of any judgment or order entered against a servicemember; and

2. vacate or stay any attachment or garnishment of the servicemember's property or assets, whether before or after judgment if it finds that the servicemember's ability to comply with the judgment or garnishment is materially affected by military service.

The stay of execution may be ordered for any part of the servicemember's military service plus 90 days after discharge from the service. The court may also order the servicemember to make installment payments during any stay ordered.

ADDITIONAL RIGHTS UNDER THE SCRA

Several additional rights are available under the SCRA. For example, when an action for compliance with a contract is stayed under the SCRA, contractual penalties do not accrue during the period of the stay.

The SCRA also generally provides that a landlord cannot evict a servicemember or the servicemember's dependants from a primary residence without a court order. In an eviction proceeding, the court may also adjust the lease obligations to protect the interests of the parties. If the court stays the eviction proceeding, it may provide equitable relief to the landlord by ordering garnishment of a portion of the servicemember's pay.

In addition, under the SCRA, a servicemember may terminate residential and automotive leases if he or she is transferred after the lease is made.

APPENDIX 1:
DIRECTORY OF UNITED STATES
BANKRUPTCY COURTS—MAIN OFFICES

COURTHOUSE	ADDRESS	TELEPHONE	WEBSITE
Alabama Middle Bankruptcy Court	One Church Street, Montgomery, AL 36104	334-954-3800	www.almb.uscourts.gov
Alabama Northern Bankruptcy Court	1800 Fifth Avenue North, Birmingham, AL 35203	205-714-4002	www.alnb.uscourts.gov
Alabama Southern Bankruptcy Court	201 St. Louis Street, Mobile, AL 36602	251-441-5391	www.alsb.uscourts.gov
Alaska Bankruptcy Court	605 West Fourth Avenue, Anchorage, AK 99501	907-271-2655	www.akb.uscourts.gov
Arizona Bankruptcy Court	230 North First Avenue, Phoenix, AZ 85003	602-682-4000	www.azb.uscourts.gov

COURTHOUSE	ADDRESS	TELEPHONE	WEBSITE
Arkansas Eastern, Western Bankruptcy Court	300 West Second Street, Little Rock, AR 72201	501-918-5500	www.areb.uscourts.gov
California Central Bankruptcy Court	255 East Temple Street, Los Angeles, CA 90012	213-894-3118	www.cacb.uscourts.gov
California Eastern Bankruptcy Court	501 I Street, Sacramento, CA 95814	916-930-4400	www.caeb.uscourts.gov
California Northern Bankruptcy Court	235 Pine Street, San Francisco, CA 94104	415-268-2300	www.canb.uscourts.gov
California Southern Bankruptcy Court	325 West F Street, San Diego, CA 92101	619-557-5620	www.casb.uscourts.gov
Colorado Bankruptcy Court	721 19th Street, Denver, CO 80202	303-844-4045	www.cob.uscourts.gov
Connecticut Bankruptcy Court	450 Main Street, Hartford, CT 06103	860-240-3675	www.ctb.uscourts.gov
Delaware Bankruptcy Court	824 North Market Street, Wilmington, DE 19801	302-252-2900	www.deb.uscourts.gov
District of Columbia Bankruptcy Court	333 Constitution Avenue N.W., Washington, DC 20001	202-565-2500	www.dcb.uscourts.gov
Florida Middle Bankruptcy Court	801 North Florida Avenue, Tampa, FL33602	813-301-5162	www.flmb.uscourts.gov
Florida Northern Bankruptcy Court	110 East Park Avenue, Tallahassee, FL 32301	850-521-5001	www.flnb.uscourts.gov
Florida Southern Bankruptcy Court	51 Southwest First Avenue, Miami, FL 33130	305-714-1800	www.flsb.uscourts.gov

COURTHOUSE	ADDRESS	TELEPHONE	WEBSITE
Georgia Middle Bankruptcy Court	433 Cherry Street, Macon, GA 31201	478-752-3506	www.gamb.uscourts.gov
Georgia Northern Bankruptcy Court	75 Spring Street SW, Atlanta, GA 30303	404-215-1000	www.ganb.uscourts.gov
Georgia Southern Bankruptcy Court	125 Bull Street, Savannah, GA 31402	912-650-4100	www.gasb.uscourts.gov
Hawaii Bankruptcy Court	1132 Bishop Street, Honolulu, HI 96813	808-522-8100	www.hib.uscourts.gov
Idaho Bankruptcy Court	550 West Fort Street, Boise, ID 83724	208-334-1361	www.id.uscourts.gov
Illinois Central Bankruptcy Court	600 East Monroe Street, Springfield, IL 62701	217-492-4551	www.ilcb.uscourts.gov
Illinois Northern Bankruptcy Court	219 South Dearborn Street, Chicago, IL 60604	312-435-5694	www.ilnb.uscourts.gov
Illinois Southern Bankruptcy Court	750 Missouri Avenue, East St. Louis, IL 62201	618-482-9400	www.ilsb.uscourts.gov
Indiana Northern Bankruptcy Court	401 South Michigan Street, South Bend, IN 46601	574-968-2100	www.innb.uscourts.gov
Indiana Southern Bankruptcy Court	46 East Ohio Street, Indianapolis, IN 46204	317-229-3800	www.insb.uscourts.gov
Iowa Northern Bankruptcy Court	425 Second Street Southeast, Cedar Rapids, IA 52401	319-286-2200	www.ianb.uscourts.gov
Iowa Southern Bankruptcy Court	110 East Court Avenue, Des Moines, IA 50309	515-284-6230	www.iasb.uscourts.gov

COURTHOUSE	ADDRESS	TELEPHONE	WEBSITE
Kansas Bankruptcy Court	401 North Market Street, Wichita, KS 67202	316-269-6486	www.ksb.uscourts.gov
Kentucky Eastern Bankruptcy Court	100 East Vine Street, Lexington, KY 40507	859-233-2608	www.kyeb.uscourts.gov
Kentucky Western Bankruptcy Court	601 West Broadway, Louisville, KY 40202	502-627-5800	www.kywb.uscourts.gov
Louisiana Eastern Bankruptcy Court	500 Poydras Street, New Orleans, LA 70130	504-589-7878	www.laeb.uscourts.gov
Louisiana Middle Bankruptcy Court	707 Florida Street, Baton Rouge, LA 70801	225-389-0211	www.lamb.uscourts.gov
Louisiana Western Bankruptcy Court	300 Fannin Street, Shreveport, LA 71101	318-676-4267	www.lawb.uscourts.gov
Maine Bankruptcy Court	537 Congress Street, Portland, ME 04101-3306	207-780-3482	www.meb.uscourts.gov
Maryland Bankruptcy Court	101 West Lombard Street, Baltimore, MD 21201	410-962-2688	www.mdb.uscourts.gov
Massachusetts Bankruptcy Court	10 Causeway Street, Boston, MA 02222	617-565-8950	www.mab.uscourts.gov
Michigan Eastern Bankruptcy Court	211 West Fort Street, Detroit, MI 48226	313-234-0068	www.mieb.uscourts.gov
Michigan Western Bankruptcy Court	One Division Street NW, Grand Rapids, MI 49503	616-456-2693	www.miwb.uscourts.gov
Minnesota Bankruptcy Court	300 South Fourth Street, Minneapolis, MN 55415	612-664-5200	www.mnb.uscourts.gov

COURTHOUSE	ADDRESS	TELEPHONE	WEBSITE
Mississippi Northern Bankruptcy Court	703 Highway 145 North, Aberdeen, MS 39730	662-369-2596	www.msnb.uscourts.gov
Mississippi Southern Bankruptcy Court	100 East Capitol Street, Jackson, MS 39201	601-965-5301	www.mssb.uscourts.gov
Missouri Eastern Bankruptcy Court	111 South Tenth Street, St. Louis, MO 63102	314-244-4500	www.moeb.uscourts.gov
Missouri Western Bankruptcy Court	400 East Ninth Street, Kansas City, MO 64106	816-512-5000	www.mow.uscourts.gov
Montana Bankruptcy Court	400 North Main Street, Butte, MT 59701	406-782-3354	www.mtb.uscourts.gov
Nebraska Bankruptcy Court	111 South 18th Plaza, Omaha, NE 68102	402-661-7444	www.neb.uscourts.gov
Nevada Bankruptcy Court	300 Las Vegas Boulevard South, Las Vegas, NV 89101	702-388-6257	www.nvb.uscourts.gov
New Hampshire Bankruptcy Court	1000 Elm Street, Manchester, NH 03101	603-222-2600	www.nhb.uscourts.gov
New Jersey Bankruptcy Court	50 Walnut Street, Newark, NJ 07102	973-645-4764	www.njb.uscourts.gov
New Mexico Bankruptcy Court	500 Gold Avenue SW, Albuquerque, NM 87102	505-348-2500	www.nmcourt.fed.us
New York Eastern Bankruptcy Court	271 Cadman Plaza East, Brooklyn, NY 11201	347-394-1700	www.nyeb.uscourts.gov
New York Northern Bankruptcy Court	445 Broadway, Albany, NY 12207	518-257-1661	www.nynb.uscourts.gov

COURTHOUSE	ADDRESS	TELEPHONE	WEBSITE
New York Southern Bankruptcy Court	One Bowling Green, New York, NY 10004	212-668-2870	www.nysb.uscourts.gov
New York Western Bankruptcy Court	100 State Street, Rochester, NY 14614	585-613-4200	www.nywb.uscourts.gov
North Carolina Eastern Bankruptcy Court	1760 Parkwood Boulevard West, Wilson, NC 27893	252-237-0248	www.nceb.uscourts.gov
North Carolina Middle Bankruptcy Court	101 South Edgeworth Street, Greensboro, NC 27401	336-333-5647	www.ncmb.uscourts.gov
North Carolina Western Bankruptcy Court	401 West Trade Street, Charlotte, NC 28202	704-350-7500	www.ncwb.uscourts.gov
North Dakota Bankruptcy Court	655 First Avenue North, Fargo, ND 58102	701-297-7100	www.ndb.uscourts.gov
Ohio Northern Bankruptcy Court	201 Superior Avenue, Cleveland, OH 44114	216-615-4300	www.ohnb.uscourts.gov
Ohio Southern Bankruptcy Court	120 West Third Street, Dayton, OH 45402	937-225-2516	www.ohsb.uscourts.gov
Oklahoma Eastern Bankruptcy Court	111 West Fourth Street, Okmulgee, OK 74447	918-758-0126	www.okeb.uscourts.gov
Oklahoma Northern Bankruptcy Court	224 South Boulder Avenue, Tulsa, OK 74103	918-699-4000	www.oknb.uscourts.gov
Oklahoma Western Bankruptcy Court	215 Dean A. McGee Avenue, Oklahoma City, OK 73102	405-609-5700	www.okwb.uscourts.gov
Oregon Bankruptcy Court	1001 Southwest Fifth Avenue, Portland, OR 97204	503-326-2231	www.orb.uscourts.gov

COURTHOUSE	ADDRESS	TELEPHONE	WEBSITE
Pennsylvania Eastern Bankruptcy Court	900 Market Street, Philadelphia, PA 19107	215-408-2800	www.paeb.uscourts.gov
Pennsylvania Middle Bankruptcy Court	197 South Main Street, Wilkes Barre, PA 18701	570-826-6450	www.pamb.uscourts.gov
Pennsylvania Western Bankruptcy Court	600 Grant Street, Pittsburgh, PA 15219	412-644-4060	www.pawb.uscourts.gov
Puerto Rico Bankruptcy Court	300 Calle Del Recinto Sur, San Juan, PR 00901	787-977-6000	www.prb.uscourts.gov
Rhode Island Bankruptcy Court	380 Westminster Mall, Providence, RI 02903	401-528-4477	www.rib.uscourts.gov
South Carolina Bankruptcy Court	1100 Laurel Street, Columbia, SC 29201	803-765-5436	www.scb.uscourts.gov
South Dakota Bankruptcy Court	400 South Phillips Avenue, Sioux Falls, SD 57104	605-330-4541	www.sdb.uscourts.gov
Tennessee Eastern Bankruptcy Court	31 East 11th Street, Chattanooga, TN 37402	423-752-5163	www.tneb.uscourts.gov
Tennessee Middle Bankruptcy Court	701 Broadway, Nashville, TN 37203	615-736-5590	www.tnmb.uscourts.gov
Tennessee Western Bankruptcy Court	200 Jefferson Avenue, Memphis, TN 38103	901-328-3500	www.tnwb.uscourts.gov
Texas Eastern Bankruptcy Court	110 North College Avenue, Tyler, TX 75702	903-590-3200	www.txeb.uscourts.gov
Texas Northern Bankruptcy Court	1100 Commerce Street, Dallas, TX 75242	214-753-2000	www.tnxb.uscourts.gov

COURTHOUSE	ADDRESS	TELEPHONE	WEBSITE
Texas Southern Bankruptcy Court	515 Rusk Street, Houston, TX 77002	713-250-5500	www.txsb.uscourts.gov
Texas Western Bankruptcy Court	615 East Houston Street, San Antonio, TX 78205	210-472-5187	www.txwb.uscourts.gov
Utah Bankruptcy Court	350 South Main Street, Salt Lake City, UT 84101	801-524-6687	www.utb.uscourts.gov
Vermont Bankruptcy Court	67 Merchants Row, Rutland, VT 05701	802-776-2000	www.vtb.uscourts.gov
Virginia Eastern Bankruptcy Court	1100 East Main Street, Richmond, VA 23219	804-916-2400	www.vaeb.uscourts.gov
Virginia Western Bankruptcy Court	210 Church Avenue SW, Roanoke, VA 24011	540-857-2391	www.vawb.uscourts.gov
Washington Eastern Bankruptcy Court	904 West Riverside Avenue, Spokane, WA 99201	509-353-2404	www.waeb.uscourts.gov
Washington Western Bankruptcy Court	700 Stewart Street, Seattle, WA 98101	206-370-5200	www.wawb.uscourts.gov
West Virginia Northern Bankruptcy Court	1125 Chapline Street, Wheeling, WV 26003	304-233-1655	www.wvnb.uscourts.gov
West Virginia Southern Bankruptcy Court	300 Virginia Street East, Charleston, WV 25301	304-347-3003	www.wvsb.uscourts.gov
Wisconsin Eastern Bankruptcy Court	517 East Wisconsin Avenue, Milwaukee, WI 53202	414-297-3291	www.wieb.uscourts.gov
Wisconsin Western Bankruptcy Court	120 North Henry Street, Madison, WI 53703	608-264-5178	www.wiw.uscourts.gov

COURTHOUSE	ADDRESS	TELEPHONE	WEBSITE
Wyoming Bankruptcy Court	2120 Capitol Avenue, Cheyenne, WY 82001	307-433-2200	www.wyb.uscourts.gov

Source: Administrative Office of the U.S. Courts

APPENDIX 2:
DEBTOR'S CERTIFICATION OF COMPLETION OF INSTRUCTIONAL COURSE CONCERNING FINANCIAL MANAGEMENT (FORM B23)

United States Bankruptcy Court
_____ District Of _____

In re _____,   Case No. _____
                Debtor   Chapter _____

DEBTOR'S CERTIFICATION OF COMPLETION OF INSTRUCTIONAL COURSE CONCERNING PERSONAL FINANCIAL MANAGEMENT

[Complete one of the following statements.]

☐ I/We, _____. the debtor(s) in the above-
         (Printed Name(s) of Debtor and Joint Debtor, if any)
styled case hereby certify that on _____ I/we completed an instructional
                                 (Date)
course in personal financial management provided by _____,
                                              (Name of Provider)
an approved personal financial management instruction provider. If the provider furnished a
document attesting to the completion of the personal financial management instructional
course, a copy of that document is attached.

☐ I/We, _____, the debtor(s) in the above-
styled
        (Printed Names of Debtor and Joint Debtor, if any)
case, hereby certify that no personal financial management course is required because:
[Check the appropriate box.]
☐ I am/We are incapacitated or disabled, as defined in 11 U.S.C. § 109(h);
☐ I am/We are on active military duty in a military combat zone; or
☐ I/We reside in a district in which the United States trustee (or bankruptcy administrator) has
determined that the approved instructional courses are not adequate at this time to serve the
additional individuals who would otherwise be required to complete such courses.

Signature of Debtor: _____

Date: _____

Signature of Joint Debtor: _____

Date: _____

APPENDIX 3:
DEBTOR'S VOLUNTARY PETITION
(OFFICIAL FORM 1)

(Official Form 1) (10/05)

United States Bankruptcy Court _____District of_____	Voluntary Petition

Name of Debtor (if individual, enter Last, First, Middle):	Name of Joint Debtor (Spouse) (Last, First, Middle):
All Other Names used by the Debtor in the last 8 years (include married, maiden, and trade names):	All Other Names used by the Joint Debtor in the last 8 years (include married, maiden, and trade names):
Last four digits of Soc. Sec./Complete EIN or other Tax I.D. No. (if more than one, state all):	Last four digits of Soc. Sec./Complete EIN or other Tax I.D. No. (if more than one, state all):
Street Address of Debtor (No. & Street, City, and State): ZIPCODE	Street Address of Joint Debtor (No. & Street, City, and State): ZIPCODE
County of Residence or of the Principal Place of Business:	County of Residence or of the Principal Place of Business:
Mailing Address of Debtor (if different from street address): ZIPCODE	Mailing Address of Joint Debtor (if different from street address): ZIPCODE
Location of Principal Assets of Business Debtor (if different from street address above): ZIPCODE	

Type of Debtor (Form of Organization) (Check **one** box.)	Nature of Business (Check **all** applicable boxes.)	Chapter of Bankruptcy Code Under Which the Petition is Filed (Check one box)
☐ Individual (includes Joint Debtors) ☐ Corporation (includes LLC and LLP) ☐ Partnership ☐ Other (If debtor is not one of the above entities, check this box and provide the information requested below.) State type of entity: _____	☐ Health Care Business ☐ Single Asset Real Estate as defined in 11 U.S.C. § 101 (51B) ☐ Railroad ☐ Stockbroker ☐ Commodity Broker ☐ Clearing Bank ☐ Nonprofit Organization qualified under 26 U.S.C. § 501(c)(3)	☐ Chapter 7 ☐ Chapter 11 ☐ Chapter 15 Petition for Recognition of a Foreign Main Proceeding ☐ Chapter 9 ☐ Chapter 12 ☐ Chapter 15 Petition for Recognition of a Foreign Nonmain Proceeding ☐ Chapter 13 **Nature of Debts** (Check one box) ☐ Consumer/Non-Business ☐ Business

Filing Fee (Check one box) ☐ Full Filing Fee attached ☐ Filing Fee to be paid in installments (Applicable to individuals only) Must attach signed application for the court's consideration certifying that the debtor is unable to pay fee except in installments. Rule 1006(b). See Official Form 3A. ☐ Filing Fee waiver requested (Applicable to chapter 7 individuals only). Must attach signed application for the court's consideration. See Official Form 3B.	**Chapter 11 Debtors** Check one box: ☐ Debtor is a small business debtor as defined in 11 U.S.C. § 101(51D). ☐ Debtor is not a small business debtor as defined in 11 U.S.C. § 101(51D). Check if: ☐ Debtor's aggregate noncontingent liquidated debts owed to non-insiders or affiliates are less than $2 million.

Statistical/Administrative Information   THIS SPACE IS FOR COURT USE ONLY

☐ Debtor estimates that funds will be available for distribution to unsecured creditors.
☐ Debtor estimates that, after any exempt property is excluded and administrative expenses paid, there will be no funds available for distribution to unsecured creditors.

Estimated Number of Creditors	1-49	50-99	100-199	200-999	1,000-5,000	5,001-10,000	10,001-25,000	25,001-50,000	50,001-100,000	OVER 100,000
	☐	☐	☐	☐	☐	☐	☐	☐	☐	☐

Estimated Assets	$0 to $50,000	$50,001 to $100,000	$100,001 to $500,000	$500,001 to $1 million	$1,000,001 to $10 million	$10,000,001 to $50 million	$50,000,001 to $100 million	More than $100 million
	☐	☐	☐	☐	☐	☐	☐	☐

Estimated Debts	$0 to $50,000	$50,001 to $100,000	$100,001 to $500,000	$500,001 to $1 million	$1,000,001 to $10 million	$10,000,001 to $50 million	$50,000,001 to $100 million	More than $100 million
	☐	☐	☐	☐	☐	☐	☐	☐

DEBTOR'S VOLUNTARY PETITION

(Official Form 1) (10/05)

FORM B1, Page 2

Voluntary Petition *(This page must be completed and filed in every case)*	Name of Debtor(s):	
Prior Bankruptcy Case Filed Within Last 8 Years (If more than one, attach additional sheet)		
Location Where Filed:	Case Number:	Date Filed:
Pending Bankruptcy Case Filed by any Spouse, Partner or Affiliate of this Debtor (If more than one, attach additional sheet)		
Name of Debtor:	Case Number:	Date Filed:
District:	Relationship:	Judge:

Exhibit A	**Exhibit B**
(To be completed if debtor is required to file periodic reports (e.g., forms 10K and 10Q) with the Securities and Exchange Commission pursuant to Section 13 or 15(d) of the Securities Exchange Act of 1934 and is requesting relief under chapter 11.)	(To be completed if debtor is an individual whose debts are primarily consumer debts.) I, the attorney for the petitioner named in the foregoing petition, declare that I have informed the petitioner that [he or she] may proceed under chapter 7, 11, 12, or 13 of title 11, United States Code, and have explained the relief available under each such chapter. I further certify that I delivered to the debtor the notice required by § 342(b) of the Bankruptcy Code.
☐ Exhibit A is attached and made a part of this petition.	X _____ Signature of Attorney for Debtor(s) Date
Exhibit C	**Certification Concerning Debt Counseling by Individual/Joint Debtor(s)**
Does the debtor own or have possession of any property that poses or is alleged to pose a threat of imminent and identifiable harm to public health or safety? ☐ Yes, and Exhibit C is attached and made a part of this petition. ☐ No	☐ I/we have received approved budget and credit counseling during the 180-day period preceding the filing of this petition. ☐ I/we request a waiver of the requirement to obtain budget and credit counseling prior to filing based on exigent circumstances. (Must attach certification describing.)

Information Regarding the Debtor (Check the Applicable Boxes)

Venue (Check any applicable box)

☐ Debtor has been domiciled or has had a residence, principal place of business, or principal assets in this District for 180 days immediately preceding the date of this petition or for a longer part of such 180 days than in any other District.

☐ There is a bankruptcy case concerning debtor's affiliate, general partner, or partnership pending in this District.

☐ Debtor is a debtor in a foreign proceeding and has its principal place of business or principal assets in the United States in this District, or has no principal place of business or assets in the United States but is a defendant in an action or proceeding [in a federal or state court] in this District, or the interests of the parties will be served in regard to the relief sought in this District.

Statement by a Debtor Who Resides as a Tenant of Residential Property
Check all applicable boxes.

☐ Landlord has a judgment against the debtor for possession of debtor's residence. (If box checked, complete the following.)

_____
(Name of landlord that obtained judgment)

_____
(Address of landlord)

☐ Debtor claims that under applicable nonbankruptcy law, there are circumstances under which the debtor would be permitted to cure the entire monetary default that gave rise to the judgment for possession, after the judgment for possession was entered, and

☐ Debtor has included in this petition the deposit with the court of any rent that would become due during the 30-day period after the filing of the petition.

(Official Form 1) (10/05)	FORM B1, Page 3
Voluntary Petition *(This page must be completed and filed in every case)*	Name of Debtor(s):

Signatures

Signature(s) of Debtor(s) (Individual/Joint)	**Signature of a Foreign Representative**
I declare under penalty of perjury that the information provided in this petition is true and correct. [If petitioner is an individual whose debts are primarily consumer debts and has chosen to file under chapter 7] I am aware that I may proceed under chapter 7, 11, 12 or 13 of title 11, United States Code, understand the relief available under each such chapter, and choose to proceed under chapter 7. [If no attorney represents me and no bankruptcy petition preparer signs the petition] I have obtained and read the notice required by § 342(b) of the Bankruptcy Code. I request relief in accordance with the chapter of title 11, United States Code, specified in this petition.	I declare under penalty of perjury that the information provided in this petition is true and correct, that I am the foreign representative of a debtor in a foreign proceeding, and that I am authorized to file this petition. (Check only one box.) ☐ I request relief in accordance with chapter 15 of title 11, United States Code. Certified copies of the documents required by § 1515 of title 11 are attached. ☐ Pursuant to § 1511 of title 11, United States Code, I request relief in accordance with the chapter of title 11 specified in this petition. A certified copy of the order granting recognition of the foreign main proceeding is attached.
X_____ Signature of Debtor X_____ Signature of Joint Debtor _____ Telephone Number (If not represented by attorney) _____ Date	X_____ (Signature of Foreign Representative) _____ (Printed Name of Foreign Representative) _____ Date
Signature of Attorney	**Signature of Non-Attorney Bankruptcy Petition Preparer**
X_____ Signature of Attorney for Debtor(s) _____ Printed Name of Attorney for Debtor(s) _____ Firm Name _____ Address _____ Telephone Number _____ Date	I declare under penalty of perjury that: (1) I am a bankruptcy petition preparer as defined in 11 U.S.C. § 110; (2) I prepared this document for compensation and have provided the debtor with a copy of this document and the notices and information required under 11 U.S.C. §§ 110(b), 110(h), and 342(b); and, (3) if rules or guidelines have been promulgated pursuant to 11 U.S.C. § 110(h) setting a maximum fee for services chargeable by bankruptcy petition preparers, I have given the debtor notice of the maximum amount before preparing any document for filing for a debtor or accepting any fee from the debtor, as required in that section. Official Form 19B is attached. _____ Printed Name and title, if any, of Bankruptcy Petition Preparer _____ Social Security number (If the bankrutpcy petition preparer is not an individual, state the Social Security number of the officer, principal, responsible person or partner of the bankruptcy petition preparer.)(Required by 11 U.S.C. § 110.)
Signature of Debtor (Corporation/Partnership) I declare under penalty of perjury that the information provided in this petition is true and correct, and that I have been authorized to file this petition on behalf of the debtor. The debtor requests relief in accordance with the chapter of title 11, United States Code, specified in this petition. X_____ Signature of Authorized Individual _____ Printed Name of Authorized Individual _____ Title of Authorized Individual _____ Date	Address X_____ _____ Date Signature of Bankruptcy Petition Preparer or officer, principal, responsible person, or partner whose social security number is provided above. Names and Social Security numbers of all other individuals who prepared or assisted in preparing this document unless the bankruptcy petition preparer is not an individual: If more than one person prepared this document, attach additional sheets conforming to the appropriate official form for each person. *A bankruptcy petition preparer's failure to comply with the provisions of title 11 and the Federal Rules of Bankruptcy Procedure may result in fines or imprisonment or both 11 U.S.C. §110; 18 U.S.C. §156.*

APPENDIX 4:
SCHEDULE A—DEBTOR'S REAL
PROPERTY (FORM B6A)

Form B6A
(10/05)

In re _____,   Case No. _____
         Debtor   (If known)

SCHEDULE A - REAL PROPERTY

Except as directed below, list all real property in which the debtor has any legal, equitable, or future interest, including all property owned as a co-tenant, community property, or in which the debtor has a life estate. Include any property in which the debtor holds rights and powers exercisable for the debtor's own benefit. If the debtor is married, state whether husband, wife, or both own the property by placing an "H," "W," "J," or "C" in the column labeled "Husband, Wife, Joint, or Community." If the debtor holds no interest in real property, write "None" under "Description and Location of Property."

Do not include interests in executory contracts and unexpired leases on this schedule. List them in Schedule G - Executory Contracts and Unexpired Leases.

If an entity claims to have a lien or hold a secured interest in any property, state the amount of the secured claim. See Schedule D. If no entity claims to hold a secured interest in the property, write "None" in the column labeled "Amount of Secured Claim."

If the debtor is an individual or if a joint petition is filed, state the amount of any exemption claimed in the property only in Schedule C - Property Claimed as Exempt.

DESCRIPTION AND LOCATION OF PROPERTY	NATURE OF DEBTOR'S INTEREST IN PROPERTY	HUSBAND, WIFE, JOINT, OR COMMUNITY	CURRENT VALUE OF DEBTOR'S INTEREST IN PROPERTY, WITHOUT DEDUCTING ANY SECURED CLAIM OR EXEMPTION	AMOUNT OF SECURED CLAIM
		Total ▶		

(Report also on Summary of Schedules.)

APPENDIX 5:
SCHEDULE B—DEBTOR'S PERSONAL PROPERTY (FORM B6B)

Form B6B
(10/05)

In re _____ ,   Case No. _____
         Debtor   (If known)

SCHEDULE B - PERSONAL PROPERTY

Except as directed below, list all personal property of the debtor of whatever kind. If the debtor has no property in one or more of the categories, place an "x" in the appropriate position in the column labeled "None." If additional space is needed in any category, attach a separate sheet properly identified with the case name, case number, and the number of the category. If the debtor is married, state whether husband, wife, or both own the property by placing an "H," "W," "J," or "C" in the column labeled "Husband, Wife, Joint, or Community." If the debtor is an individual or a joint petition is filed, state the amount of any exemptions claimed only in Schedule C - Property Claimed as Exempt.

Do not list interests in executory contracts and unexpired leases on this schedule. List them in Schedule G - Executory Contracts and Unexpired Leases.

If the property is being held for the debtor by someone else, state that person's name and address under "Description and Location of Property." In providing the information requested in this schedule, do not include the name or address of a minor child. Simply state "a minor child."

TYPE OF PROPERTY	N O N E	DESCRIPTION AND LOCATION OF PROPERTY	HUSBAND, WIFE, JOINT, OR COMMUNITY	CURRENT VALUE OF DEBTOR'S INTEREST IN PROPERTY, WITH-OUT DEDUCTING ANY SECURED CLAIM OR EXEMPTION
1. Cash on hand.				
2. Checking, savings or other financial accounts, certificates of deposit, or shares in banks, savings and loan, thrift, building and loan, and homestead associations, or credit unions, brokerage houses, or cooperatives.				
3. Security deposits with public utilities, telephone companies, landlords, and others.				
4. Household goods and furnishings, including audio, video, and computer equipment.				
5. Books; pictures and other art objects; antiques; stamp, coin, record, tape, compact disc, and other collections or collectibles.				
6. Wearing apparel.				
7. Furs and jewelry.				
8. Firearms and sports, photographic, and other hobby equipment.				
9. Interests in insurance policies. Name insurance company of each policy and itemize surrender or refund value of each.				
10. Annuities. Itemize and name each issuer.				
11. Interests in an education IRA as defined in 26 U.S.C. § 530(b)(1) or under a qualified State tuition plan as defined in 26 U.S.C. § 529(b)(1). Give particulars. (File separately the record(s) of any such interest(s). 11 U.S.C. § 521(c); Rule 1007(b)).				

Form B6B-Cont.
(10/05)

In re _____ ,   Case No. _____
                Debtor   (If known)

SCHEDULE B - PERSONAL PROPERTY
(Continuation Sheet)

TYPE OF PROPERTY	N O N E	DESCRIPTION AND LOCATION OF PROPERTY	HUSBAND, WIFE, JOINT, OR COMMUNITY	CURRENT VALUE OF DEBTOR'S INTEREST IN PROPERTY, WITH-OUT DEDUCTING ANY SECURED CLAIM OR EXEMPTION
12. Interests in IRA, ERISA, Keogh, or other pension or profit sharing plans. Give particulars.				
13. Stock and interests in incorporated and unincorporated businesses. Itemize.				
14. Interests in partnerships or joint ventures. Itemize.				
15. Government and corporate bonds and other negotiable and non-negotiable instruments.				
16. Accounts receivable.				
17. Alimony, maintenance, support, and property settlements to which the debtor is or may be entitled. Give particulars.				
18. Other liquidated debts owed to debtor including tax refunds. Give particulars.				
19. Equitable or future interests, life estates, and rights or powers exercisable for the benefit of the debtor other than those listed in Schedule A – Real Property.				
20. Contingent and noncontingent interests in estate of a decedent, death benefit plan, life insurance policy, or trust.				
21. Other contingent and unliquidated claims of every nature, including tax refunds, counterclaims of the debtor, and rights to setoff claims. Give estimated value of each.				

Form B6B-cont.
(10/05)

In re _____, Case No. _____
                    Debtor   (If known)

SCHEDULE B -PERSONAL PROPERTY
(Continuation Sheet)

TYPE OF PROPERTY	N O N E	DESCRIPTION AND LOCATION OF PROPERTY	HUSBAND, WIFE, JOINT, OR COMMUNITY	CURRENT VALUE OF DEBTOR'S INTEREST IN PROPERTY, WITH-OUT DEDUCTING ANY SECURED CLAIM OR EXEMPTION
22. Patents, copyrights, and other intellectual property. Give particulars.				
23. Licenses, franchises, and other general intangibles. Give particulars.				
24. Customer lists or other compilations containing personally identifiable information (as defined in 11 U.S.C. § 101(41A)) provided to the debtor by individuals in connection with obtaining a product or service from the debtor primarily for personal, family, or household purposes.				
25. Automobiles, trucks, trailers, and other vehicles and accessories.				
26. Boats, motors, and accessories.				
27. Aircraft and accessories.				
28. Office equipment, furnishings, and supplies.				
29. Machinery, fixtures, equipment, and supplies used in business.				
30. Inventory.				
31. Animals.				
32. Crops - growing or harvested. Give particulars.				
33. Farming equipment and implements.				
34. Farm supplies, chemicals, and feed.				
35. Other personal property of any kind not already listed. Itemize.				

_____continuation sheets attached   Total▶ $ _____

(Include amounts from any continuation
sheets attached. Report total also on
Summary of Schedules.)

Individual Bankruptcy and Restructuring   **97**

APPENDIX 6:
SCHEDULE C—PROPERTY CLAIMED AS EXEMPT (FORM B6C)

Form B6C
(10/05)

In re _____,   Case No. _____
         Debtor   **(If known)**

SCHEDULE C - PROPERTY CLAIMED AS EXEMPT

Debtor claims the exemptions to which debtor is entitled under: ☐ Check if debtor claims a homestead exemption that exceeds
(Check one box) $125,000.
☐ 11 U.S.C. § 522(b)(2)
☐ 11 U.S.C. § 522(b)(3)

DESCRIPTION OF PROPERTY	SPECIFY LAW PROVIDING EACH EXEMPTION	VALUE OF CLAIMED EXEMPTION	CURRENT VALUE OF PROPERTY WITHOUT DEDUCTING EXEMPTION

APPENDIX 7:
FEDERAL EXEMPTIONS UNDER § 522(D)
OF THE BANKRUPTCY CODE

1. Debtor's aggregate interest, not to exceed $18,450 in value, in real property or personal property that the debtor, or a dependent of the debtor, uses as a residence, in a cooperative that owns property that the debtor or a dependent of the debtor uses as a residence, or in a burial plot for the debtor or a dependent of the debtor.

2. The debtor's interest, not to exceed $2,950 in value, in one motor vehicle.

3. The debtor's interest, not to exceed $425 in value in any particular item or $9,850 in aggregate value, in household furnishings, household goods, wearing apparel, appliances, books, animals, crops, or musical instruments, that are held primarily for the personal, family, or household use of the debtor or a dependent of the debtor.

4. The debtor's aggregate interest, not to exceed $1,225 in value, in jewelry held primarily for the personal, family, or household use of the debtor or a dependent of the debtor.

5. The debtor's aggregate interest in any property, not to exceed in value $975 plus up to $9,250 of any unused amount of the exemption provided under paragraph (1) of this subsection.

6. The debtor's aggregate interest, not to exceed $1,850 in value, in any implements, professional books, or tools, of the trade of the debtor or the trade of a dependent of the debtor.

7. Any unmatured life insurance contract owned by the debtor, other than a credit life insurance contract.

8. The debtor's aggregate interest, not to exceed in value $9,850 less any amount of property of the estate transferred in the manner specified in section 542(d) of this title, in any accrued dividend or interest under, or loan value of, any un-matured life insurance contract owned by the debtor

under which the insured is the debtor or an individual of whom the debtor is a dependent.

9. Professionally prescribed health aids for the debtor or a dependent of the debtor.

10. The debtor's right to receive:

(a) A social security benefit, unemployment compensation, or a local public assistance benefit;

(b) A veterans' benefit;

(c) A disability, illness, or unemployment benefit;

(d) Alimony, support, or separate maintenance, to the extent reasonably necessary for the support of the debtor and any dependent of the debtor;

(e) A payment under a stock bonus, pension, profit-sharing, annuity, or similar plan or contract on account of illness, disability, death, age, or length of service, to the extent reasonably necessary for the support of the debtor and any dependent of the debtor, unless: (i) such plan or contract was established by or under the auspices of an insider that employed the debtor at the time the debtor's rights under such plan or contract arose; (ii) such payment is on account of age or length of service; and (iii) such plan or contract does not qualify under section 401(a), 403(a), 403(b), 408, or 409 of the Internal Revenue Code of 1986 (26 U.S.C. 401(a), 403(a), 403(b), 408, or 409).

11. The debtor's right to receive, or property that is traceable to:

(a) An award under a crime victim's reparation law;

(b) A payment on account of the wrongful death of an individual of whom the debtor was a dependent, to the extent reasonably necessary for the support of the debtor and any dependent of the debtor;

(c) A payment under a life insurance contract that insured the life of an individual of whom the debtor was a dependent on the date of such individual's death, to the extent reasonably necessary for the support of the debtor and any dependent of the debtor;

(d) A payment, not to exceed $18,450, on account of personal bodily injury, not including pain and suffering or compensation for actual pecuniary loss, of the debtor or an individual of whom the debtor is a dependent; or

(e) A payment in compensation of loss of future earnings of the debtor or an individual of whom the debtor is or was a dependent, to the extent reasonably necessary for the support of the debtor and any dependent of the debtor.

APPENDIX 8:
TABLE OF STATE STATUTES GOVERNING BANKRUPTCY EXEMPTIONS

STATE	STATUTE
Alabama	Alabama Code § 6-10-2 (homestead); § 6-10-5 (burial place); § 6-10-6 (personal property)
Alaska	Alaska Statutes § 09.38.010 (homestead); § 09.38.017 (retirement benefits); §§ 09.38.015 et. seq. (personal property)
Arizona	Arizona Revised Statutes Annotated § 33-101 (homestead); §§ 33-1121 et. seq. (personal property)
Arkansas	Arkansas Statutes Annotated §§ 16-66-210 and 16-66-218b (homestead); § 16-22-218a (property); § 16-66-218b (personal property)
California	California Civil Code § 704.730 (homestead); §§ 704.010 et. seq. (personal property)
Colorado	Colorado Revised Statutes §§ 38-41-201 et. seq. (homestead); § 13-54-102 (personal property)
Connecticut	Connecticut General Statutes Annotated § 52-352b (personal property)
Delaware	Delaware Code Annotated Title 10 §§ 4902 et. seq. (personal property)
District of Columbia	D.C. Code Annotated § 15-501 (personal property)
Florida	Florida Const. Art. X § 4 (homestead/personal property); Florida Statutes §§ 222.11 et. seq. (miscellaneous)
Georgia	Georgia Code Annotated §§ 44-13-1 et. seq. (real/personal property); § 44-13-100 (another option)
Hawaii	Hawaii Revised Statutes § 651-92 (homestead); § 651-121 (personal property)
Idaho	Idaho Code §§ 55-1001 et. seq. (homestead); §§ 11-603 et. seq. (personal property)

STATE	STATUTE
Illinois	Illinois Annotated Statutes Chapter 110 §§ 12-901 et. seq. (homestead); §§ 12-1001 et. seq. (personal property)
Indiana	Indiana Code Annotated § 34-2-28-1 (real/personal property)
Iowa	Iowa Code Annotated §§ 561.1 et. seq. (homestead); §§ 627.1 et. seq. (personal property)
Kansas	Kansas Constitution Art. 15 § 9 and Kansas Statutes Annotated §§ 60-2301 et. seq. (homestead); § 60-2304 (personal property)
Kentucky	Kentucky Revised Statutes Annotated §§ 427.060 et. seq. (homestead); §§ 4287.010 et. seq. (personal property)
Louisiana	Louisiana Revised Statutes Annotated § 20:1 (homestead); § 13:3881 (personal property)
Maine	Maine Revised Statutes Annotated Title 14 § 4422 (homestead/personal property)
Maryland	Annotated Code of Maryland § 11-504 (personal property)
Massachusetts	Massachusetts General Laws Annotated; Chapter 188 §§ 1 et. seq. (homestead); Chapter 235 § 34 (personal property)
Michigan	Michigan Constitution Article X § 3 and Michigan Compiled Laws Annotated § 27A.6023(h) (homestead); § 600.6023 (personal property)
Minnesota	Minnesota Statutes Annotated §§ 510.01 et. seq. (homestead); § 550.37 (personal property)
Mississippi	Mississippi Code Annotated §§ 85-3-21 et. seq. (homestead); § 85-3-1 (other property)
Missouri	Missouri Annotated Statutes §§ 513.475 et seq. (homestead); §§ 513.430 et. seq. (personal property)
Montana	Montana Code Annotated §§ 70-32-101 et. seq. (homestead); §§ 25-13-608 et. seq. (personal property)
Nebraska	Nebraska Revised Statutes §§ 40-101 et. seq. (homestead); §§ 25-1552 et. seq. (personal property)
Nevada	Nevada Constitution Art. 4 § 30 and Nevada Revised Statutes Annotated §§ 115.005 et. seq. (homestead); Nevada Constitution Art. 1 § 14 and Nevada Revised Statutes Annotated §§ 21.090 et. seq. (personal property)
New Hampshire	New Hampshire Revised Statutes Annotated § 480:1 (homestead); § 511:2 (personal property)
New Jersey	New Jersey Statutes Annotated § 2A:17-19 (personal property)

STATE	STATUTE
New Mexico	New Mexico Statutes Annotated § 42-10-9 (homestead); §§ 42-10-1 et. seq. (personal property)
New York	New York Civil Practice Law and Rules § 5206 (homestead); § 5205 (personal property); Debtor and Creditor Law § 282 et. seq. (bankruptcy exemptions)
North Carolina	North Carolina Constitution Art. X § 2 and North Carolina General Statutes §§ 1C-1601 et. seq. (homestead); North Carolina Constitution Art. X § 1 and North Carolina General Statutes § 1C-1601 (personal property)
North Dakota	North Dakota Cent. Code §§ 47-18-01 et. seq. (homestead); §§ 28-22-02 et. seq. (personal property)
Ohio	Ohio Revised Code Annotated § 2329.66 (homestead/personal property)
Oklahoma	Oklahoma Statutes Annotated Title 31 § 2 (homestead); Title 31 § 1 (other property)
Oregon	Oregon Revised Statutes §§ 23.240 et. seq. (homestead); § 23.160 (personal property)
Pennsylvania	23 Pennsylvania Cons. Statutes Annotated 42 § 8124 (personal property); 42 § 8123 (general monetary)
Rhode Island	Rhode Island General Laws § 9-26-4 (personal property)
South Carolina	South Carolina Code Annotated § 15-41-30(1) (homestead); § 15-42-30 (personal property)
South Dakota	South Dakota Codified Laws Annotated § 43-45-3 and §§ 43-31-1 et. seq. (homestead); §§ 43-45-1 et. seq. (personal property)
Tennessee	Tennessee State Constitution Art. XI § 11 and Tennessee Code Annotated §§ 26-2-301 et. seq. (homestead); §§ 26-2-102 et. seq. (personal property)
Texas	Texas Codes Annotated §§ 41.001 et. seq. (homestead); §§ 2.001 et. seq. (personal property)
Utah	Utah Constitution Art. XXII § 1 and Utah Code Annotated §§ 78-23-3 et. seq. (homestead); §§ 78-23-5 et. seq. (personal property)
Vermont	Vermont Statutes Annotated Title 27 §§ 101 et. seq. (homestead); Title 27 § 2740 (personal property)
Virginia	Virginia Code Annotated §§ 34-4 et. seq. (homestead); § 34-26 (personal property)
Washington	Washington Revised Code Annotated §§ 6.13.010 et. seq. (homestead); § 6.15.010 (personal property)
West Virginia	West Virginia Code §§ 38-9-1 et. seq. (homestead); §§ 38-8-1 et. seq. (personal property); 38-10-4 (bankruptcy exemptions)

STATE	STATUTE
Wisconsin	Wisconsin Statutes Annotated § 815.20 and § 990.01(14) (homestead); § 815.18 (personal property)
Wyoming	Wyoming Constitution Art. 19 § 9 and Wyoming Statutes Annotated §§ 1-20-101 et. seq. (homestead); §§ 1-20-105 et. seq. (personal property)

APPENDIX 9:
SCHEDULE D—CREDITOR'S HOLDING SECURED CLAIMS (FORM B6D)

Form B6D

(10/05)   In re _____,   Case No. _____
                Debtor   (If known)

SCHEDULE D – CREDITORS HOLDING SECURED CLAIMS

State the name, mailing address, including zip code, and last four digits of any account number of all entities holding claims secured by property of the debtor as of the date of filing of the petition. The complete account number of any account the debtor has with the creditor is useful to the trustee and the creditor and may be provided if the debtor chooses to do so. List creditors holding all types of secured interests such as judgment liens, garnishments, statutory liens, mortgages, deeds of trust, and other security interests.

List creditors in alphabetical order to the extent practicable. If a minor child is a creditor, indicate that by stating "a minor child and do not disclose the child's name. See 11 U.S.C. § 112; Fed. R. Bankr. P. 1007(m). If all secured creditors will not fit on this page, use the continuation sheet provided.

If any entity other than a spouse in a joint case may be jointly liable on a claim, place an "X" in the column labeled "Codebtor, include the entity on the appropriate schedule of creditors, and complete Schedule H – Codebtors. If a joint petition is filed, state whether husband, wife, both of them, or the marital community may be liable on each claim by placing an "H, "W, "J, or "C" in the column labeled "Husband, Wife, Joint, or Community.

If the claim is contingent, place an "X" in the column labeled "Contingent. If the claim is unliquidated, place an "X" in the column labeled "Unliquidated. If the claim is disputed, place an "X" in the column labeled "Disputed. (You may need to place an "X" in more than one of these three columns.)

Report the total of all claims listed on this schedule in the box labeled "Total" on the last sheet of the completed schedule. Report this total also on the Summary of Schedules.

☐   Check this box if debtor has no creditors holding secured claims to report on this Schedule D.

CREDITOR'S NAME AND MAILING ADDRESS INCLUDING ZIP CODE AND AN ACCOUNT NUMBER (See Instructions Above)	CODEBTOR	HUSBAND, WIFE, JOINT, OR COMMUNITY	DATE CLAIM WAS INCURRED, NATURE OF LIEN, AND DESCRIPTION AND VALUE OF PROPERTY SUBJECT TO LIEN	CONTINGENT	UNLIQUIDATED	DISPUTED	AMOUNT OF CLAIM WITHOUT DEDUCTING VALUE OF COLLATERAL	UNSECURED PORTION, IF ANY
ACCOUNT NO.								
			VALUE $					
ACCOUNT NO.								
			VALUE $					
ACCOUNT NO.								
			VALUE $					
ACCOUNT NO.								
			VALUE $					
____ continuation sheets attached			Subtotal ▶ (Total of this page)				$	
			Total ▶ (Use only on last page)				$	

(Report total also on Summary of Schedules)

Form B6D – Cont.
(10/05)

In re _____ , Case No. _____
            Debtor   (If known)

SCHEDULE D – CREDITORS HOLDING SECURED CLAIMS
(Continuation Sheet)

CREDITOR'S NAME AND MAILING ADDRESS INCLUDING ZIP CODE AND AN ACCOUNT NUMBER (See Instructions Above)	CODEBTOR	HUSBAND, WIFE, JOINT, OR COMMUNITY	DATE CLAIM WAS INCURRED, NATURE OF LIEN , AND DESCRIPTION AND VALUE OF PROPERTY SUBJECT TO LIEN	CONTINGENT	UNLIQUIDATED	DISPUTED	AMOUNT OF CLAIM WITHOUT DEDUCTING VALUE OF COLLATERAL	UNSECURED PORTION, IF ANY
ACCOUNT NO.								
			VALUE $					
ACCOUNT NO.								
			VALUE $					
ACCOUNT NO.								
			VALUE $					
ACCOUNT NO.								
			VALUE $					
ACCOUNT NO.								
			VALUE $					

Sheet no.___ of ___ continuation sheets attached to Schedule of Creditors Holding Secured Claims

Subtotal ▶ (Total of this page) $ _____

Total ▶ (Use only on last page) $ _____

APPENDIX 10:
SCHEDULE E—CREDITORS HOLDING UNSECURED PRIORITY CLAIMS (FORM B6E)

In re _____,   Case No._____
              Debtor   (if known)

SCHEDULE E - CREDITORS HOLDING UNSECURED PRIORITY CLAIMS

A complete list of claims entitled to priority, listed separately by type of priority, is to be set forth on the sheets provided. Only holders of unsecured claims entitled to priority should be listed in this schedule. In the boxes provided on the attached sheets, state the name, mailing address, including zip code, and last four digits of the account number, if any, of all entities holding priority claims against the debtor or the property of the debtor, as of the date of the filing of the petition. Use a separate continuation sheet for each type of priority and label each with the type of priority.

The complete account number of any account the debtor has with the creditor is useful to the trustee and the creditor and may be provided if the debtor chooses to do so. If a minor child is a creditor, indicate that by stating "a minor child" and do not disclose the child's name. See 11 U.S.C. § 112; Fed.R.Bankr.P. 1007(m).

If any entity other than a spouse in a joint case may be jointly liable on a claim, place an "X" in the column labeled "Codebtor," include the entity on the appropriate schedule of creditors, and complete Schedule H-Codebtors. If a joint petition is filed, state whether husband, wife, both of them or the marital community may be liable on each claim by placing an "H," "W," "J," or "C" in the column labeled "Husband, Wife, Joint, or Community." If the claim is contingent, place an "X" in the column labeled "Contingent." If the claim is unliquidated, place an "X" in the column labeled "Unliquidated." If the claim is disputed, place an "X" in the column labeled "Disputed." (You may need to place an "X" in more than one of these three columns.)

Report the total of claims listed on each sheet in the box labeled "Subtotal" on each sheet. Report the total of all claims listed on this Schedule E in the box labeled "Total" on the last sheet of the completed schedule. Report this total also on the Summary of Schedules.

Report the total of amounts entitled to priority listed on each sheet in the box labeled "Subtotal" on each sheet. Report the total of all amounts entitled to priority listed on this Schedule E in the box labeled "Total" on the last sheet of the completed schedule. If applicable, also report this total on the Means Test form.

☐ Check this box if debtor has no creditors holding unsecured priority claims to report on this Schedule E.

TYPES OF PRIORITY CLAIMS (Check the appropriate box(es) below if claims in that category are listed on the attached sheets)

☐ **Domestic Support Obligations**

Claims for domestic support that are owed to or recoverable by a spouse, former spouse, or child of the debtor, or the parent, legal guardian, or responsible relative of such a child, or a governmental unit to whom such a domestic support claim has been assigned to the extent provided in 11 U.S.C. § 507(a)(1).

☐ **Extensions of credit in an involuntary case**

Claims arising in the ordinary course of the debtor's business or financial affairs after the commencement of the case but before the earlier of the appointment of a trustee or the order for relief. 11 U.S.C. § 507(a)(3).

☐ **Wages, salaries, and commissions**

Wages, salaries, and commissions, including vacation, severance, and sick leave pay owing to employees and commissions owing to qualifying independent sales representatives up to $10,000* per person earned within 180 days immediately preceding the filing of the original petition, or the cessation of business, whichever occurred first, to the extent provided in 11 U.S.C. § 507(a)(4).

☐ **Contributions to employee benefit plans**

Money owed to employee benefit plans for services rendered within 180 days immediately preceding the filing of the original petition, or the cessation of business, whichever occurred first, to the extent provided in 11 U.S.C. § 507(a)(5).

SCHEDULE E—CREDITORS HOLDING UNSECURED PRIORITY CLAIMS

Form B6E Contd.
(10/05)

In re _____ , Case No._____
   Debtor   (if known)

☐ **Certain farmers and fishermen**

   Claims of certain farmers and fishermen, up to $4,925* per farmer or fisherman, against the debtor, as provided in 11 U.S.C. § 507(a)(6).

☐ **Deposits by individuals**

   Claims of individuals up to $2,225* for deposits for the purchase, lease, or rental of property or services for personal, family, or household use, that were not delivered or provided. 11 U.S.C. § 507(a)(7).

☐ **Taxes and Certain Other Debts Owed to Governmental Units**

   Taxes, customs duties, and penalties owing to federal, state, and local governmental units as set forth in 11 U.S.C. § 507(a)(8).

☐ **Commitments to Maintain the Capital of an Insured Depository Institution**

   Claims based on commitments to the FDIC, RTC, Director of the Office of Thrift Supervision, Comptroller of the Currency, or Board of Governors of the Federal Reserve System, or their predecessors or successors, to maintain the capital of an insured depository institution. 11 U.S.C. § 507 (a)(9).

☐ **Claims for Death or Personal Injury While Debtor Was Intoxicated**

   Claims for death or personal injury resulting from the operation of a motor vehicle or vessel while the debtor was intoxicated from using alcohol, a drug, or another substance. 11 U.S.C. § 507(a)(10).

* Amounts are subject to adjustment on April 1, 2007, and every three years thereafter with respect to cases commenced on or after the date of adjustment.

____ continuation sheets attached

Form B6E - Cont.
(10/05)

In re _____,   Case No. _____
          Debtor   (If known)

SCHEDULE E - CREDITORS HOLDING UNSECURED PRIORITY CLAIMS
(Continuation Sheet)

TYPE OF PRIORITY

CREDITOR'S NAME, MAILING ADDRESS INCLUDING ZIP CODE, AND ACCOUNT NUMBER (See instructions.)	CODEBTOR	HUSBAND, WIFE, JOINT, OR COMMUNITY	DATE CLAIM WAS INCURRED AND CONSIDERATION FOR CLAIM	CONTINGENT	UNLIQUIDATED	DISPUTED	AMOUNT OF CLAIM	AMOUNT ENTITLED TO PRIORITY
Account No.								
Account No.								
Account No.								
Account No.								
Account No.								

Sheet no. ___ of ___ sheets attached to Schedule of Creditors Holding Priority Claims

Subtotal ▶ (Total of this page) $ _____ $ _____

Total ▶ (Use only on last page of the completed Schedule E.) (Report total also on Summary of Schedules) $ _____ $ _____

APPENDIX 11:
CREDITORS HOLDING UNSECURED NONPRIORITY CLAIMS (FORM B6F)

Form B6F (10/05)

In re _____, Case No. _____

              Debtor   **(If known)**

SCHEDULE F- CREDITORS HOLDING UNSECURED NONPRIORITY CLAIMS

State the name, mailing address, including zip code, and last four digits of any account number, of all entities holding unsecured claims without priority against the debtor or the property of the debtor, as of the date of filing of the petition. The complete account number of any account the debtor has with the creditor is useful to the trustee and the creditor and may be provided if the debtor chooses to do so. If a minor child is a creditor, indicate that by stating "a minor child" and do not disclose the child's name. See 11 U.S.C. § 112; Fed.R.Bankr.P. 1007(m). Do not include claims listed in Schedules D and E. If all creditors will not fit on this page, use the continuation sheet provided.

If any entity other than a spouse in a joint case may be jointly liable on a claim, place an "X" in the column labeled "Codebtor," include the entity on the appropriate schedule of creditors, and complete Schedule H - Codebtors. If a joint petition is filed, state whether husband, wife, both of them, or the marital community maybe liable on each claim by placing an "H," "W," "J," or "C" in the column labeled "Husband, Wife, Joint, or Community."

If the claim is contingent, place an "X" in the column labeled "Contingent." If the claim is unliquidated, place an "X" in the column labeled "Unliquidated." If the claim is disputed, place an "X" in the column labeled "Disputed." (You may need to place an "X" in more than one of these three columns.)

Report the total of all claims listed on this schedule in the box labeled "Total" on the last sheet of the completed schedule. Report this total also on the Summary of Schedules.

☐ Check this box if debtor has no creditors holding unsecured claims to report on this Schedule F.

CREDITOR'S NAME, MAILING ADDRESS INCLUDING ZIP CODE, AND ACCOUNT NUMBER (See instructions above.)	CODEBTOR	HUSBAND, WIFE, JOINT, OR COMMUNITY	DATE CLAIM WAS INCURRED AND CONSIDERATION FOR CLAIM. IF CLAIM IS SUBJECT TO SETOFF, SO STATE.	CONTINGENT	UNLIQUIDATED	DISPUTED	AMOUNT OF CLAIM
ACCOUNT NO.							
ACCOUNT NO.							
ACCOUNT NO.							
ACCOUNT NO.							
			Subtotal ►				$
_____continuation sheets attached			Total ► (Use only on last page of the completed Schedule F.) (Report also on Summary of Schedules.)				$

In re _____,   Case No. _____
                 Debtor   (If known)

SCHEDULE F - CREDITORS HOLDING UNSECURED NONPRIORITY CLAIMS
(Continuation Sheet)

CREDITOR'S NAME, MAILING ADDRESS INCLUDING ZIP CODE, AND ACCOUNT NUMBER (See instructions above.)	CODEBTOR	HUSBAND, WIFE, JOINT, OR COMMUNITY	DATE CLAIM WAS INCURRED AND CONSIDERATION FOR CLAIM. IF CLAIM IS SUBJECT TO SETOFF, SO STATE.	CONTINGENT	UNLIQUIDATED	DISPUTED	AMOUNT OF CLAIM
ACCOUNT NO.							
ACCOUNT NO.							
ACCOUNT NO.							
ACCOUNT NO.							
ACCOUNT NO.							

Sheet no.___of___sheets attached to Schedule of Creditors Holding Unsecured Nonpriority Claims

Subtotal▶ $

Total▶ $
(Use only on last page of the completed Schedule F.)
(Report also on Summary of Schedules.)

APPENDIX 12:
SCHEDULE G—EXECUTORY CONTRACTS
AND UNEXPIRED LEASES (FORM B6G)

In re _____ .　　　　Case No._____
　　　　Debtor　　　　　　　　　　　　　　　　　　　　(if known)

SCHEDULE G - EXECUTORY CONTRACTS AND UNEXPIRED LEASES

Describe all executory contracts of any nature and all unexpired leases of real or personal property. Include any timeshare interests. State nature of debtor's interest in contract, i.e., "Purchaser," "Agent," etc. State whether debtor is the lessor or lessee of a lease. Provide the names and complete mailing addresses of all other parties to each lease or contract described. If a minor child is a party to one of the leases or contracts, indicate that by stating "a minor child" and do not disclose the child's name. See 11 U.S.C. § 112; Fed.R. Bankr. P. 1007(m).

☐ Check this box if debtor has no executory contracts or unexpired leases.

NAME AND MAILING ADDRESS, INCLUDING ZIP CODE, OF OTHER PARTIES TO LEASE OR CONTRACT.	DESCRIPTION OF CONTRACT OR LEASE AND NATURE OF DEBTOR'S INTEREST. STATE WHETHER LEASE IS FOR NONRESIDENTIAL REAL PROPERTY. STATE CONTRACT NUMBER OF ANY GOVERNMENT CONTRACT.

APPENDIX 13:
SCHEDULE H—DEBTOR'S LIST OF CO-DEBTORS (FORM B6H)

Form B6H
(10/05)

In re _____ ,   Case No. _____
                    Debtor   (if known)

SCHEDULE H - CODEBTORS

Provide the information requested concerning any person or entity, other than a spouse in a joint case, that is also liable on any debts listed by debtor in the schedules of creditors. Include all guarantors and co-signers. If the debtor resides or resided in a community property state, commonwealth, or territory (including Alaska, Arizona, California, Idaho, Louisiana, Nevada, New Mexico, Puerto Rico, Texas, Washington, or Wisconsin) within the eight year period immediately preceding the commencement of the case, identify the name of the debtor's spouse and of any former spouse who resides or resided with the debtor in the community property state, commonwealth, or territory. Include all names used by the nondebtor spouse during the eight years immediately preceding the commencement of this case. If a minor child is a codebtor or a creditor, indicate that by stating "a minor child" and do not disclose the child's name. See 11 U.S.C. § 112; Fed. Bankr. P. 1007(m).

☐ Check this box if debtor has no codebtors.

NAME AND ADDRESS OF CODEBTOR	NAME AND ADDRESS OF CREDITOR

APPENDIX 14:
SCHEDULE I—CURRENT INCOME OF
INDIVIDUAL DEBTOR (FORM B6I)

'orm B6I
10/05)

In re _____ ,   Case No._____
      Debtor   (if known)

SCHEDULE I - CURRENT INCOME OF INDIVIDUAL DEBTOR(S)

The column labeled "Spouse" must be completed in all cases filed by joint debtors and by a married debtor in a chapter 7, 11, 12, or 13 case whether or not a joint petition is filed, unless the spouses are separated and a joint petition is not filed. Do not state the name of any minor child.

Debtor's Marital Status:	DEPENDENTS OF DEBTOR AND SPOUSE	
	RELATIONSHIP:	AGE:

Employment: Occupation	DEBTOR	SPOUSE
Name of Employer		
How long employed		
Address of Employer		

INCOME: (Estimate of average monthly income)   DEBTOR   SPOUSE

1. Current monthly gross wages, salary, and commissions $_____ $_____
    (Prorate if not paid monthly.)
2. Estimate monthly overtime $_____ $_____

3. SUBTOTAL $_____ $_____

4. LESS PAYROLL DEDUCTIONS
    a. Payroll taxes and social security $_____ $_____
    b. Insurance $_____ $_____
    c. Union dues $_____ $_____
    d. Other (Specify): _____ $_____ $_____

5. SUBTOTAL OF PAYROLL DEDUCTIONS $_____ $_____

6. TOTAL NET MONTHLY TAKE HOME PAY $_____ $_____

7. Regular income from operation of business or profession or farm. $_____ $_____
    (Attach detailed statement)
8. Income from real property $_____ $_____
9. Interest and dividends $_____ $_____
10. Alimony, maintenance or support payments payable to the debtor for $_____ $_____
    the debtor's use or that of dependents listed above.
11. Social security or government assistance
    (Specify):_____ $_____ $_____
12. Pension or retirement income $_____ $_____
13. Other monthly income $_____ $_____
    (Specify):_____

14. SUBTOTAL OF LINES 7 THROUGH 13
15. TOTAL MONTHLY INCOME (Add amounts shown on lines 6 and 14) $_____ $_____

16. TOTAL COMBINED MONTHLY INCOME: $_____
    (Report also on Summary of Schedules.)

17. Describe any increase or decrease in income reasonably anticipated to occur within the year following the filing of this document:
_____
_____

APPENDIX 15:
SCHEDULE J—CURRENT EXPENDITURES
OF INDIVIDUAL DEBTOR (FORM B6J)

Form B6J
(10/05)

In re _____ ,   Case No._____
                 Debtor   (if known)

SCHEDULE J - CURRENT EXPENDITURES OF INDIVIDUAL DEBTOR(S)

Complete this schedule by estimating the average monthly expenses of the debtor and the debtor's family. Pro rate any payments made bi-weekly, quarterly, semi-annually, or annually to show monthly rate.

☐ Check this box if a joint petition is filed and debtor's spouse maintains a separate household. Complete a separate schedule of expenditures labeled "Spouse."

1. Rent or home mortgage payment (include lot rented for mobile home) $ _____
   a. Are real estate taxes included?   Yes _____ No _____
   b. Is property insurance included?   Yes _____ No _____
2. Utilities: a. Electricity and heating fuel $ _____
        b. Water and sewer $ _____
        c. Telephone $ _____
        d. Other _____ $ _____
3. Home maintenance (repairs and upkeep) $ _____
4. Food $ _____
5. Clothing $ _____
6. Laundry and dry cleaning $ _____
7. Medical and dental expenses $ _____
8. Transportation (not including car payments) $ _____
9. Recreation, clubs and entertainment, newspapers, magazines, etc. $ _____
10.Charitable contributions $ _____
11.Insurance (not deducted from wages or included in home mortgage payments)
      a. Homeowner's or renter's $ _____
      b. Life $ _____
      c. Health $ _____
      d. Auto $ _____
      e. Other _____ $ _____
12.Taxes (not deducted from wages or included in home mortgage payments)
(Specify) _____ $ _____
13. Installment payments: (In chapter 11, 12, and 13 cases, do not list payments to be included in the plan)
      a. Auto $ _____
      b. Other _____ $ _____
      c. Other _____ $ _____
14. Alimony, maintenance, and support paid to others $ _____
15. Payments for support of additional dependents not living at your home $ _____
16. Regular expenses from operation of business, profession, or farm (attach detailed statement) $ _____
17. Other _____ $ _____
18. TOTAL MONTHLY EXPENSES (Report also on Summary of Schedules)
19. Describe any increase or decrease in expenditures reasonably anticipated to occur within the year following the filing of $ _____
this document: _____

20. STATEMENT OF MONTHLY NET INCOME
   a. Total monthly income from Line 16 of Schedule I $ _____
   b. Total monthly expenses from Line 18 above $ _____
   c. Monthly net income (a. minus b.) $ _____

APPENDIX 16:
DEBTOR'S STATEMENT OF FINANCIAL AFFAIRS (FORM B7)

Official Form 7
(10/05)

UNITED STATES BANKRUPTCY COURT

_____ DISTRICT OF _____

In re: _____,   Case No. _____
                Debtor   (if known)

STATEMENT OF FINANCIAL AFFAIRS

This statement is to be completed by every debtor. Spouses filing a joint petition may file a single statement on which the information for both spouses is combined. If the case is filed under chapter 12 or chapter 13, a married debtor must furnish information for both spouses whether or not a joint petition is filed, unless the spouses are separated and a joint petition is not filed. An individual debtor engaged in business as a sole proprietor, partner, family farmer, or self-employed professional, should provide the information requested on this statement concerning all such activities as well as the individual's personal affairs. Do not include the name or address of a minor child in this statement. Indicate payments, transfers and the like to minor children by stating "a minor child." See 11 U.S.C. § 112; Fed. R. Bankr. P. 1007(m).

Questions 1 - 18 are to be completed by all debtors. Debtors that are or have been in business, as defined below, also must complete Questions 19 - 25. **If the answer to an applicable question is "None," mark the box labeled "None."** If additional space is needed for the answer to any question, use and attach a separate sheet properly identified with the case name, case number (if known), and the number of the question.

DEFINITIONS

"In business." A debtor is "in business" for the purpose of this form if the debtor is a corporation or partnership. An individual debtor is "in business" for the purpose of this form if the debtor is or has been, within six years immediately preceding the filing of this bankruptcy case, any of the following: an officer, director, managing executive, or owner of 5 percent or more of the voting or equity securities of a corporation; a partner, other than a limited partner, of a partnership; a sole proprietor or self-employed full-time or part-time. An individual debtor also may be "in business" for the purpose of this form if the debtor engages in a trade, business, or other activity, other than as an employee, to supplement income from the debtor's primary employment.

"Insider." The term "insider" includes but is not limited to: relatives of the debtor; general partners of the debtor and their relatives; corporations of which the debtor is an officer, director, or person in control; officers, directors, and any owner of 5 percent or more of the voting or equity securities of a corporate debtor and their relatives; affiliates of the debtor and insiders of such affiliates; any managing agent of the debtor. 11 U.S.C. § 101.

1. **Income from employment or operation of business**

None
☐   State the gross amount of income the debtor has received from employment, trade, or profession, or from operation of the debtor's business, including part-time activities either as an employee or in independent trade or business, from the beginning of this calendar year to the date this case was commenced. State also the gross amounts received during the **two years** immediately preceding this calendar year. (A debtor that maintains, or has maintained, financial records on the basis of a fiscal rather than a calendar year may report fiscal year income. Identify the beginning and ending dates of the debtor's fiscal year.) If a joint petition is filed, state income for each spouse separately. (Married debtors filing under chapter 12 or chapter 13 must state income of both spouses whether or not a joint petition is filed, unless the spouses are separated and a joint petition is not filed.)

AMOUNT   SOURCE

DEBTOR'S STATEMENT OF FINANCIAL AFFAIRS (FORM B7)

2

2. Income other than from employment or operation of business

None ☐

State the amount of income received by the debtor other than from employment, trade, profession, operation of the debtor's business during the **two years** immediately preceding the commencement of this case. Give particulars. If a joint petition is filed, state income for each spouse separately. (Married debtors filing under chapter 12 or chapter 13 must state income for each spouse whether or not a joint petition is filed, unless the spouses are separated and a joint petition is not filed.)

AMOUNT   SOURCE

3. Payments to creditors

Complete a. or b., as appropriate, and c.

None ☐

a. *Individual or joint debtor(s) with primarily consumer debts:* List all payments on loans, installment purchases of goods or services, and other debts to any creditor made within **90 days** immediately preceding the commencement of this case if the aggregate value of all property that constitutes or is affected by such transfer is not less than $600. Indicate with an asterisk (*) any payments that were made to a creditor on account of a domestic support obligation or as part of an alternative repayment schedule under a plan by an approved nonprofit budgeting and creditor counseling agency. (Married debtors filing under chapter 12 or chapter 13 must include payments by either or both spouses whether or not a joint petition is filed, unless the spouses are separated and a joint petition is not filed.)

NAME AND ADDRESS OF CREDITOR	DATES OF PAYMENTS	AMOUNT PAID	AMOUNT STILL OWING

None ☐

b. *Debtor whose debts are not primarily consumer debts:* List each payment or other transfer to any creditor made within **90** days immediately preceding the commencement of the case if the aggregate value of all property that constitutes or is affected by such transfer is not less than $5,000. (Married debtors filing under chapter 12 or chapter 13 must include payments and other transfers by either or both spouses whether or not a joint petition is filed, unless the spouses are separated and a joint petition is not filed.)

NAME AND ADDRESS OF CREDITOR	DATES OF PAYMENTS/ TRANSFERS	AMOUNT PAID OR VALUE OF TRANSFERS	AMOUNT STILL OWING

None ☐

c. *All debtors:* List all payments made within **one year** immediately preceding the commencement of this case to or for the benefit of creditors who are or were insiders. (Married debtors filing under chapter 12 or chapter 13 must include payments by either or both spouses whether or not a joint petition is filed, unless the spouses are separated and a joint petition is not filed.)

NAME AND ADDRESS OF CREDITOR AND RELATIONSHIP TO DEBTOR	DATE OF PAYMENT	AMOUNT PAID	AMOUNT STILL OWING

4. Suits and administrative proceedings, executions, garnishments and attachments

3

None
☐
a. List all suits and administrative proceedings to which the debtor is or was a party within **one year** immediately preceding the filing of this bankruptcy case. (Married debtors filing under chapter 12 or chapter 13 must include information concerning either or both spouses whether or not a joint petition is filed, unless the spouses are separated and a joint petition is not filed.)

CAPTION OF SUIT AND CASE NUMBER	NATURE OF PROCEEDING	COURT OR AGENCY AND LOCATION	STATUS OR DISPOSITION

None
☐
b. Describe all property that has been attached, garnished or seized under any legal or equitable process within **one year** immediately preceding the commencement of this case. (Married debtors filing under chapter 12 or chapter 13 must include information concerning property of either or both spouses whether or not a joint petition is filed, unless the spouses are separated and a joint petition is not filed.)

NAME AND ADDRESS OF PERSON FOR WHOSE BENEFIT PROPERTY WAS SEIZED	DATE OF SEIZURE	DESCRIPTION AND VALUE OF PROPERTY

5. Repossessions, foreclosures and returns

None
☐
List all property that has been repossessed by a creditor, sold at a foreclosure sale, transferred through a deed in lieu of foreclosure or returned to the seller, within **one year** immediately preceding the commencement of this case. (Married debtors filing under chapter 12 or chapter 13 must include information concerning property of either or both spouses whether or not a joint petition is filed, unless the spouses are separated and a joint petition is not filed.)

NAME AND ADDRESS OF CREDITOR OR SELLER	DATE OF REPOSSESSION, FORECLOSURE SALE, TRANSFER OR RETURN	DESCRIPTION AND VALUE OF PROPERTY

6. Assignments and receiverships

None
☐
a. Describe any assignment of property for the benefit of creditors made within **120 days** immediately preceding the commencement of this case. (Married debtors filing under chapter 12 or chapter 13 must include any assignment by either or both spouses whether or not a joint petition is filed, unless the spouses are separated and a joint petition is not filed.)

NAME AND ADDRESS OF ASSIGNEE	DATE OF ASSIGNMENT	TERMS OF ASSIGNMENT OR SETTLEMENT

DEBTOR'S STATEMENT OF FINANCIAL AFFAIRS (FORM B7)

4

None ☐ b. List all property which has been in the hands of a custodian, receiver, or court-appointed official within **one year** immediately preceding the commencement of this case. (Married debtors filing under chapter 12 or chapter 13 must include information concerning property of either or both spouses whether or not a joint petition is filed, unless the spouses are separated and a joint petition is not filed.)

NAME AND ADDRESS OF CUSTODIAN	NAME AND LOCATION OF COURT CASE TITLE & NUMBER	DATE OF ORDER	DESCRIPTION AND VALUE Of PROPERTY

7. Gifts

None ☐ List all gifts or charitable contributions made within **one year** immediately preceding the commencement of this case except ordinary and usual gifts to family members aggregating less than $200 in value per individual family member and charitable contributions aggregating less than $100 per recipient. (Married debtors filing under chapter 12 or chapter 13 must include gifts or contributions by either or both spouses whether or not a joint petition is filed, unless the spouses are separated and a joint petition is not filed.)

NAME AND ADDRESS OF PERSON OR ORGANIZATION	RELATIONSHIP TO DEBTOR, IF ANY	DATE OF GIFT	DESCRIPTION AND VALUE OF GIFT

8. Losses

None ☐ List all losses from fire, theft, other casualty or gambling within **one year** immediately preceding the commencement of this case **or since the commencement of this case**. (Married debtors filing under chapter 12 or chapter 13 must include losses by either or both spouses whether or not a joint petition is filed, unless the spouses are separated and a joint petition is not filed.)

DESCRIPTION AND VALUE OF PROPERTY	DESCRIPTION OF CIRCUMSTANCES AND, IF LOSS WAS COVERED IN WHOLE OR IN PART BY INSURANCE, GIVE PARTICULARS	DATE OF LOSS

9. Payments related to debt counseling or bankruptcy

None ☐ List all payments made or property transferred by or on behalf of the debtor to any persons, including attorneys, for consultation concerning debt consolidation, relief under the bankruptcy law or preparation of a petition in bankruptcy within **one year** immediately preceding the commencement of this case.

NAME AND ADDRESS OF PAYEE	DATE OF PAYMENT, NAME OF PAYER IF OTHER THAN DEBTOR	AMOUNT OF MONEY OR DESCRIPTION AND VALUE OF PROPERTY

10. Other transfers

Individual Bankruptcy and Restructuring

5

None ☐

a. List all other property, other than property transferred in the ordinary course of the business or financial affairs of the debtor, transferred either absolutely or as security within **two years** immediately preceding the commencement of this case. (Married debtors filing under chapter 12 or chapter 13 must include transfers by either or both spouses whether or not a joint petition is filed, unless the spouses are separated and a joint petition is not filed.)

NAME AND ADDRESS OF TRANSFEREE, RELATIONSHIP TO DEBTOR	DATE	DESCRIBE PROPERTY TRANSFERRED AND VALUE RECEIVED

None ☐

b. List all property transferred by the debtor within **ten years** immediately preceding the commencement of this case to a self-settled trust or similar device of which the debtor is a beneficiary.

NAME OF TRUST OR OTHER DEVICE	DATE(S) OF TRANSFER(S)	AMOUNT OF MONEY OR DESCRIPTION AND VALUE OF PROPERTY OR DEBTOR'S INTEREST IN PROPERTY

11. Closed financial accounts

None ☐

List all financial accounts and instruments held in the name of the debtor or for the benefit of the debtor which were closed, sold, or otherwise transferred within **one year** immediately preceding the commencement of this case. Include checking, savings, or other financial accounts, certificates of deposit, or other instruments; shares and share accounts held in banks, credit unions, pension funds, cooperatives, associations, brokerage houses and other financial institutions. (Married debtors filing under chapter 12 or chapter 13 must include information concerning accounts or instruments held by or for either or both spouses whether or not a joint petition is filed, unless the spouses are separated and a joint petition is not filed.)

NAME AND ADDRESS OF INSTITUTION	TYPE OF ACCOUNT, LAST FOUR DIGITS OF ACCOUNT NUMBER, AND AMOUNT OF FINAL BALANCE	AMOUNT AND DATE OF SALE OR CLOSING

12. Safe deposit boxes

None ☐

List each safe deposit or other box or depository in which the debtor has or had securities, cash, or other valuables within **one year** immediately preceding the commencement of this case. (Married debtors filing under chapter 12 or chapter 13 must include boxes or depositories of either or both spouses whether or not a joint petition is filed, unless the spouses are separated and a joint petition is not filed.)

NAME AND ADDRESS OF BANK OR OTHER DEPOSITORY	NAMES AND ADDRESSES OF THOSE WITH ACCESS TO BOX OR DEPOSITORY	DESCRIPTION OF CONTENTS	DATE OF TRANSFER OR SURRENDER, IF ANY

13. Setoffs

6

None
☐
List all setoffs made by any creditor, including a bank, against a debt or deposit of the debtor within **90 days** preceding the commencement of this case. (Married debtors filing under chapter 12 or chapter 13 must include information concerning either or both spouses whether or not a joint petition is filed, unless the spouses are separated and a joint petition is not filed.)

NAME AND ADDRESS OF CREDITOR	DATE OF SETOFF	AMOUNT OF SETOFF

---

14. Property held for another person

None
☐
List all property owned by another person that the debtor holds or controls.

NAME AND ADDRESS OF OWNER	DESCRIPTION AND VALUE OF PROPERTY	LOCATION OF PROPERTY

---

15. Prior address of debtor

None
☐
If debtor has moved within **three years** immediately preceding the commencement of this case, list all premises which the debtor occupied during that period and vacated prior to the commencement of this case. If a joint petition is filed, report also any separate address of either spouse.

ADDRESS	NAME USED	DATES OF OCCUPANCY

---

16. Spouses and Former Spouses

None
☐
If the debtor resides or resided in a community property state, commonwealth, or territory (including Alaska, Arizona, California, Idaho, Louisiana, Nevada, New Mexico, Puerto Rico, Texas, Washington, or Wisconsin) within **eight years** immediately preceding the commencement of the case, identify the name of the debtor's spouse and of any former spouse who resides or resided with the debtor in the community property state.

NAME

7

17. Environmental Information.

For the purpose of this question, the following definitions apply:

"Environmental Law" means any federal, state, or local statute or regulation regulating pollution, contamination, releases of hazardous or toxic substances, wastes or material into the air, land, soil, surface water, groundwater, or other medium, including, but not limited to, statutes or regulations regulating the cleanup of these substances, wastes, or material.

"Site" means any location, facility, or property as defined under any Environmental Law, whether or not presently or formerly owned or operated by the debtor, including, but not limited to, disposal sites.

"Hazardous Material" means anything defined as a hazardous waste, hazardous substance, toxic substance, hazardous material, pollutant, or contaminant or similar term under an Environmental Law.

None ☐   a. List the name and address of every site for which the debtor has received notice in writing by a governmental unit that it may be liable or potentially liable under or in violation of an Environmental Law. Indicate the governmental unit, the date of the notice, and, if known, the Environmental Law:

SITE NAME AND ADDRESS	NAME AND ADDRESS OF GOVERNMENTAL UNIT	DATE OF NOTICE	ENVIRONMENTAL LAW

None ☐   b. List the name and address of every site for which the debtor provided notice to a governmental unit of a release of Hazardous Material. Indicate the governmental unit to which the notice was sent and the date of the notice.

SITE NAME AND ADDRESS	NAME AND ADDRESS OF GOVERNMENTAL UNIT	DATE OF NOTICE	ENVIRONMENTAL LAW

None ☐   c. List all judicial or administrative proceedings, including settlements or orders, under any Environmental Law with respect to which the debtor is or was a party. Indicate the name and address of the governmental unit that is or was a party to the proceeding, and the docket number.

NAME AND ADDRESS OF GOVERNMENTAL UNIT	DOCKET NUMBER	STATUS OR DISPOSITION

18 . Nature, location and name of business

None ☐   a. *If the debtor is an individual*, list the names, addresses, taxpayer identification numbers, nature of the businesses, and beginning and ending dates of all businesses in which the debtor was an officer, director, partner, or managing executive of a corporation, partner in a partnership, sole proprietor, or was self-employed in a trade, profession, or other activity either full- or part-time within **six years** immediately preceding the commencement of this case, or in which the debtor owned 5 percent or more of the voting or equity securities within **six years** immediately preceding the commencement of this case.

If the debtor is a partnership, list the names, addresses, taxpayer identification numbers, nature of the businesses, and beginning and ending dates of all businesses in which the debtor was a partner or owned 5 percent or more of the voting or equity securities, within **six years** immediately preceding the commencement of this case.

If the debtor is a corporation, list the names, addresses, taxpayer identification numbers, nature of the businesses, and beginning and ending dates of all businesses in which the debtor was a partner or owned 5 percent or more of the voting or equity securities within **six years** immediately preceding the commencement of this case.

ʃ

NAME	LAST FOUR DIGITS OF SOC. SEC. NO./ COMPLETE EIN OR OTHER TAXPAYER I.D. NO.	ADDRESS	NATURE OF BUSINESS	BEGINNING AND ENDING DATES

None ☐   b. Identify any business listed in response to subdivision a., above, that is "single asset real estate" as defined in 11 U.S.C. § 101.

     NAME   ADDRESS

     The following questions are to be completed by every debtor that is a corporation or partnership and by any individual debtor who is or has been, within **six years** immediately preceding the commencement of this case, any of the following: an officer, director, managing executive, or owner of more than 5 percent of the voting or equity securities of a corporation; a partner, other than a limited partner, of a partnership, a sole proprietor, or self-employed in a trade, profession, or other activity, either full- or part-time.

     *(An individual or joint debtor should complete this portion of the statement **only** if the debtor is or has been in business, as defined above, within six years immediately preceding the commencement of this case. A debtor who has not been in business within those six years should go directly to the signature page.)*

     19. Books, records and financial statements

None ☐   a. List all bookkeepers and accountants who within **two years** immediately preceding the filing of this bankruptcy case kept or supervised the keeping of books of account and records of the debtor.

     NAME AND ADDRESS   DATES SERVICES RENDERED

None ☐   b. List all firms or individuals who within **two years** immediately preceding the filing of this bankruptcy case have audited the books of account and records, or prepared a financial statement of the debtor.

     NAME   ADDRESS   DATES SERVICES RENDERED

None ☐   c. List all firms or individuals who at the time of the commencement of this case were in possession of the books of account and records of the debtor. If any of the books of account and records are not available, explain.

     NAME   ADDRESS

9

None ☐   d. List all financial institutions, creditors and other parties, including mercantile and trade agencies, to whom a financial statement was issued by the debtor within **two years** immediately preceding the commencement of this case.

          NAME AND ADDRESS   DATE ISSUED

---

20. Inventories

None ☐   a. List the dates of the last two inventories taken of your property, the name of the person who supervised the taking of each inventory, and the dollar amount and basis of each inventory.

                                                   DOLLAR AMOUNT
                                                 OF INVENTORY
         DATE OF INVENTORY   INVENTORY SUPERVISOR   (Specify cost, market or other basis)

None ☐   b. List the name and address of the person having possession of the records of each of the inventories reported in a., above.

                                                   NAME AND ADDRESSES
                                                 OF CUSTODIAN
         DATE OF INVENTORY   OF INVENTORY RECORDS

---

21. Current Partners, Officers, Directors and Shareholders

None ☐   a. If the debtor is a partnership, list the nature and percentage of partnership interest of each member of the partnership.

          NAME AND ADDRESS   NATURE OF INTEREST   PERCENTAGE OF INTEREST

None ☐   b. If the debtor is a corporation, list all officers and directors of the corporation, and each stockholder who directly or indirectly owns, controls, or holds 5 percent or more of the voting or equity securities of the corporation.

                                                   NATURE AND PERCENTAGE
          NAME AND ADDRESS   TITLE   OF STOCK OWNERSHIP

---

22. Former partners, officers, directors and shareholders

None ☐   a. If the debtor is a partnership, list each member who withdrew from the partnership within **one year** immediately preceding the commencement of this case.

          NAME   ADDRESS   DATE OF WITHDRAWAL

10

None ☐ b. If the debtor is a corporation, list all officers, or directors whose relationship with the corporation terminated within **one year** immediately preceding the commencement of this case.

NAME AND ADDRESS   TITLE   DATE OF TERMINATION

23. Withdrawals from a partnership or distributions by a corporation

None ☐ If the debtor is a partnership or corporation, list all withdrawals or distributions credited or given to an insider, including compensation in any form, bonuses, loans, stock redemptions, options exercised and any other perquisite during **one year** immediately preceding the commencement of this case.

NAME & ADDRESS   AMOUNT OF MONEY
OF RECIPIENT,   DATE AND PURPOSE   OR DESCRIPTION
RELATIONSHIP TO DEBTOR   OF WITHDRAWAL   AND VALUE OF PROPERTY

24. Tax Consolidation Group.

None ☐ If the debtor is a corporation, list the name and federal taxpayer identification number of the parent corporation of any consolidated group for tax purposes of which the debtor has been a member at any time within **six years** immediately preceding the commencement of the case.

NAME OF PARENT CORPORATION   TAXPAYER IDENTIFICATION NUMBER (EIN)

25. Pension Funds.

None ☐ If the debtor is not an individual, list the name and federal taxpayer identification number of any pension fund to which the debtor, as an employer, has been responsible for contributing at any time within **six years** immediately preceding the commencement of the case.

NAME OF PENSION FUND   TAXPAYER IDENTIFICATION NUMBER (EIN)

* * * * * *

11

[If completed by an individual or individual and spouse]

I declare under penalty of perjury that I have read the answers contained in the foregoing statement of financial affairs and any attachments thereto and that they are true and correct.

Date _____   Signature _____
                                  of Debtor

Date _____   Signature_____
                                  of Joint Debtor
                                  (if any)

[If completed on behalf of a partnership or corporation]

I, declare under penalty of perjury that I have read the answers contained in the foregoing statement of financial affairs and any attachments thereto and that they are true and correct to the best of my knowledge, information and belief.

Date _____   Signature _____

                                  _____
                                  Print Name and Title

[An individual signing on behalf of a partnership or corporation must indicate position or relationship to debtor.]

_____ continuation sheets attached

Penalty for making a false statement: Fine of up to $500,000 or imprisonment for up to 5 years, or both. 18 U.S.C. §§ 152 and 3571

DECLARATION AND SIGNATURE OF NON-ATTORNEY BANKRUPTCY PETITION PREPARER (See 11 U.S.C. § 110)

I declare under penalty of perjury that: (1) I am a bankruptcy petition preparer as defined in 11 U.S.C. § 110; (2) I prepared this document for compensation and have provided the debtor with a copy of this document and the notices and information required under 11 U.S.C. §§ 110(b), 110(h), and 12(b); and, (3) if rules or guidelines have been promulgated pursuant to 11 U.S.C. § 110(h) setting a maximum fee for services chargeable by bankruptcy petition preparers, I have given the debtor notice of the maximum amount before preparing any document for filing for a debtor or accepting any fee from the debtor, as required by that section.

_____   _____
rinted or Typed Name and Title, if any, of Bankruptcy Petition Preparer   Social Security No.(Required by 11 U.S.C. § 110.)

the bankruptcy petition preparer is not an individual, state the name, title (if any), address, and social security number of the officer, principal, responsible rson, or partner who signs this document.

_____

ddress

_____   _____
iignature of Bankruptcy Petition Preparer   Date

ames and Social Security numbers of all other individuals who prepared or assisted in preparing this document unless the bankruptcy petition preparer is t an individual:

more than one person prepared this document, attach additional signed sheets conforming to the appropriate Official Form for each person.

bankruptcy petition preparer's failure to comply with the provisions of title 11 and the Federal Rules of Bankruptcy Procedure may result in nes or imprisonment or both. 18 U.S.C. § 156.

Individual Bankruptcy and Restructuring   133

APPENDIX 17:
DEBTOR'S APPLICATION AND ORDER TO PAY FILING FEE IN INSTALLMENTS (FORM B3A)

Form 3A
(10/05)

United States Bankruptcy Court
_____ District Of _____

In re _____ ,   Case No. _____
                    Debtor
                                                    Chapter _____

APPLICATION TO PAY FILING FEE IN INSTALLMENTS

1.   In accordance with Fed. R. Bankr. P. 1006, I apply for permission to pay the filing fee amounting to $_____ in installments.

2.   I am unable to pay the filing fee except in installments.

3.   Until the filing fee is paid in full, I will not make any additional payment or transfer any additional property to an attorney or any other person for services in connection with this case.

4.   I propose the following terms for the payment of the Filing Fee.*

       $ _____   Check one ☐   With the filing of the petition, or
                                            ☐   On or before _____

       $ _____ on or before _____

       $ _____ on or before _____

       $ _____ on or before _____

*   The number of installments proposed shall not exceed four (4), and the final installment shall be payable not later than 120 days after filing the petition. For cause shown, the court may extend the time of any installment, provided the last installment is paid not later than 180 days after filing the petition. Fed. R. Bankr. P. 1006(b)(2).

5.   I understand that if I fail to pay any installment when due, my bankruptcy case may be dismissed and I may not receive a discharge of my debts.

_____   _____   _____   _____
Signature of Attorney   Date   Signature of Debtor   Date
                                                             (In a joint case, both spouses must sign.)

_____   _____   _____   _____
Name of Attorney   Signature of Joint Debtor (if any)   Date

DECLARATION AND SIGNATURE OF NON-ATTORNEY BANKRUPTCY PETITION PREPARER (See 11 U.S.C. § 110)

       I declare under penalty of perjury that: (1) I am a bankruptcy petition preparer as defined in 11 U.S.C. § 110; (2) I prepared this document for compensation and have provided the debtor with a copy of this document and the notices and information required under 11 U.S.C. §§ 110(b), 110(h), and 342(b); (3) if rules or guidelines have been promulgated pursuant to 11 U.S.C. § 110(h) setting a maximum fee for services chargeable by bankruptcy petition preparers, I have given the debtor notice of the maximum amount before preparing any document for filing for a debtor or accepting any fee from the debtor, as required under that section; and (4) I will not accept any additional money or other property from the debtor before the filing fee is paid in full.

_____   _____
Printed or Typed Name and Title, if any, of Bankruptcy Petition Preparer   Social Security No. (Required by 11 U.S.C. § 110.)
If the bankruptcy petition preparer is not an individual, state the name, title (if any), address, and social security number of the officer, principal, responsible person, or partner who signs the document.

_____
Address

x_____   _____
Signature of Bankruptcy Petition Preparer   Date

Names and Social Security numbers of all other individuals who prepared or assisted in preparing this document, unless the bankruptcy petition preparer is not an individual:

If more than one person prepared this document, attach additional signed sheets conforming to the appropriate Official Form for each person.
A bankruptcy petition preparer's failure to comply with the provisions of title 11 and the Federal Rules of Bankruptcy Procedure may result in fines or imprisonment or both. 11 U.S.C. § 110; 18 U.S.C. § 156.

DEBTOR'S APPLICATION AND ORDER TO PAY FILING FEE IN INSTALLMENTS

Form 3A Contd.
(10/05)

United States Bankruptcy Court
_____ District Of _____

In re _____,
　　　　　　　　Debtor

Case No. _____

Chapter _____

ORDER APPROVING PAYMENT OF FILING FEE IN INSTALLMENTS

☐　　IT IS ORDERED that the debtor(s) may pay the filing fee in installments on the terms proposed in the foregoing application.

☐　　IT IS ORDERED that the debtor(s) shall pay the filing fee according to the following terms:

$ _____　Check one ☐　With the filing of the petition, or
　　　　　　　　　　　　　　☐　On or before _____

$ _____ on or before _____

$ _____ on or before _____

$ _____ on or before _____

☐　　IT IS FURTHER ORDERED that until the filing fee is paid in full the debtor(s) shall not make any additional payment or transfer any additional property to an attorney or any other person for services in connection with this case.

BY THE COURT

Date: _____

_____
United States Bankruptcy Judge

　　　　　　Individual Bankruptcy and Restructuring

APPENDIX 18:
DEBTOR'S APPLICATION FOR WAIVER OF CHAPTER 7 FILING FEE (FORM B3B)

Form B3B
(04/09/06)

APPLICATION FOR WAIVER OF THE CHAPTER 7 FILING FEE
FOR INDIVIDUALS WHO CANNOT PAY THE FILING FEE
IN FULL OR IN INSTALLMENTS

The court fee for filing a case under chapter 7 of the Bankruptcy Code is $299.

If you cannot afford to pay the full fee at the time of filing, you may apply to pay the fee in installments. A form, which is available from the bankruptcy clerk's office, must be completed to make that application. If your application to pay in installments is approved, you will be permitted to file your petition, completing payment of the fee over the course of four to six months.

If you cannot afford to pay the fee either in full at the time of filing or in installments, then you may request a waiver of the filing fee by completing this application and filing it with the Clerk of Court. A judge will decide whether you have to pay the fee. By law, the judge may waive the fee only if your income is less than 150 percent of the official poverty line applicable to your family size and you are unable to pay the fee in installments. You may obtain information about the poverty guidelines at www.uscourts.gov or in the bankruptcy clerk's office.

Required information. Complete all items in the application, and attach requested schedules. Then sign the application on the last page. If you and your spouse are filing a joint bankruptcy petition, you both must provide information as requested and sign the application.

Form B3B
(04/09/06)

United States Bankruptcy Court
_____ District of _____

In re: _____   Case No. _____
    Debtor(s)   (if known)

APPLICATION FOR WAIVER OF THE CHAPTER 7 FILING FEE
FOR INDIVIDUALS WHO CANNOT PAY THE FILING FEE IN FULL OR IN INSTALLMENTS

Part A. Family Size and Income

1. Including yourself, your spouse, and dependents you have listed or will list on Schedule I (Current Income of Individual Debtors(s)), how many people are in your family? (Do not include your spouse if you are separated AND are not filing a joint petition.) _____

2. Restate the following information that you provided, or will provide, on Line 16 of Schedule I. Attach a completed copy of Schedule I, if it is available.

   Total Combined Monthly Income (Line 16 of Schedule I): $_____

3. State the monthly net income, if any, of dependents included in Question 1 above. Do not include any income already reported in Item 2. If none, enter $0.

   $_____

4. Add the "Total Combined Monthly Income" reported in Question 2 to your dependents' monthly net income from Question 3.

   $_____

5. Do you expect the amount in Question 4 to increase or decrease by more than 10% during the next 6 months? Yes ___ No ___

   If yes, explain.

Part B: Monthly Expenses

6. EITHER (a) attach a completed copy of Schedule J (Schedule of Monthly Expenses), and state your total monthly expenses reported on Line 18 of that Schedule, OR (b) if you have not yet completed Schedule J, provide an estimate of your total monthly expenses.

   $ _____

7. Do you expect the amount in Question 6 to increase or decrease by more than 10% during the next 6 months? Yes ___ No ___
   If yes, explain.

Part C. Real and Personal Property

EITHER (1) attach completed copies of Schedules A (Real Property) and Schedule B (Personal Property), OR (2) if you have not yet completed those schedules, answer the following questions.

8. State the amount of cash you have on hand: $ _____

9. State below any money you have in savings, checking, or other accounts in a bank or other financial institution.

Bank or Other Financial Institution:	Type of Account such as savings, checking, CD:	Amount:
_____	_____	$ _____
_____	_____	$ _____

Form B3B Cont.
(04/09/06)
10. State below the assets owned by you. **Do not list ordinary household furnishings and clothing.**

Home   Address: _____   Value: $ _____

Amount owed on mortgages and liens: $ _____

Other real estate   Address: _____   Value: $ _____

Amount owed on mortgages and liens: $ _____

Motor vehicle   Model/Year: _____   Value: $ _____

Amount owed: $ _____

Motor vehicle   Model/Year: _____   Value: $ _____

Amount owed: $ _____

Other   Description _____   Value: $ _____

Amount owed: $ _____

11. State below any person, business, organization, or governmental unit that owes you money and the amount that is owed.

Name of Person, Business, or Organization that Owes You Money   Amount Owed

_____ $ _____

_____ $ _____

Part D. Additional Information.

12. Have you paid an **attorney** any money for services in connection with this case, including the completion of this form, the bankruptcy petition, or schedules? Yes ___ No ___
If yes, how much have you paid? $ _____

13. Have you promised to pay or do you anticipate paying an **attorney** in connection with your bankruptcy case? Yes ___ No ___
If yes, how much have you promised to pay or do you anticipate paying? $ _____

14. Have you paid **anyone other than an attorney** (such as a bankruptcy petition preparer, paralegal, typing service, or another person) any money for services in connection with this case, including the completion of this form, the bankruptcy petition, or schedules? Yes ___ No ___
If yes, how much have you paid? $ _____

15. Have you promised to pay or do you anticipate paying **anyone other than an attorney** (such as a bankruptcy petition preparer, paralegal, typing service, or another person) any money for services in connection with this case, including the completion of this form, the bankruptcy petition, or schedules? Yes ___ No ___
If yes, how much have you promised to pay or do you anticipate paying? $ _____

16. Has anyone paid an attorney or other person or service in connection with this case, on your behalf? Yes ___ No ___

If yes, explain.

Form B3B Cont.
(04/09/06)
17. Have you previously filed for bankruptcy relief during the past eight years? Yes ___ No ___

Case Number (if known)	Year filed	Location of filing	Did you obtain a discharge? (if known)
_____	_____	_____	Yes ____ No ____ Don't know ____
_____	_____	_____	Yes ____ No ____ Don't know ____

18. Please provide any other information that helps to explain why you are unable to pay the filing fee in installments.

19. I (we) declare under penalty of perjury that I (we) cannot currently afford to pay the filing fee in full or in installments and that the foregoing information is true and correct.

Executed on: _____   _____
                     Date   Signature of Debtor

_____   _____
          Date   Signature of Co-debtor

DECLARATION AND SIGNATURE OF BANKRUPTCY PETITION PREPARER (See 11 U.S.C. § 110)

I declare under penalty of perjury that: (1) I am a bankruptcy petition preparer as defined in 11 U.S.C. § 110; (2) I prepared this document for compensation and have provided the debtor with a copy of this document and the notices and information required under 11 U.S.C. §§ 110(b), 110(h), and 342(b); and (3) if rules or guidelines have been promulgated pursuant to 11 U.S.C. § 110(h) setting a maximum fee for services chargeable by bankruptcy petition preparers, I have given the debtor notice of the maximum amount before preparing any document for filing for a debtor or accepting any fee from the debtor, as required under that section.

_____
Printed or Typed Name and Title, if any, of Bankruptcy Petition Preparer   Social Security No. (Required by
                                                                                                                       11 U.S.C. §110.)
If the bankruptcy petition preparer is not an individual, state the name, title (if any), address, and social security number of the officer, principal, responsible person, or partner who signs the document.

_____

_____
Address

x_____   _____
Signature of Bankruptcy Petition Preparer   Date

Names and Social Security numbers of all other individuals who prepared or assisted in preparing this document, unless the bankruptcy petition preparer is not an individual:

If more than one person prepared this document, attach additional signed sheets conforming to the appropriate Official Form for each person.
A bankruptcy petition preparer's failure to comply with the provisions of title 11 and the Federal Rules of Bankruptcy Procedure may result in fines or imprisonment or both. 11 U.S.C. § 110; 18 U.S.C. § 156.

Form B3B
(04/09/06)

United States Bankruptcy Court
_____ District of _____

In re: _____   Case No. _____
    Debtor(s)

ORDER ON DEBTOR'S APPLICATION FOR WAIVER OF THE CHAPTER 7 FILING FEE

Upon consideration of the debtor's "Application for Waiver of the Chapter 7 Filing Fee," the court orders that the application be:

[ ] GRANTED.

    This order is subject to being vacated at a later time if developments in the administration of the bankruptcy case demonstrate that the waiver was unwarranted.

[ ] DENIED.

    The debtor shall pay the chapter 7 filing fee according to the following terms:

    $ _____ on or before _____

    $ _____ on or before _____

    $ _____ on or before _____

    $ _____ on or before _____

    Until the filing fee is paid in full, the debtor shall not make any additional payment or transfer any additional property to an attorney or any other person for services in connection with this case.

    IF THE DEBTOR FAILS TO TIMELY PAY THE FILING FEE IN FULL OR TO TIMELY MAKE INSTALLMENT PAYMENTS, THE COURT MAY DISMISS THE DEBTOR'S CHAPTER 7 CASE.

[ ] SCHEDULED FOR HEARING.

    A hearing to consider the debtor's "Application for Waiver of the Chapter 7 Filing Fee" shall be held on _____ at _____ am/pm at _____.
                                                     (address of courthouse)

    IF THE DEBTOR FAILS TO APPEAR AT THE SCHEDULED HEARING, THE COURT MAY DEEM SUCH FAILURE TO BE THE DEBTOR'S CONSENT TO THE ENTRY OF AN ORDER DENYING THE FEE WAIVER APPLICATION BY DEFAULT.

                                    BY THE COURT:

DATE: _____   _____
                                      United States Bankruptcy Judge

APPENDIX 19: STATEMENT OF CURRENT MONTHLY INCOME AND MEANS TEST CALCULATION— CHAPTER 7 CASE (FORM B22A)

Form B22A (Chapter 7) (10/05)

In re _____
             Debtor(s)

Case Number: _____
           (If known)

According to the calculations required by this statement:
  ☐ **The presumption arises.**
  ☐ **The presumption does not arise.**
(Check the box as directed in Parts I, III, and VI of this statement.)

STATEMENT OF CURRENT MONTHLY INCOME AND MEANS TEST CALCULATION
FOR USE IN CHAPTER 7 ONLY

In addition to Schedule I and J, this statement must be completed by every individual Chapter 7 debtor, whether or not filing jointly, whose debts are primarily consumer debts. Joint debtors may complete one statement only.

	Part I. EXCLUSION FOR DISABLED VETERANS
1	If you are a disabled veteran described in the Veteran's Declaration in this Part I, (1) check the box at the beginning of the Veteran's Declaration, (2) check the box for "The presumption does not arise" at the top of this statement, and (3) complete the verification in Part VIII. Do not complete any of the remaining parts of this statement. ☐ **Veteran's Declaration.** By checking this box, I declare under penalty of perjury that I am a disabled veteran (as defined in 38 U.S.C. § 3741(1)) whose indebtedness occurred primarily during a period in which I was on active duty (as defined in 10 U.S.C. § 101(d)(1)) or while I was performing a homeland defense activity (as defined in 32 U.S.C. §901(1)).

	Part II. CALCULATION OF MONTHLY INCOME FOR § 707(b)(7) EXCLUSION		
2	**Marital/filing status.** Check the box that applies and complete the balance of this part of this statement as directed. a. ☐ Unmarried. **Complete only Column A ("Debtor's Income") for Lines 3-11.** b. ☐ Married, not filing jointly, with declaration of separate households. By checking this box, debtor declares under penalty of perjury: "My spouse and I are legally separated under applicable non-bankruptcy law or my spouse and I are living apart other than for the purpose of evading the requirements of § 707(b)(2)(A) of the Bankruptcy Code." **Complete only Column A ("Debtor's Income") for Lines 3-11.** c. ☐ Married, not filing jointly, without the declaration of separate households set out in Line 2.b above. **Complete both Column A ("Debtor's Income") and Column B (Spouse's Income) for Lines 3-11.** d. ☐ Married, filing jointly. **Complete both Column A ("Debtor's Income") and Column B ("Spouse's Income") for Lines 3-11.**		
	All figures must reflect average monthly income for the six calendar months prior to filing the bankruptcy case, ending on the last day of the month before the filing. If you received different amounts of income during these six months, you must total the amounts received during the six months, divide this total by six, and enter the result on the appropriate line.	**Column A** Debtor's Income	**Column B** Spouse's Income
3	Gross wages, salary, tips, bonuses, overtime, commissions.	$	$
4	Income from the operation of a business, profession or farm. Subtract Line b from Line a and enter the difference on Line 4. Do not enter a number less than zero. **Do not include any part of the business expenses entered on Line b as a deduction in Part V.**		
	a. Gross receipts $		
	b. Ordinary and necessary business expenses $		
	c. Business income Subtract Line b from Line a	$	$
5	Rent and other real property income. Subtract Line b from Line a and enter the difference on Line 5. Do not enter a number less than zero. **Do not include any part of the operating expenses entered on Line b as a deduction in Part V.**		
	a. Gross receipts $		
	b. Ordinary and necessary operating expenses $		
	c. Rental income Subtract Line b from Line a	$	$
6	Interest, dividends and royalties.	$	$
7	Pension and retirement income.	$	$
8	Regular contributions to the household expenses of the debtor or the debtor's dependents, including child or spousal support. Do not include contributions from the debtor's spouse if Column B is completed.	$	$

STATEMENT OF CURRENT MONTHLY INCOME AND MEANS TEST CALCULATION

Form B 22A (Chapter 7) (10/05)   2

9	Unemployment compensation. Enter the amount in Column A and, if applicable, Column B. However, if you contend that unemployment compensation received by you or your spouse was a benefit under the Social Security Act, do not list the amount of such compensation in Column A or B, but instead state the amount in the space below: Unemployment compensation claimed to be a benefit under the Social Security Act Debtor \$ _____ Spouse \$ _____	\$	\$
10	Income from all other sources. If necessary, list additional sources on a separate page. **Do not include** any benefits received under the Social Security Act or payments received as a victim of a war crime, crime against humanity, or as a victim of international or domestic terrorism. Specify source and amount. a. _____ \$ _____ b. _____ \$ _____ Total and enter on Line 10	\$	\$
11	**Subtotal of Current Monthly Income for § 707(b)(7).** Add Lines 3 thru 10 in Column A, and, if Column B is completed, add Lines 3 through 10 in Column B. Enter the total(s).	\$	\$
12	**Total Current Monthly Income for § 707(b)(7).** If Column B has been completed, add Line 11, Column A to Line 11, Column B, and enter the total. If Column B has not been completed, enter the amount from Line 11, Column A.	\$	

Part III. APPLICATION OF § 707(b)(7) EXCLUSION

13	**Annualized Current Monthly Income for § 707(b)(7).** Multiply the amount from Line 12 by the number 12 and enter the result.	\$
14	**Applicable median family income.** Enter the median family income for the applicable state and household size. (This information is available by family size at www.usdoj.gov/ust/ or from the clerk of the bankruptcy court.) a. Enter debtor's state of residence: _____ b. Enter debtor's household size: _____	\$
15	**Application of Section 707(b)(7).** Check the applicable box and proceed as directed. ☐ **The amount on Line 13 is less than or equal to the amount on Line 14.** Check the box for "The presumption does not arise" at the top of page 1 of this statement, and complete Part VIII; do not complete Parts IV, V, VI or VII. ☐ **The amount on Line 13 is more than the amount on Line 14.** Complete the remaining parts of this statement.	

Complete Parts IV, V, VI, and VII of this statement only if required. (See Line 15.)

Part IV. CALCULATION OF CURRENT MONTHLY INCOME FOR § 707(b)(2)

16	Enter the amount from Line 12.	\$
17	**Marital adjustment.** If you checked the box at Line 2.c, enter the amount of the income listed in Line 11, Column B that was NOT regularly contributed to the household expenses of the debtor or the debtor's dependents. If you did not check box at Line 2.c, enter zero.	\$
18	**Current monthly income for § 707(b)(2).** Subtract Line 17 from Line 16 and enter the result.	\$

Part V. CALCULATION OF DEDUCTIONS ALLOWED UNDER § 707(b)(2)

Subpart A: Deductions under Standards of the Internal Revenue Service (IRS)

19	**National Standards: food, clothing, household supplies, personal care, and miscellaneous.** Enter "Total" amount from IRS National Standards for Allowable Living Expenses for the applicable family size and income level. (This information is available at www.usdoj.gov/ust/ or from the clerk of the bankruptcy court.)	\$
20A	**Local Standards: housing and utilities; non-mortgage expenses.** Enter the amount of the IRS Housing and Utilities Standards; non-mortgage expenses for the applicable county and family size.	\$

Form B 22A (Chapter 7) (10/05) 3

(This information is available at www.usdoj.gov/ust/ or from the clerk of the bankruptcy court).

20B	**Local Standards: housing and utilities; mortgage / rent expense.** Enter, in Line a below, the amount of the IRS Housing and Utilities Standards; mortgage/rent expense for your county and family size (this information is available at www.usdoj.gov/ust/ or from the clerk of the bankruptcy court); enter on Line b the total of the Average Monthly Payments for any debts secured by your home, as stated in Line 42; subtract Line b from Line a and enter the result in Line 20B. **Do not enter an amount less than zero.**		
	a.	IRS Housing and Utilities Standards; mortgage/rental expense	$
	b.	Average Monthly Payment for any debts secured by your home, if any, as stated in Line 42	$
	c.	Net mortgage/rental expense	Subtract Line b from Line a. $

21	**Local Standards: housing and utilities; adjustment.** if you contend that the process set out in Lines 20A and 20B does not accurately compute the allowance to which you are entitled under the IRS Housing and Utilities Standards, enter any additional amount to which you contend you are entitled, and state the basis for your contention in the space below: _____ _____ _____	$

22	**Local Standards: transportation; vehicle operation / public transportation expense.** You are entitled to an expense allowance in this category regardless of whether you pay the expenses of operating a vehicle and regardless of whether you use public transportation. Check the number of vehicles for which you pay the operating expenses or for which the operating expenses are included as a contribution to your household expenses in Line 8. ☐ 0 ☐ 1 ☐ 2 or more. Enter the amount from IRS Transportation Standards, Operating Costs & Public Transportation Costs for the applicable number of vehicles in the applicable Metropolitan Statistical Area or Census Region. (This information is available at www.usdoj.gov/ust/ or from the clerk of the bankruptcy court.)	$

23	**Local Standards: transportation ownership / lease expense; Vehicle 1.** Check the number of vehicles for which you claim an ownership/lease expense. (You may not claim an ownership/lease expense for more than two vehicles.) ☐ 1 ☐ 2 or more. Enter, in Line a below, the amount of the IRS Transportation Standards, Ownership Costs, First Car (available at www.usdoj.gov/ust/ or from the clerk of the bankruptcy court); enter in Line b the total of the Average Monthly Payments for any debts secured by Vehicle 1, as stated in Line 42; subtract Line b from Line a and enter the result in Line 23. **Do not enter an amount less than zero.**		
	a.	IRS Transportation Standards, Ownership Costs, First Car	$
	b.	Average Monthly Payment for any debts secured by Vehicle 1, as stated in Line 42	$
	c.	Net ownership/lease expense for Vehicle 1	Subtract Line b from Line a. $

24	**Local Standards: transportation ownership / lease expense; Vehicle 2.** Complete this Line only if you checked the "2 or more" Box in Line 23. Enter, in Line a below, the amount of the IRS Transportation Standards, Ownership Costs, Second Car (available at www.usdoj.gov/ust/ or from the clerk of the bankruptcy court); enter in Line b the total of the Average Monthly Payments for any debts secured by Vehicle 2, as stated in Line 42; subtract Line b from Line a and enter the result in Line 24. **Do not enter an amount less than zero.**		
	a.	IRS Transportation Standards, Ownership Costs, Second Car	$
	b.	Average Monthly Payment for any debts secured by Vehicle 2, as stated in Line 42	$
	c.	Net ownership/lease expense for Vehicle 2	Subtract Line b from Line a. $

25	**Other Necessary Expenses: taxes.** Enter the total average monthly expense that you actually incur for all federal, state and local taxes, other than real estate and sales taxes, such as income taxes, self employment taxes, social security taxes, and Medicare taxes. **Do not include real estate or sales taxes.**	

26	**Other Necessary Expenses: mandatory payroll deductions.** Enter the total average monthly payroll deductions that are required for your employment, such as mandatory retirement contributions, union dues, and uniform costs. **Do not include discretionary amounts, such as non-mandatory 401(k) contributions.**	$

Individual Bankruptcy and Restructuring 145

STATEMENT OF CURRENT MONTHLY INCOME AND MEANS TEST CALCULATION

Form B 22A (Chapter 7) (10/05) 4

27	**Other Necessary Expenses: life insurance.** Enter average monthly premiums that you actually pay for term life insurance for yourself. **Do not include premiums for insurance on your dependents, for whole life or for any other form of insurance.**	$
28	**Other Necessary Expenses: court-ordered payments.** Enter the total monthly amount that you are required to pay pursuant to court order, such as spousal or child support payments. **Do not include payments on past due support obligations included in Line 44.**	$
29	**Other Necessary Expenses: education for employment or for a physically or mentally challenged child.** Enter the total monthly amount that you actually expend for education that is a condition of employment and for education that is required for a physically or mentally challenged dependent child for whom no public education providing similar services is available.	$
30	**Other Necessary Expenses: childcare.** Enter the average monthly amount that you actually expend on childcare. **Do not include payments made for children's education.**	$
31	**Other Necessary Expenses: health care.** Enter the average monthly amount that you actually expend on health care expenses that are not reimbursed by insurance or paid by a health savings account. **Do not include payments for health insurance listed in Line 34.**	$
32	**Other Necessary Expenses: telecommunication services.** Enter the average monthly expenses that you actually pay for cell phones, pagers, call waiting, caller identification, special long distance or internet services necessary for the health and welfare of you or your dependents. **Do not include any amount previously deducted.**	$
33	**Total Expenses Allowed under IRS Standards.** Enter the total of Lines 19 through 32.	$

Subpart B: Additional Expense Deductions under § 707(b)

Note: Do not include any expenses that you have listed in Lines 19-32

34	**Health Insurance, Disability Insurance and Health Savings Account Expenses.** List the average monthly amounts that you actually expend in each of the following categories and enter the total.		
	a. Health Insurance	$	
	b. Disability Insurance	$	
	c. Health Savings Account	$	
		Total: Add Lines a, b and c	$
35	**Continued contributions to the care of household or family members.** Enter the actual monthly expenses that you will continue to pay for the reasonable and necessary care and support of an elderly, chronically ill, or disabled member of your household or member of your immediate family who is unable to pay for such expenses.	$
36	**Protection against family violence.** Enter any average monthly expenses that you actually incurred to maintain the safety of your family under the Family Violence Prevention and Services Act or other applicable federal law.	$
37	**Home energy costs in excess of the allowance specified by the IRS Local Standards.** Enter the average monthly amount by which your home energy costs exceed the allowance in the IRS Local Standards for Housing and Utilities. **You must provide your case trustee with documentation demonstrating that the additional amount claimed is reasonable and necessary.**	$
38	**Education expenses for dependent children less than 18.** Enter the average monthly expenses that you actually incur, not to exceed $125 per child, in providing elementary and secondary education for your dependent children less than 18 years of age. **You must provide your case trustee with documentation demonstrating that the amount claimed is reasonable and necessary and not already accounted for in the IRS Standards.**	$
39	**Additional food and clothing expense.** Enter the average monthly amount by which your food and clothing expenses exceed the combined allowances for food and apparel in the IRS National Standards, not to exceed five percent of those combined allowances. (This information is available at www.usdoj.gov/ust/ or from the clerk of the bankruptcy court.) **You must provide your case trustee with documentation demonstrating that the additional amount claimed is reasonable and necessary.**	$
40	**Continued charitable contributions.** Enter the amount that you will continue to contribute in the form of cash or financial instruments to a charitable organization as defined in 26 U.S.C. § 170(c)(1)-(2).	$
41	**Total Additional Expense Deductions under § 707(b).** Enter the total of Lines 34 through 40	$

STATEMENT OF CURRENT MONTHLY INCOME AND MEANS TEST CALCULATION

Form B 22A (Chapter 7) (10/05)   5

Subpart C: Deductions for Debt Payment			

Future payments on secured claims. For each of your debts that is secured by an interest in property that you own, list the name of the creditor, identify the property securing the debt, and state the Average Monthly Payment. The Average Monthly Payment is the total of all amounts contractually due to each Secured Creditor in the 60 months following the filing of the bankruptcy case, divided by 60. Mortgage debts should include payments of taxes and insurance required by the mortgage. If necessary, list additional entries on a separate page.

42

	Name of Creditor	Property Securing the Debt	60-month Average Payment	
a.			$	
b.			$	
c.			$	
			Total: Add Lines a, b and c.	$

Past due payments on secured claims. If any of the debts listed in Line 42 are in default, and the property securing the debt is necessary for your support or the support of your dependents, you may include in your deductions 1/60th of the amount that you must pay the creditor as a result of the default (the "cure amount") in order to maintain possession of the property. List any such amounts in the following chart and enter the total. If necessary, list additional entries on a separate page.

43

	Name of Creditor	Property Securing the Debt in Default	1/60th of the Cure Amount	
a.			$	
b.			$	
c.			$	
			Total: Add Lines a, b and c	$

44 | **Payments on priority claims.** Enter the total amount of all priority claims (including priority child support and alimony claims), divided by 60. | | | $ |

Chapter 13 administrative expenses. If you are eligible to file a case under Chapter 13, complete the following chart, multiply the amount in line a by the amount in line b, and enter the resulting administrative expense.

45

	a.	Projected average monthly Chapter 13 plan payment.	$	
	b.	Current multiplier for your district as determined under schedules issued by the Executive Office for United States Trustees. (This information is available at www.usdoj.gov/ust/ or from the clerk of the bankruptcy court.)	x	
	c.	Average monthly administrative expense of Chapter 13 case		
			Total: Multiply Lines a and b	$

46 | **Total Deductions for Debt Payment.** Enter the total of Lines 42 through 45. | | | $ |

Subpart D: Total Deductions Allowed under § 707(b)(2)			

47 | **Total of all deductions allowed under § 707(b)(2).** Enter the total of Lines 33, 41, and 46. | | | $ |

Part VI. DETERMINATION OF § 707(b)(2) PRESUMPTION

48	Enter the amount from Line 18 (Current monthly income for § 707(b)(2))	$
49	Enter the amount from Line 47 (Total of all deductions allowed under § 707(b)(2))	$
50	**Monthly disposable income under § 707(b)(2).** Subtract Line 49 from Line 48 and enter the result	$
51	**60-month disposable income under § 707(b)(2).** Multiply the amount in Line 50 by the number 60 and enter the result.	$

Form B 22A (Chapter 7) (10/05)   6

	Initial presumption determination. Check the applicable box and proceed as directed.
52	☐ **The amount on Line 51 is less than $6,000** Check the box for "The presumption does not arise" at the top of page 1 of this statement, and complete the verification in Part VIII. Do not complete the remainder of Part VI. ☐ **The amount set forth on Line 51 is more than $10,000.** Check the box for "The presumption arises" at the top of page 1 of this statement, and complete the verification in Part VIII. You may also complete Part VII. Do not complete the remainder of Part VI. ☐ **The amount on Line 51 is at least $6,000, but not more than $10,000.** Complete the remainder of Part VI (Lines 53 through 55).

53	Enter the amount of your total non-priority unsecured debt	$
54	**Threshold debt payment amount.** Multiply the amount in Line 53 by the number 0.25 and enter the result.	$

55	**Secondary presumption determination.** Check the applicable box and proceed as directed. ☐ **The amount on Line 51 is less than the amount on Line 54.** Check the box for "The presumption does not arise" at the top of page 1 of this statement, and complete the verification in Part VIII. ☐ **The amount on Line 51 is equal to or greater than the amount on Line 54.** Check the box for "The presumption arises" at the top of page 1 of this statement, and complete the verification in Part VIII. You may also complete Part VII.

Part VII: ADDITIONAL EXPENSE CLAIMS

56	**Other Expenses.** List and describe any monthly expenses, not otherwise stated in this form, that are required for the health and welfare of you and your family and that you contend should be an additional deduction from your current monthly income under § 707(b)(2)(A)(ii)(I). If necessary, list additional sources on a separate page. All figures should reflect your average monthly expense for each item. Total the expenses.

	Expense Description	Monthly Amount
a.		$
b.		$
c.		$
	Total: Add Lines a, b and c	$

Part VIII: VERIFICATION

57	I declare under penalty of perjury that the information provided in this statement is true and correct. *(If this a joint case, both debtors must sign.)* Date: _____ Signature: _____ (Debtor) Date: _____ Signature: _____ (Joint Debtor, if any)

APPENDIX 20:
NOTICE OF CHAPTER 7 BANKRUPTCY CASE, MEETING OF CREDITORS AND DEADLINES IN A NO-ASSET CASE (FORM B9A)

FORM B9A (Chapter 7 Individual or Joint Debtor No Asset Case (10/05))

UNITED STATES BANKRUPTCY COURT_____District of_____

Notice of
Chapter 7 Bankruptcy Case, Meeting of Creditors, & Deadlines

[A chapter 7 bankruptcy case concerning the debtor(s) listed below was filed on _____(date).]
or [A bankruptcy case concerning the debtor(s) listed below was originally filed under chapter_____on _____(date) and was converted to a case under chapter 7 on_____.]

You may be a creditor of the debtor. **This notice lists important deadlines.** You may want to consult an attorney to protect your rights. All documents filed in the case may be inspected at the bankruptcy clerk's office at the address listed below. NOTE: The staff of the bankruptcy clerk's office cannot give legal advice.

See Reverse Side for Important Explanations

Debtor(s) (name(s) and address):	Case Number:
	Last four digits of Social Security No./Complete EIN or other Taxpayer ID No.
All other names used by the Debtor(s) in the last 8 years (include married, maiden, and trade names):	Bankruptcy Trustee (name and address):
Attorney for Debtor(s) (name and address):	
Telephone number:	Telephone number:

Meeting of Creditors

Date: / /   Time: (   ) A. M.   Location:
                              (   ) P. M.

Presumption of Abuse under 11 U.S.C. § 707(b)
See "Presumption of Abuse" on the reverse side.

Depending on the documents filed with the petition, one of the following statements will appear.

    The presumption of abuse does not arise.
       Or
    The presumption of abuse arises.
       Or
    Insufficient information has been filed to date to permit the clerk to make any determination concerning the presumption of abuse. If more complete information, when filed, shows that the presumption has arisen, creditors will be notified.

Deadlines:
Papers must be *received* by the bankruptcy clerk's office by the following deadlines:
Deadline to File a Complaint Objecting to Discharge of the Debtor or to Determine Dischargeability of Certain Debts:

Deadline to Object to Exemptions:
Thirty (30) days after the *conclusion* of the meeting of creditors.

Creditors May Not Take Certain Actions:
In most instances, the filing of the bankruptcy case automatically stays certain collection and other actions against the debtor and the debtor's property. Under certain circumstances, the stay may be limited to 30 days or not exist at all, although the debtor can request the court to extend or impose a stay. If you attempt to collect a debt or take other action in violation of the Bankruptcy Code, you may be penalized. Consult a lawyer to determine your rights in this case.

Please Do Not File A Proof of Claim Unless You Receive a Notice To Do So.

Foreign Creditors
A creditor to whom this notice is sent at a foreign address should read the information under "Do Not File a Proof of Claim at This Time" on the reverse side.

Address of the Bankruptcy Clerk's Office:	For the Court:
	Clerk of the Bankruptcy Court:
Telephone number:	
Hours Open:	Date:

EXPLANATIONS	Form B9A (10/05)
Filing of Chapter 7 Bankruptcy Case	A bankruptcy case under Chapter 7 of the Bankruptcy Code (title 11, United States Code) has been filed in this court by or against the debtor(s) listed on the front side, and an order for relief has been entered.
Legal Advice	The staff of the bankruptcy clerk's office cannot give legal advice. Consult a lawyer to determine your rights in this case.
Creditors Generally May Not Take Certain Actions	Prohibited collection actions are listed in Bankruptcy Code § 362. Common examples of prohibited actions include contacting the debtor by telephone, mail, or otherwise to demand repayment; taking actions to collect money or obtain property from the debtor; repossessing the debtor's property; starting or continuing lawsuits or foreclosures; and garnishing or deducting from the debtor's wages. Under certain circumstances, the stay may be limited to 30 days or not exist at all, although the debtor can request the court to extend or impose a stay.
Presumption of Abuse	If the presumption of abuse arises, creditors may have the right to file a motion to dismiss the case under § 707(b) of the Bankruptcy Code. The debtor may rebut the presumption by showing special circumstances.
Meeting of Creditors	A meeting of creditors is scheduled for the date, time, and location listed on the front side. *The debtor (both spouses in a joint case) must be present at the meeting to be questioned under oath by the trustee and by creditors.* Creditors are welcome to attend, but are not required to do so. The meeting may be continued and concluded at a later date without further notice.
Do Not File a Proof of Claim at This Time	There does not appear to be any property available to the trustee to pay creditors. *You therefore should not file a proof of claim at this time.* If it later appears that assets are available to pay creditors, you will be sent another notice telling you that you may file a proof of claim, and telling you the deadline for filing your proof of claim. If this notice is mailed to a creditor at a foreign address, the creditor may file a motion requesting the court to extend the deadline.
Discharge of Debts	The debtor is seeking a discharge of most debts, which may include your debt. A discharge means that you may never try to collect the debt from the debtor. If you believe that the debtor is not entitled to receive a discharge under Bankruptcy Code § 727 (a) *or* that a debt owed to you is not dischargeable under Bankruptcy Code § 523 (a) (2), (4), or (6), you must start a lawsuit by filing a complaint in the bankruptcy clerk's office by the "Deadline to File a Complaint Objecting to Discharge of the Debtor or to Determine Dischargeability of Certain Debts" listed on the front side. The bankruptcy clerk's office must receive the complaint and any required filing fee by that Deadline.
Exempt Property	The debtor is permitted by law to keep certain property as exempt. Exempt property will not be sold and distributed to creditors. The debtor must file a list of all property claimed as exempt. You may inspect that list at the bankruptcy clerk's office. If you believe that an exemption claimed by the debtor is not authorized by law, you may file an objection to that exemption. The bankruptcy clerk's office must receive the objections by the "Deadline to Object to Exemptions" listed on the front side.
Bankruptcy Clerk's Office	Any paper that you file in this bankruptcy case should be filed at the bankruptcy clerk's office at the address listed on the front side. You may inspect all papers filed, including the list of the debtor's property and debts and the list of the property claimed as exempt, at the bankruptcy clerk's office.
Foreign Creditors	Consult a lawyer familiar with United States bankruptcy law if you have any questions regarding your rights in this case.

Refer To Other Side For Important Deadlines and Notices

Individual Bankruptcy and Restructuring

APPENDIX 21:
PROOF OF CLAIM (FORM B10)

Form B10 (Official Form 10) (10/05)

United States Bankruptcy Court Central District of California		PROOF OF CLAIM
Name of Debtor	Case Number	

NOTE: This form should not be used to make a claim for an administrative expense arising after the commencement of the case. A "request" for payment of an administrative expense may be filed pursuant to 11 U.S.C. § 503.

Name of Creditor (The person or other entity to whom the debtor owes money or property):	☐ Check box if you are aware that anyone else has filed a proof of claim relating to your claim. Attach copy of statement giving particulars.	
Name and address where notices should be sent:	☐ Check box if you have never received any notices from the bankruptcy court in this case.	
Telephone number:	☐ Check box if the address differs from the address on the envelope sent to you by the court.	**This space is for Court use only.**
Last four digits of account or other number by which creditor identifies debtor:	Check here ☐ replaces if this claim ☐ amends a previously filed claim, dated: _____	

1. Basis for Claim
- ☐ Goods sold
- ☐ Services performed
- ☐ Money loaned
- ☐ Personal injury/wrongful death
- ☐ Taxes
- ☐ Other _____

☐ Retire benefits as defined in 11 U.S.C. § 1114(a)
☐ Wages, salaries, and compensation (Fill out below)
    Last four digits of your Social Security number: _____
    Unpaid compensation for services performed
    from _____ to _____
        (date)   (date)

2. Date debt was incurred:

3. If court judgment, date obtained:

4. Total Amount of Claim at Time Case Filed: $_____ (unsecured) $_____ (secured) $_____ (priority) $_____ (Total)

If all or part of your claim is secured or entitled to priority, also complete Item 5 or 7 below.

☐ Check this box if claim includes interest or other charges in addition to the principal amount of the claim. Attach itemized statement of all interest or additional charges.

5. Secured Claim.
☐ Check this box if your claim is secured by collateral (including a right of setoff).

Brief Description of Collateral:
☐ Real Estate   ☐ Motor Vehicle
☐ Other _____

Value of Collateral: $_____

Amount of arrearage and other charges <u>at time case filed</u> included in secured claim, if any $_____

6. Unsecured Nonpriority Claim. $_____
☐ Check this box if (a) there is no collateral or lien securing your claim, or (b) your claim exceeds the value of the property securing it or (c) none or only part of your claim is entitled to priority.

7. Unsecured Priority Claim.
☐ Check this box if you have an unsecured priority claim, all or part of which is entitled to priority.
Amount entitled to priority $_____
Specify the priority of the claim:
☐ Wages, salaries, or commissions (up to $10,000),* earned within 180 days before filing of the bankruptcy petition or cessation of the debtor's business, whichever is earlier - 11 U.S.C. § 507(a)(4).
☐ Contributions to an employee benefit plan - 11 U.S.C. § 507(a)(5).
☐ Up to $2,225* of deposits toward purchase, lease or rental of property or services for personal, family, or household use - 11 U.S.C. § 507(a)(7).
☐ Domestic support obligations under - 11 U.S.C. § 507(a)(1)(A) or (a)(1)(B).
☐ Taxes or penalties owed to governmental units - 11 U.S.C. § 507(a)(8).
☐ Other - Specify applicable paragraph of 11 U.S.C. § 507(a)(_____).
*Amounts are subject to adjustment on 4/1/07 and every 3 years thereafter with respect to cases commenced on or after the date of adjustment. $10,000 and 180-day limits apply to cases filed on or after 4/20/05. Pub. L. 109-8

8. Credits: The amount of all payments on this claim has been credited and deducted for the purpose of making this proof of claim.

9. Supporting Documents: Attach copies of supporting documents, such as promissory notes, purchase orders, invoices, itemized statements of running accounts, contracts, court judgments, mortgages, security agreements, and evidence of perfection of lien. DO NOT SEND ORIGINAL DOCUMENTS. If the documents are not available, explain. If the documents are voluminous, attach a summary.

10. Date-Stamped Copy: To receive an acknowledgment of the filing of your claim, enclose a stamped, self-addressed envelope and copy of this proof of claim.

This space is for Court use only.

Date	Sign and print the name and title, if any, of the creditor or other person authorized to file this claim (attach copy of power of attorney, if any):

Penalty for presenting fraudulent claim: Fine of up to $500,000 or imprisonment for up to 5 years, or both. 18 U.S.C. §§ 152 and 3571.

Form B10 (Official Form 10) (10/05)

INSTRUCTIONS FOR PROOF OF CLAIM FORM

The instructions and definitions below are general explanations of the law. In particular types of cases or circumstances, such as bankruptcy cases that are not filed voluntarily by a debtor, there may be exceptions to these general rules.

----- DEFINITIONS -----

Debtor
The person, corporation, or other entity that has filed a bankruptcy case is called the debtor.

Creditor
A creditor is any person, corporation, or other entity to whom the debtor owed a debt on the date that the bankruptcy case was filed.

Proof of Claim
A form telling the bankruptcy court how much the debtor owed a creditor at the time the bankruptcy case was filed (the amount of the creditor's claim). This form must be filed with the clerk of the bankruptcy court where the bankruptcy case was filed.

Secured Claim
A claim is a secured claim to the extent that the creditor has a lien on property of the debtor (collateral) that gives the creditor the right to be paid from that property before creditors who do not have liens on the property.

Examples of liens are a mortgage on real estate and a security interest in a car, truck, boat, television set, or other item of property. A lien may have been obtained through a court proceeding before the bankruptcy case began; in some states a court judgment is a lien. In addition, to the extent a creditor also owes money to the debtor (has a right of setoff), the creditor's claim may be a secured claim. (See also *Unsecured Claim.*)

Unsecured Claim
If a claim is not a secured claim it is an unsecured claim. A claim may be partly secured and partly unsecured if the property on which a creditor has a lien is not worth enough to pay the creditor in full.

Unsecured Priority Claim
Certain types of unsecured claims are given priority, so they are to be paid in bankruptcy cases before most other unsecured claims (if there is sufficient money or property available to pay these claims). The most common types of priority claims are listed on the proof of claim form. Unsecured claims that are not specifically given priority status by the bankruptcy laws are classified as *Unsecured Nonpriority claims.*

Items to be completed in Proof of Claim form (if not already filled in)

Court, Name of Debtor, and Case Number:
Fill in the name of the federal judicial district where the bankruptcy case was filed (*for example:* Central District of California), the name of the debtor in the bankruptcy case, and the bankruptcy case number. If you received a notice of the case from the court, all of this information is near the top of the notice.

Information about Creditor:
Complete the section giving the name, address, and telephone number of the creditor to whom the debtor owes money or property, and the debtor's account number, if any. If anyone else has already filed a proof of claim relating to this debt, if you never received notices from the bankruptcy court about this case, if your address differs from that to which the court sent notice, or if this proof of claim replaces or changes a proof of claim that was already filed, check the appropriate box on the form.

1. Basis for Claim:
Check the type of debt for which the proof of claim is being filed. If the type of debt is not listed, check "Other" and briefly describe the type of debt. If you were an employee of the debtor, fill in the last four digits of your Social Security number and the dates of work for which you were not paid.

2. Date Debt Incurred:
Fill in the date when the debt first was owed by the debtor.

3. Court Judgments:
If you have a court judgment for this debt, state the date the court entered the judgment.

4. Total Amount of Claim at Time Case Filed:
Fill in the total amount of the entire claim. If interest or other charges in addition to the principal amount of the claim are included, check the appropriate place on the form and attach an itemization of the interest and charges.

5. Secured Claim:
Check the appropriate place if the claim is a secured claim. You must state the type and value of property that is collateral for the claim, attach copies of the documentation of your lien, and state the amount past due on the claim as of the date the bankruptcy case was filed. A claim may be partly secured and partly unsecured. (See DEFINITIONS, above.)

6. Unsecured Nonpriority Claim:
Check the appropriate place if you have an unsecured nonpriority claim, sometimes referred to as a "general unsecured claim." (See DEFINITIONS, above.) If your claim is partly secured and partly unsecured, state here the amount that is unsecured. If part of your claim is entitled to priority, state here the amount **not** entitled to priority.

7. Unsecured Priority Claim:
Check the appropriate place if you have an unsecured priority claim, and state the amount entitled to priority. (See DEFINITIONS, above.) A claim may be partly priority and partly nonpriority if, for example, the claim is for more than the amount given priority by the law. Check the appropriate place to specify the type of priority claim.

8. Credits:
By signing this proof of claim, you are stating under oath that in calculating the amount of your claim you have given the debtor credit for all payments received from the debtor.

9. Supporting Documents:
You must attach to this proof of claim form copies of documents that show the debtor owes the debt claimed or, if the documents are too lengthy, a summary of those documents. If documents are not available, you must attach an explanation of why they are not available.

Individual Bankruptcy and Restructuring

APPENDIX 22:
NOTICE OF CHAPTER 7 BANKRUPTCY CASE, MEETING OF CREDITORS AND DEADLINES IN AN ASSET CASE (FORM B9C)

FORM B9C (Chapter 7 Individual or Joint Debtor Asset Case (10/05))

UNITED STATES BANKRUPTCY COURT_____District of_____

Notice of
Chapter 7 Bankruptcy Case, Meeting of Creditors, & Deadlines

[A chapter 7 bankruptcy case concerning the debtor(s) listed below was filed on _____(date).]
or [A bankruptcy case concerning the debtor(s) listed below was originally filed under chapter_____on
_____(date) and was converted to a case under chapter 7 on_____.]

You may be a creditor of the debtor. **This notice lists important deadlines.** You may want to consult an attorney to protect your rights. All documents filed in the case may be inspected at the bankruptcy clerk's office at the address listed below. NOTE: The staff of the bankruptcy clerk's office cannot give legal advice.

See Reverse Side for Important Explanations

Debtor(s) (name(s) and address):	Case Number:
	Last four digits of Social Security No./Complete EIN or other Taxpayer ID No.:
All other names used by the Debtor(s) in the last 8 years (include married, maiden, and trade names):	Bankruptcy Trustee (name and address):
Attorney for Debtor(s) (name and address):	
Telephone number:	Telephone number:

Meeting of Creditors

Date: / /   Time: (   ) A. M.   Location:
                              (   ) P. M.

Presumption of Abuse under 11 U.S.C. § 707(b)
See "Presumption of Abuse" on the reverse side.

Depending on the documents filed with the petition, one of the following statements will appear.

The presumption of abuse does not arise.
Or
The presumption of abuse arises.
Or
Insufficient information has been filed to date to permit the clerk to make any determination concerning the presumption of abuse. If more complete information, when filed, shows that the presumption has arisen, creditors will be notified.

Deadlines:
Papers must be *received* by the bankruptcy clerk's office by the following deadlines:

Deadline to File a Proof of Claim:
For all creditors (except a governmental unit):   For a governmental unit:

Foreign Creditors:
A creditor to whom this notice is sent at a foreign address should read the information under "Claims" on the reverse side.

Deadline to File a Complaint Objecting to Discharge of the Debtor or to Determine Dischargeability of Certain Debts:

Deadline to Object to Exemptions:
Thirty (30) days after the *conclusion* of the meeting of creditors.

Creditors May Not Take Certain Actions:
In most instances, the filing of the bankruptcy case automatically stays certain collection and other actions against the debtor and the debtor's property. Under certain circumstances, the stay may be limited to 30 days or not exist at all, although the debtor can request the court to extend or impose a stay. If you attempt to collect a debt or take other action in violation of the Bankruptcy Code, you may be penalized. Consult a lawyer to determine your rights in this case.

Address of the Bankruptcy Clerk's Office:	For the Court:
	Clerk of the Bankruptcy Court:
Telephone number:	
Hours Open:	Date:

EXPLANATIONS	Form B9C (10/05)
Filing of Chapter 7 Bankruptcy Case	A bankruptcy case under Chapter 7 of the Bankruptcy Code (title 11, United States Code) has been filed in this court by or against the debtor(s) listed on the front side, and an order for relief has been entered.
Legal Advice	The staff of the bankruptcy clerk's office cannot give legal advice. Consult a lawyer to determine your rights in this case.
Creditors Generally May Not Take Certain Actions	Prohibited collection actions are listed in Bankruptcy Code § 362. Common examples of prohibited actions include contacting the debtor by telephone, mail, or otherwise to demand repayment; taking actions to collect money or obtain property from the debtor; repossessing the debtor's property; starting or continuing lawsuits or foreclosures; and garnishing or deducting from the debtor's wages. Under certain circumstances, the stay may be limited to 30 days or not exist at all, although the debtor can request the court to extend or impose a stay.
Meeting of Creditors	A meeting of creditors is scheduled for the date, time, and location listed on the front side. *The debtor (both spouses in a joint case) must be present at the meeting to be questioned under oath by the trustee and by creditors.* Creditors are welcome to attend, but are not required to do so. The meeting may be continued and concluded at a later date without further notice.
Claims	A Proof of Claim is a signed statement describing a creditor's claim. If a Proof of Claim form is not included with this notice, you can obtain one at any bankruptcy clerk's office. A secured creditor retains rights in its collateral regardless of whether that creditor files a Proof of Claim. If you do not file a Proof of Claim by the "Deadline to File a Proof of Claim" listed on the front side, you might not be paid any money on your claim from other assets in the bankruptcy case. To be paid you must file a Proof of Claim even if your claim is listed in the schedules filed by the debtor. Filing a Proof of Claim submits the creditor to the jurisdiction of the bankruptcy court, with consequences a lawyer can explain. For example, a secured creditor who files a Proof of Claim may surrender important nonmonetary rights, including the right to a jury trial. **Filing Deadline for a Foreign Creditor:** The deadlines for filing claims set forth on the front of this notice apply to all creditors. If this notice has been mailed to a creditor at a foreign address, the creditor may file a motion requesting the court to extend the deadline.
Discharge of Debts	The debtor is seeking a discharge of most debts, which may include your debt. A discharge means that you may never try to collect the debt from the debtor. If you believe that the debtor is not entitled to receive a discharge under Bankruptcy Code § 727 (a) *or* that a debt owed to you is not dischargeable under Bankruptcy Code § 523 (a) (2), (4), or (6), you must start a lawsuit by filing a complaint in the bankruptcy clerk's office by the "Deadline to File a Complaint Objecting to Discharge of the Debtor or to Determine Dischargeability of Certain Debts" listed on the front side. The bankruptcy clerk's office must receive the complaint and any required filing fee by that Deadline.
Exempt Property	The debtor is permitted by law to keep certain property as exempt. Exempt property will not be sold and distributed to creditors. The debtor must file a list of all property claimed as exempt. You may inspect that list at the bankruptcy clerk's office. If you believe that an exemption claimed by the debtor is not authorized by law, you may file an objection to that exemption. The bankruptcy clerk's office must receive the objections by the "Deadline to Object to Exemptions" listed on the front side.
Presumption of Abuse	If the presumption of abuse arises, creditors may have the right to file a motion to dismiss the case under § 707(b) of the Bankruptcy Code. The debtor may rebut the presumption by showing special circumstances.
Bankruptcy Clerk's Office	Any paper that you file in this bankruptcy case should be filed at the bankruptcy clerk's office at the address listed on the front side. You may inspect all papers filed, including the list of the debtor's property and debts and the list of the property claimed as exempt, at the bankruptcy clerk's office.
Liquidation of the Debtor's Property and Payment of Creditors' Claims	The bankruptcy trustee listed on the front of this notice will collect and sell the debtor's property that is not exempt. If the trustee can collect enough money, creditors may be paid some or all of the debts owed to them, in the order specified by the Bankruptcy Code. To make sure you receive any share of that money, you must file a Proof of Claim, as described above.
Foreign Creditors	Consult a lawyer familiar with United States bankruptcy law if you have any questions regarding your rights in this case.

Refer To Other Side For Important Deadlines and Notices

APPENDIX 23:
REAFFIRMATION AGREEMENT
(FORM B240)

B 240 - Reaffirmation Agreement
(10/05))

United States Bankruptcy Court
_____District of _____

In re _____,   Case No._____
                    Debtor   Chapter _____

REAFFIRMATION AGREEMENT

[Indicate all documents included in this filing by checking each applicable box.]

☐ Part A: Disclosures, Instructions, and   ☐ Part D: Debtor's Statement in Support of
  Notice to Debtor (Pages 1 - 5)   Reaffirmation Agreement
☐ Part B: Reaffirmation Agreement   ☐ Part E: Motion for Court Approval
☐ Part C: Certification by Debtor's   ☐ Proposed Order Approving Reaffirmation
  Attorney   Agreement

☐ *[Check this box if]* Creditor is a Credit Union as defined in §19(b)(1)(a)(iv) of the
Federal Reserve Act

PART A: DISCLOSURE STATEMENT, INSTRUCTIONS AND NOTICE TO DEBTOR

1.   DISCLOSURE STATEMENT

Before Agreeing to Reaffirm a Debt, Review These Important Disclosures:

SUMMARY OF REAFFIRMATION AGREEMENT
This Summary is made pursuant to the requirements of the Bankruptcy Code.

AMOUNT REAFFIRMED

a.   The amount of debt you have agreed to reaffirm: $_____

b.   All fees and costs accrued as of the date of this
       disclosure statement, related to the amount of debt
       shown in a., above: $_____

c.   The total amount you have agreed to reaffirm
       (Debt and fees and costs) (Add lines a. and b.): $_____

*Your credit agreement may obligate you to pay additional amounts which may come
due after the date of this disclosure. Consult your credit agreement.*
                                                          P. 2

ANNUAL PERCENTAGE RATE

[The annual percentage rate can be disclosed in different ways, depending on the type of debt.]

a. If the debt is an extension of "credit" under an "open end credit plan," as those terms are defined in § 103 of the Truth in Lending Act, such as a credit card, the creditor may disclose the annual percentage rate shown in (I) below or, to the extent this rate is not readily available or not applicable, the simple interest rate shown in (ii) below, or both.

(I) The Annual Percentage Rate disclosed, or that would have been disclosed, to the debtor in the most recent periodic statement prior to entering into the reaffirmation agreement described in Part B below or, if no such periodic statement was given to the debtor during the prior six months, the annual percentage rate as it would have been so disclosed at the time of the disclosure statement: _____%.

— And/Or ---

(ii) The simple interest rate applicable to the amount reaffirmed as of the date this disclosure statement is given to the debtor: _____%. If different simple interest rates apply to different balances included in the amount reaffirmed, the amount of each balance and the rate applicable to it are:

$_____ @ _____%;
$_____ @ _____%;
$_____ @ _____%.

b. If the debt is an extension of credit other than under than an open end credit plan, the creditor may disclose the annual percentage rate shown in (I) below, or, to the extent this rate is not readily available or not applicable, the simple interest rate shown in (ii) below, or both.

(I) The Annual Percentage Rate under §128(a)(4) of the Truth in Lending Act, as disclosed to the debtor in the most recent disclosure statement given to the debtor prior to entering into the reaffirmation agreement with respect to the debt or, if no such disclosure statement was given to the debtor, the annual percentage rate as it would have been so disclosed: _____%.

— And/Or ---

(ii) The simple interest rate applicable to the amount reaffirmed as of the date this disclosure statement is given to the debtor: _____%. If different simple interest rates apply to different balances included in the amount reaffirmed, the amount of each balance and the rate applicable to it are:

$_____ @ _____%;

$_____ @ _____%;

$_____ @ _____%.

    c. If the underlying debt transaction was disclosed as a variable rate transaction on the most recent disclosure given under the Truth in Lending Act:

    The interest rate on your loan may be a variable interest rate which changes from time to time, so that the annual percentage rate disclosed here may be higher or lower.

    d. If the reaffirmed debt is secured by a security interest or lien, which has not been waived or determined to be void by a final order of the court, the following items or types of items of the debtor's goods or property remain subject to such security interest or lien in connection with the debt or debts being reaffirmed in the reaffirmation agreement described in Part B.

Item or Type of Item   Original Purchase Price or Original Amount of Loan

Optional---*At the election of the creditor, a repayment schedule using one or a combination of the following may be provided:*

Repayment Schedule:

Your first payment in the amount of $_____ is due on _____(date), but the future payment amount may be different. Consult your reaffirmation agreement or credit agreement, as applicable.

---Or---

Your payment schedule will be: _____(number) payments in the amount of $_____ each, payable (monthly, annually, weekly, etc.) on the _____ (day) of each _____ (week, month, etc.), unless altered later by mutual agreement in writing.

---Or---

A reasonably specific description of the debtor's repayment obligations to the extent known by the creditor or creditor's representative.

P. 4

2. INSTRUCTIONS AND NOTICE TO DEBTOR

Reaffirming a debt is a serious financial decision. The law requires you to take certain steps to make sure the decision is in your best interest. If these steps are not completed, the reaffirmation agreement is not effective, even though you have signed it.

1. Read the disclosures in this Part A carefully. Consider the decision to reaffirm carefully. Then, if you want to reaffirm, sign the reaffirmation agreement in Part B (or you may use a separate agreement you and your creditor agree on).

2. Complete and sign Part D and be sure you can afford to make the payments you are agreeing to make and have received a copy of the disclosure statement and a completed and signed reaffirmation agreement.

3. If you were represented by an attorney during the negotiation of your reaffirmation agreement, the attorney must have signed the certification in Part C.

4. If you were not represented by an attorney during the negotiation of your reaffirmation agreement, you must have completed and signed Part E.

5. The original of this disclosure must be filed with the court by you or your creditor. If a separate reaffirmation agreement (other than the one in Part B) has been signed, it must be attached.

6. If the creditor is not a Credit Union and you were represented by an attorney during the negotiation of your reaffirmation agreement, your reaffirmation agreement becomes effective upon filing with the court unless the reaffirmation is presumed to be an undue hardship as explained in Part D. If the creditor is a Credit Union and you were represented by an attorney during the negotiation of your reaffirmation agreement, your reaffirmation agreement becomes effective upon filing with the court.

7. If you were not represented by an attorney during the negotiation of your reaffirmation agreement, it will not be effective unless the court approves it. The court will notify you and the creditor of the hearing on your reaffirmation agreement. You must attend this hearing in bankruptcy court where the judge will review your reaffirmation agreement. The bankruptcy court must approve your reaffirmation agreement as consistent with your best interests, except that no court approval is required if your reaffirmation agreement is for a consumer debt secured by a mortgage, deed of trust, security deed, or other lien on your real property, like your home.

P. 5

YOUR RIGHT TO RESCIND (CANCEL) YOUR REAFFIRMATION AGREEMENT

You may rescind (cancel) your reaffirmation agreement at any time before the bankruptcy court enters a discharge order, or before the expiration of the 60-day period that begins on the date your reaffirmation agreement is filed with the court, whichever occurs later. To rescind (cancel) your reaffirmation agreement, you must notify the creditor that your reaffirmation agreement is rescinded (or canceled).

Frequently Asked Questions:

What are your obligations if you reaffirm the debt? A reaffirmed debt remains your personal legal obligation. It is not discharged in your bankruptcy case. That means that if you default on your reaffirmed debt after your bankruptcy case is over, your creditor may be able to take your property or your wages. Otherwise, your obligations will be determined by the reaffirmation agreement which may have changed the terms of the original agreement. For example, if you are reaffirming an open end credit agreement, the creditor may be permitted by that agreement or applicable law to change the terms of that agreement in the future under certain conditions.

Are you required to enter into a reaffirmation agreement by any law? No, you are not required to reaffirm a debt by any law. Only agree to reaffirm a debt if it is in your best interest. Be sure you can afford the payments you agree to make.

What if your creditor has a security interest or lien? Your bankruptcy discharge does not eliminate any lien on your property. A "lien" is often referred to as a security interest, deed of trust, mortgage or security deed. Even if you do not reaffirm and your personal liability on the debt is discharged, because of the lien your creditor may still have the right to take the security property if you do not pay the debt or default on it. If the lien is on an item of personal property that is exempt under your State's law or that the trustee has abandoned, you may be able to redeem the item rather than reaffirm the debt. To redeem, you make a single payment to the creditor equal to the current value of the security property, as agreed by the parties or determined by the court.

NOTE: When this disclosure refers to what a creditor "may" do, it does not use the word "may" to give the creditor specific permission. The word "may" is used to tell you what might occur if the law permits the creditor to take the action. If you have questions about your reaffirming a debt or what the law requires, consult with the attorney who helped you negotiate this agreement reaffirming a debt. If you don't have an attorney helping you, the judge will explain the effect of your reaffirming a debt when the hearing on the reaffirmation agreement is held.

P. 6

PART B: REAFFIRMATION AGREEMENT.

I (we) agree to reaffirm the debts arising under the credit agreement described below.

1. Brief description of credit agreement:

2. Description of any changes to the credit agreement made as part of this reaffirmation agreement:

SIGNATURE(S):

Borrower: Co-borrower, if also reaffirming these debts:

_____   _____
(Print Name)   (Print Name)

_____   _____
(Signature)   (Signature)
Date: _____   Date: _____

Accepted by creditor:

_____
(Print Name)

_____
(Signature)
Date of creditor acceptance: _____

P. 7

PART C: CERTIFICATION BY DEBTOR'S ATTORNEY (IF ANY).

[Check each applicable box.]

☐ I hereby certify that (1) this agreement represents a fully informed and voluntary agreement by the debtor; (2) this agreement does not impose an undue hardship on the debtor or any dependent of the debtor; and (3) I have fully advised the debtor of the legal effect and consequences of this agreement and any default under this agreement.

☐ *[If applicable and the creditor is not a Credit Union.]* A presumption of undue hardship has been established with respect to this agreement. In my opinion, however, the debtor is able to make the required payment.

Printed Name of Debtor's Attorney: _____

Signature of Debtor's Attorney: _____

Date: _____

P. 8

PART D: DEBTOR'S STATEMENT IN SUPPORT OF REAFFIRMATION AGREEMENT

[Read and complete numbered paragraphs 1 and 2, OR, if the creditor is a Credit Union and the debtor is represented by an attorney, read the unnumbered paragraph below. Sign the appropriate signature line(s) and date your signature.]

1. I believe this reaffirmation agreement will not impose an undue hardship on my dependents or me. I can afford to make the payments on the reaffirmed debt because my monthly income (take home pay plus any other income received) is $_____, and my actual current monthly expenses including monthly payments on post-bankruptcy debt and other reaffirmation agreements total $_____, leaving $_____ to make the required payments on this reaffirmed debt. I understand that if my income less my monthly expenses does not leave enough to make the payments, this reaffirmation agreement is presumed to be an undue hardship on me and must be reviewed by the court. However, this presumption may be overcome if I explain to the satisfaction of the court how I can afford to make the payments here: _____.

2. I received a copy of the Reaffirmation Disclosure Statement in Part A and a completed and signed reaffirmation agreement.

Signed: _____
      (Debtor)

_____
(Joint Debtor, if any)
Date: _____

— Or

[If the creditor is a Credit Union and the debtor is represented by an attorney]

I believe this reaffirmation agreement is in my financial interest. I can afford to make the payments on the reaffirmed debt. I received a copy of the Reaffirmation Disclosure Statement in Part A and a completed and signed reaffirmation agreement.

Signed: _____
      (Debtor)

_____
(Joint Debtor, if any)
Date: _____

P. 9

PART E: MOTION FOR COURT APPROVAL
(To be completed only if the debtor is not represented by an attorney.)

MOTION FOR COURT APPROVAL OF REAFFIRMATION AGREEMENT

I (we), the debtor(s), affirm the following to be true and correct:

I am not represented by an attorney in connection with this reaffirmation agreement.

I believe this reaffirmation agreement is in my best interest based on the income and expenses I have disclosed in my Statement in Support of this reaffirmation agreement, and because (provide any additional relevant reasons the court should consider):

Therefore, I ask the court for an order approving this reaffirmation agreement.

Signed:_____
       (Debtor)

       _____
       (Joint Debtor, if any)

Date: _____

United States Bankruptcy Court
_____District of _____

In re _____,   Case No._____
                Debtor   Chapter _____

ORDER APPROVING REAFFIRMATION AGREEMENT

The debtor(s) _____ have filed a motion for approval of the
                (Name(s) of debtor(s))

reaffirmation agreement dated _____ made between the debtor(s) and
                   (Date of agreement)
_____. The court held the hearing required by 11 U.S.C. § 524(d)
    (Name of creditor)
on notice to the debtor(s) and the creditor on _____.
                       (Date)

COURT ORDER: The court grants the debtor's motion and approves the reaffirmation
                  agreement described above.

BY THE COURT

Date: _____   _____
                                United States Bankruptcy Judge

APPENDIX 24:
DISCHARGE ORDER (FORM 18)

Form 18
(10/05)

United States Bankruptcy Court

_____ District Of _____

In re _____,)
    [Set forth here all names including married,)
    maiden, and trade names used by debtor within)
    last 8 years.])
                    Debtor) Case No. _____
)
)
Address _____)
)
        _____) Chapter 7
)
Last four digits of Social Security No(s).: _____)
_____)
Employer's Tax Identification No(s). *[if any]:*_____)
_____)

DISCHARGE OF DEBTOR

    It appearing that the debtor is entitled to a discharge, **IT IS ORDERED:** The debtor is granted a discharge under section 727 of title 11, United States Code, (the Bankruptcy Code).

Dated: _____

                                BY THE COURT

                                _____
                                United States Bankruptcy Judge

SEE THE BACK OF THIS ORDER FOR IMPORTANT INFORMATION.

Official Form 18 - Contd.
(10/05)

EXPLANATION OF BANKRUPTCY DISCHARGE
IN A CHAPTER 7 CASE

This court order grants a discharge to the person named as the debtor. It is not a dismissal of the case and it does not determine how much money, if any, the trustee will pay to creditors.

Collection of Discharged Debts Prohibited
The discharge prohibits any attempt to collect from the debtor a debt that has been discharged. For example, a creditor is not permitted to contact a debtor by mail, phone, or otherwise, to file or continue a lawsuit, to attach wages or other property, or to take any other action to collect a discharged debt from the debtor. *[In a case involving community property:* There are also special rules that protect certain community property owned by the debtor's spouse, even if that spouse did not file a bankruptcy case.] A creditor who violates this order can be required to pay damages and attorney's fees to the debtor.

However, a creditor may have the right to enforce a valid lien, such as a mortgage or security interest, against the debtor's property after the bankruptcy, if that lien was not avoided or eliminated in the bankruptcy case. Also, a debtor may voluntarily pay any debt that has been discharged.

Debts That are Discharged
The chapter 7 discharge order eliminates a debtor's legal obligation to pay a debt that is discharged. Most, but not all, types of debts are discharged if the debt existed on the date the bankruptcy case was filed. (If this case was begun under a different chapter of the Bankruptcy Code and converted to chapter 7, the discharge applies to debts owed when the bankruptcy case was converted.)

Debts that are Not Discharged.
Some of the common types of debts which are <u>not</u> discharged in a chapter 7 bankruptcy case are:

a. Debts for most taxes;

b. Debts incurred to pay nondischargeable taxes;

c. Debts that are domestic support obligations;

d. Debts for most student loans;

e. Debts for most fines, penalties, forfeitures, or criminal restitution obligations;

f. Debts for personal injuries or death caused by the debtor's operation of a motor vehicle, vessel, or aircraft while intoxicated;

g. Some debts which were not properly listed by the debtor;

h. Debts that the bankruptcy court specifically has decided or will decide in this bankruptcy case are not discharged;

i. Debts for which the debtor has given up the discharge protections by signing a reaffirmation agreement in compliance with the Bankruptcy Code requirements for reaffirmation of debts.

j. Debts owed to certain pension, profit sharing, stock bonus, other retirement plans, or to the Thrift Savings Plan for federal employees for certain types of loans from these plans.

This information is only a general summary of the bankruptcy discharge. There are exceptions to these general rules. Because the law is complicated, you may want to consult an attorney to determine the exact effect of the discharge in this case.

APPENDIX 25:
NOTICE OF CHAPTER 13 BANKRUPTCY CASE, MEETING OF CREDITORS AND DEADLINES (FORM B9I)

FORM B9I (Chapter 13 Case (10/05))

UNITED STATES BANKRUPTCY COURT_____District of_____

Notice of
Chapter 13 Bankruptcy Case, Meeting of Creditors, & Deadlines

[The debtor(s) listed below filed a chapter 13 bankruptcy case on _____ (date).]
or [A bankruptcy case concerning the debtor(s) listed below was originally filed under chapter_____
on _____ (date) and was converted to a case under chapter 13 on_____.]

You may be a creditor of the debtor. **This notice lists important deadlines.** You may want to consult an attorney to protect your rights. All documents filed in the case may be inspected at the bankruptcy clerk's office at the address listed below.
NOTE: The staff of the bankruptcy clerk's office cannot give legal advice.

See Reverse Side for Important Explanations

Debtor(s) (name(s) and address):	Case Number:
Telephone number:	Last four digits of Social Security No./Complete EIN or other Taxpayer ID No.:
All other names used by the Debtor(s) in the last 8 years (include married, maiden, and trade names):	Bankruptcy Trustee (name and address):
Attorney for Debtor(s) (name and address):	
Telephone number:	Telephone number:

Meeting of Creditors

Date: / /   Time: (   ) A. M.   Location:
                                 (   ) P. M.

Deadlines:
Papers must be *received* by the bankruptcy clerk's office by the following deadlines:

Deadline to File a Proof of Claim:
For all creditors(except a governmental unit):   For a governmental unit:

Foreign Creditors
A creditor to whom this notice is sent at a foreign address should read the information under "Claims" on the reverse side.

Deadline to File a Complaint to Determine Dischargeability of Certain Debts:

Deadline to Object to Exemptions:
Thirty (30) days after the *conclusion* of the meeting of creditors.

Filing of Plan, Hearing on Confirmation of Plan
[The debtor has filed a plan. The plan or a summary of the plan is enclosed. The hearing on confirmation will be held:
Date:_____Time:_____Location:_____]
or [The debtor has filed a plan. The plan or a summary of the plan and notice of confirmation hearing will be sent separately.]
or [The debtor has not filed a plan as of this date. You will be sent separate notice of the hearing on confirmation of the plan.]

Creditors May Not Take Certain Actions:
In most instances, the filing of the bankruptcy case automatically stays certain collection and other actions against the debtor, the debtor's property, and certain codebtors. Under certain circumstances, the stay may be limited to 30 days or not exist at all, although the debtor can request the court to extend or impose a stay. If you attempt to collect a debt or take other action in violation of the Bankruptcy Code, you may be penalized. Consult a lawyer to determine your rights in this case.

Address of the Bankruptcy Clerk's Office:	For the Court:
	Clerk of the Bankruptcy Court:
Telephone number:	
Hours Open:	Date:

Individual Bankruptcy and Restructuring   **167**

EXPLANATIONS	Form B9I (10/05)
Filing of Chapter 13 Bankruptcy Case	A bankruptcy case under Chapter 13 of the Bankruptcy Code (title 11, United States Code) has been filed in this court by the debtor(s) listed on the front side, and an order for relief has been entered. Chapter 13 allows an individual with regular income and debts below a specified amount to adjust debts pursuant to a plan. A plan is not effective unless confirmed by the bankruptcy court. You may object to confirmation of the plan and appear at the confirmation hearing. A copy or summary of the plan [is included with this notice] *or* [will be sent to you later], and [the confirmation hearing will be held on the date indicated on the front of this notice] *or* [you will be sent notice of the confirmation hearing]. The debtor will remain in possession of the debtor's property and may continue to operate the debtor's business, if any, unless the court orders otherwise.
Legal Advice	The staff of the bankruptcy clerk's office cannot give legal advice. Consult a lawyer to determine your rights in this case.
Creditors Generally May Not Take Certain Actions	Prohibited collection actions against the debtor and certain codebtors are listed in Bankruptcy Code § 362 and § 1301. Common examples of prohibited actions include contacting the debtor by telephone, mail, or otherwise to demand repayment; taking actions to collect money or obtain property from the debtor; repossessing the debtor's property; starting or continuing lawsuits or foreclosures; and garnishing or deducting from the debtor's wages. Under certain circumstances, the stay may be limited to 30 days or not exist at all, although the debtor can request the court to exceed or impose a stay.
Meeting of Creditors	A meeting of creditors is scheduled for the date, time, and location listed on the front side. *The debtor (both spouses in a joint case) must be present at the meeting to be questioned under oath by the trustee and by creditors.* Creditors are welcome to attend, but are not required to do so. The meeting may be continued and concluded at a later date without further notice
Claims	A Proof of Claim is a signed statement describing a creditor's claim. If a Proof of Claim form is not included with this notice, you can obtain one at any bankruptcy clerk's office. A secured creditor retains rights in its collateral regardless of whether that creditor files a Proof of Claim. If you do not file a Proof of Claim by the "Deadline to File a Proof of Claim" listed on the front side, you might not be paid any money on your claim from other assets in the bankruptcy case. To be paid you must file a Proof of Claim even if your claim is listed in the schedules filed by the debtor. Filing a Proof of Claim submits the creditor to the jurisdiction of the bankruptcy court, with consequences a lawyer can explain. For example, a secured creditor who files a Proof of Claim may surrender important nonmonetary rights, including the right to a jury trial. **Filing Deadline for a Foreign Creditor:** The deadlines for filing claims set forth on the front of this notice apply to all creditors. If this notice has been mailed to a creditor at a foreign address, the creditor may file a motion requesting the court to extend the deadline.
Discharge of Debts	The debtor is seeking a discharge of most debts, which may include your debt. A discharge means that you may never try to collect the debt from the debtor. If you believe that a debt owed to you is not dischargeable under Bankruptcy Code § 523 (a) (2) or (4), you must start a lawsuit by filing a complaint in the bankruptcy clerk's office by the "Deadline to File a Complaint to Determine Dischargeability of Certain Debts" listed on the front side. The bankruptcy clerk's office must receive the complaint and any required filing fee by that deadline.
Exempt Property	The debtor is permitted by law to keep certain property as exempt. Exempt property will not be sold and distributed to creditors, even if the debtor's case is converted to chapter 7. The debtor must file a list of all property claimed as exempt. You may inspect that list at the bankruptcy clerk's office. If you believe that an exemption claimed by the debtor is not authorized by law, you may file an objection to that exemption. The bankruptcy clerk's office must receive the objection by the "Deadline to Object to Exemptions" listed on the front side.
Bankruptcy Clerk's Office	Any paper that you file in this bankruptcy case should be filed at the bankruptcy clerk's office at the address listed on the front side. You may inspect all papers filed, including the list of the debtor's property and debts and the list of the property claimed as exempt, at the bankruptcy clerk's office.
Foreign Creditors	Consult a lawyer familiar with United States bankruptcy law if you have any questions regarding your rights in this case.

Refer To Other Side For Important Deadlines and Notices

Individual Bankruptcy and Restructuring

APPENDIX 26:
CHAPTER 13 REPAYMENT PLAN
(CA FORM F-3015-1.1)

Name _____

Address _____

_____

Telephone _____ (FAX) _____

☐ Attorney for Debtor(s)   Attorney's
☐ Debtor(s) in Pro Se   State Bar I.D. No.
                            _____

UNITED STATES BANKRUPTCY COURT
CENTRAL DISTRICT OF CALIFORNIA

List all names including trade names used by Debtor(s) within last   Chapter 13 Case No.:
6 years:

CHAPTER 13 PLAN

CREDITORS MEETING:
Date:
Time:
Place:
CONFIRMATION HEARING:
Date:
Time:
Place:

NOTICE

This plan is proposed by the above debtor.* The debtor attests, under penalty of perjury, that the information stated in this plan is accurate. Creditors cannot vote on this plan. However, creditors may object to this plan being confirmed pursuant to 11 U.S.C. § 1324. Any objection must be in writing and must be filed with the court and served upon the debtor, debtor's attorney (if any), and the chapter 13 trustee not less than 8 days before the date set for the meeting of creditors. Unless an objection is filed and served, the court may confirm this chapter 13 plan. The plan, if confirmed, modifies the rights and duties of the debtor and creditors to the treatment provided in the plan as confirmed, with the following IMPORTANT EXCEPTIONS:

Holders of secured claims will be paid on their secured claims according to this plan unless the secured creditor files a proof of claim in a different amount than that provided in the plan. If a secured creditor files a proof of claim, that creditor will be paid according to that creditor's proof of claim, unless the court orders otherwise.

HOLDERS OF ALL OTHER CLAIMS (INCLUDING PRIORITY CLAIMS, DEFICIENCY CLAIMS, ALL OTHER KINDS OF UNSECURED CLAIMS) MUST TIMELY FILE PROOFS OF CLAIM, OR THEY WILL NOT BE PAID ANY AMOUNT. A debtor who confirms a chapter 13 plan may be eligible thereafter to receive a discharge of the debts to the extent specified in 11 U.S.C. § 1328.

*Any reference to the singular shall include the plural in the case of joint debtors.

This form is mandatory by Order of the United States Bankruptcy Court for the Central District of California.

Revised December 2003   **F 3015-1.1**

CHAPTER 13 REPAYMENT PLAN

Case No.: _____

Debtor proposes the following chapter 13 plan and makes the following declarations:

I. **PROPERTIES AND FUTURE EARNINGS OR INCOME SUBJECT TO THE SUPERVISION AND CONTROL OF THE TRUSTEE:**

Debtor submits the following to the supervision and control of the trustee:

A. Payments by debtor of $_____ per month for _____ months. This monthly payment will begin within 30 days of the date the petition was filed.

Debtor will pay _____% of the allowed claims of general unsecured creditors. If that percentage is less than 100%, the debtor will pay the plan payment stated in this plan for the full term of the plan.

If the allowed general unsecured claims filed by creditors in this case total more than the amount stated in this plan, the debtor will: (1) obtain an order increasing the duration and/or amount of the monthly plan payment to provide for an amount sufficient to pay the above-stated percentage of the allowed claims filed by the unsecured creditors, or (2) obtain an order reducing the stated percentage. Failure to do one of the above may result in dismissal of the case.

If the allowed general unsecured claims filed by creditors in this case total less than the amount stated in this plan, the above monthly plan payment may be sufficient to pay higher than the stated percent to general unsecured creditors. In this event, the debtor must still make the stated plan payment for the full plan term, and the trustee shall disburse said funds in payment of allowed unsecured claims up to payment of 100% thereof.

B. Amounts necessary for the payment of postpetition claims allowed under 11 U.S.C. § 1305.

C. Other property: _____
                                    (specify property or indicate none)

Debtor will pay timely all post-confirmation tax liabilities directly to the appropriate taxing authorities.

II. **ORDER OF PAYMENTS; CLASSIFICATION AND TREATMENT OF CLAIMS:** Except as otherwise provided in the plan or by court order, the chapter 13 trustee shall disburse all available funds for the payment of claims as follows:

1. **ORDER OF PAYMENTS:**

1. The chapter 13 trustee's fee up to but not more than the amount accrued on actual payments made to date;

2. Administrative expenses (including but not limited to attorney's fees) in an amount up to but not more than _____% of each plan payment until paid in full;

3. Pro rata to all other classes up to the monthly amounts set forth in the plan, except that no payment shall be made on Class Five claims until all Class One claims have been paid in full.

Chapter 13 Plan (Rev. 12/03) - Page 3   2003 USBC, Central District of California

Case No.: _____

2. CLASSIFICATION AND TREATMENT OF CLAIMS:

1. **CLASS ONE** - Allowed unsecured claims entitled to priority under 11 U.S.C. § 507. Debtor will pay Class One claims in full in deferred payments, provided a proof of claim has been filed, as follows:

	AMOUNT OF PRIORITY CLAIM	MONTHLY PAYMENT	NUMBER OF PAYMENTS	TOTAL PAYMENT
a. Administrative Expenses				
(1) Trustee's Fee (estimated at 11% of plan payment amounts)				
(2) Attorney's Fees	$_____	$_____	#_____	$_____
(3) Other	$_____	$_____	#_____	$_____
b. Internal Revenue Service	$_____	$_____	#_____	$_____
c. Franchise Tax Board	$_____	$_____	#_____	$_____
d. Other _____	$_____	$_____	#_____	$_____
e. Other _____	$_____	$_____	#_____	$_____

2. **CLASS TWO** - Claims secured solely by real property that is the debtor's PRINCIPAL RESIDENCE.

  a. Debtor will make all postpetition payments pursuant to the promissory note and deed of trust on the following claims on which the obligation matures **AFTER** the final payment is due under this plan:

  1. ☐ Directly to Trustee: _____
      (name of creditor(s) here)

  2. ☐ Directly to Creditor: _____
      (name of creditor(s) here)

  b. Debtor will make all postpetition payments pursuant to the promissory note and deed of trust on the following claims on which the obligation matures **BEFORE** the final payment is due under this plan: _____ _____ *(name of creditor(s) here).*

  c. Debtor will cure all prepetition arrearages through the plan payment as set forth below:

Name of Creditor and Last Four Digits of Loan Number	AMOUNT OF ARREARAGES	INTEREST RATE	MONTHLY PAYMENT	NUMBER OF MONTHS	TOTAL PAYMENT
Name _____ Loan No. _____ Cure of default	$_____	%_____	$_____	#_____	$_____
Name _____ Loan No. _____ Cure of default	$_____	%_____	$_____	#_____	$_____
Name _____ Loan No. _____ Cure of default	$_____	%_____	$_____	#_____	$_____
Name _____ Loan No. _____ Cure of default	$_____	%_____	$_____	#_____	$_____

This form is mandatory by Order of the United States Bankruptcy Court for the Central District of California.
Revised December 2003   **F 3015-1.1**

CHAPTER 13 REPAYMENT PLAN

Case No.: _____

d. Pursuant to Sections 1322(c)(2) and 1325(a)(5), Debtor will pay the following claim(s) on which the obligation matures **BEFORE** the final payment is due under this plan as follows:

NAME OF CREDITOR	AMOUNT	INTEREST RATE	MONTHLY PAYMENT	NUMBER OF MONTHS	TOTAL PAYMENT
_____	$_____	____%	$_____	#____	$_____
_____	$_____	____%	$_____	#____	$_____
_____	$_____	____%	$_____	#____	$_____

Each creditor will retain its lien until its secured claim is paid in full or it is otherwise satisfied by surrender, agreement, or order of the court.

3. **CLASS THREE** - Secured claims on real or personal property which are paid in full during the term of the plan, including but not limited to a claim which is not secured solely by a security interest in the debtor's principal residence. Class Three claims will be paid in monthly payments as set forth below. Debtor is the owner of the property serving as collateral, is aware of its condition and, where the secured claim is less than the amount of the debt, believes its value is as set forth below under the heading "Amount of Secured Claim." The value as of the effective date of the plan of the series of payments to be distributed under the plan on account of each secured claim provided for by the plan is equal to the allowed amount of such claim. Any unsecured amount resulting from a deficiency in the value of the collateral is included in Class Five, or if appropriate, in Class One.

Name of Creditor and Last Four Digits of Loan Number	TOTAL AMOUNT OF CLAIM	AMOUNT OF SECURED CLAIM	INTEREST RATE ON SECURED CLAIM	AMOUNT OF UNSECURED CLAIM	MONTHLY PAYMENT	TOTAL NUMBER OF PAYMENTS	TOTAL PAYMENT
Name _____ Loan No. _____	$_____	$_____	____%	$_____	$_____	#____	$_____
Name _____ Loan No. _____	$_____	$_____	____%	$_____	$_____	#____	$_____
Name _____ Loan No. _____	$_____	$_____	____%	$_____	$_____	#____	$_____
Name _____ Loan No. _____	$_____	$_____	____%	$_____	$_____	#____	$_____
Name _____ Loan No. _____	$_____	$_____	____%	$_____	$_____	#____	$_____

Each creditor will retain its lien until (1) if oversecured, its secured claim is paid in full, or (2) if undersecured, its secured claim is paid in full and the debtor receives a discharge under chapter 13.

This form is mandatory by Order of the United States Bankruptcy Court for the Central District of California.

Revised December 2003   **F 3015-1.1**

Individual Bankruptcy and Restructuring

Chapter 13 Plan (Rev. 12/03) - Page 5   2003 USBC, Central District of California

Case No.: _____

4. **CLASS FOUR** - Claims secured by real or personal property other than the debtor's principal residence for which arrearages are paid as part of the plan payment and for which the ongoing obligation will be paid according to the terms of the agreement to the party stated below. The value as of the effective date of the plan of the series of payments to be distributed under the plan on account of each secured claim provided for by the plan is equal to the allowed amount of such claim. Defaults will be cured using the interest rate set forth below. (If more than two creditors, attach separate exhibits.)

Name of Creditor and Last Four Digits of Loan Number	AMOUNT OF ARREARAGES	INTEREST RATE ON ARREARAGES	MONTHLY PAYMENT	NUMBER OF MONTHS	TOTAL PAYMENT

Name _____

Loan No. _____
1) Cure of default $_____   _____% $_____   #_____ $_____
2) Regular monthly payment $_____   #_____ $_____

☐ To the trustee as part of the plan payment during the life of the plan and thereafter directly to the creditor.

☐ Directly to the creditor

Name _____

Loan No. _____
1) Cure of default $_____   _____% $_____   #_____ $_____
2) Regular monthly payment $_____   #_____ $_____

☐ To the trustee as part of the plan payment during the life of the plan and thereafter directly to the creditor.

☐ Directly to the creditor

Each creditor will retain its lien until (1) if oversecured, its secured claim is paid in full, or (2) if undersecured, its secured claim is paid in full and the debtor receives a discharge under chapter 13.

5. **CLASS FIVE** - Non-priority Unsecured Claims. Debtor estimates that non-priority general unsecured claims total the sum of $_____. Class Five claims will be paid as follows, subject to the terms of IA herein:

(Check one box only.)

☐ Class Five claims (including allowed unsecured amounts from Class Three) are of one class and will be paid pro rata at ____% of such claims. Unless the plan provides for payment of 100% to unsecured creditors, the debtor will pay all disposable income to the trustee for at least 36 months and will submit statements of income to the trustee on a semi-annual/annual basis. The amount of income shall be reviewed by the trustee who may petition the court to increase the monthly payments for cause.

OR

Revised December 2003   **F 3015-1.1**

Individual Bankruptcy and Restructuring   173

CHAPTER 13 REPAYMENT PLAN

Case No.: _____

☐ Class Five claims will be divided into subclasses as shown on the attached Exhibit ____ and paid pro rata in each subclass as indicated therein. The Plan provides the same treatment for each claim within each subclass of Class Five. The claims of each subclass are substantially similar and the division into subclasses does not discriminate unfairly.

6. **CLASS SIX** - Postpetition claims under 11 U.S.C. § 1305. Postpetition claims allowed under 11 U.S.C. § 1305 will be paid in full in equal monthly installments commencing no later than 30 days after entry of an order allowing such claims and concluding on the date of the last payment under the plan, provided sufficient funds are available under the plan or amended plan.

III. **COMPARISON WITH CHAPTER 7** - The value as of the effective date of the plan of property to be distributed under the plan on account of each allowed claim is not less than the amount that would be paid on such claim if the estate of the debtor were liquidated under chapter 7 of the Bankruptcy Code on such date. The percentage distribution to general unsecured creditors in chapter 7 would be (estimate) _____%.

IV. **PLAN ANALYSIS** - TOTAL PAYMENT PROVIDED FOR UNDER THE PLAN

CLASS ONE
Unpaid attorney's fee . . . . $_____
Internal Revenue Service . . . . $_____
Franchise Tax Board . . . . $_____
Other . . . . $_____
Other . . . . $_____
CLASS TWO . . . . $_____
CLASS THREE . . . . $_____
CLASS FOUR . . . . $_____
CLASS FIVE . . . . $_____
SUB-TOTAL . . . . $_____
TRUSTEE'S FEES (Estimate 11% unless advised otherwise.) . . . . $_____
TOTAL PAYMENTS . . . . $_____

V. **ENLARGEMENT OF TIME FOR PAYMENTS**

If the plan provides for payments over a period of more than 36 months, cause exists as follows:

_____ The plan proposes to pay at least 70% of unsecured claims.

_____ Other: _____

VI. **DEBTOR'S ABILITY TO MAKE PAYMENTS AND COMPLY WITH BANKRUPTCY CODE**

Debtor will be able to make all payments and comply with all provisions of the plan, based upon the availability to the debtor of the income and property the debtor proposes to use to complete the plan.

This plan complies with the provisions of chapter 13 and all other applicable provisions of the Bankruptcy Code. Any fee, charge, or amount required to be paid under the United States Code or required by the plan to be paid before confirmation has been paid or will be paid prior to confirmation. The plan has been proposed in good faith and not by any means forbidden by law.

This form is mandatory by Order of the United States Bankruptcy Court for the Central District of California.

Revised December 2003   **F 3015-1.1**

Chapter 13 Plan (Rev. 12/03) - Page 7   2003 USBC, Central District of California

Case No.: _____

VII. OTHER PROVISIONS

A. Debtor rejects the following executory contracts and unexpired leases: _____

_____

_____

B. Debtor assumes the executory contracts or unexpired leases set forth in this section. As to each contract or lease assumed, any defaults therein and debtor's proposal for cure of said default(s) is described. Evidence satisfying all requirements for assumption is provided in a separately filed pleading.

_____

_____

_____

_____

C. In addition to the payments specified in Section II herein, the debtor will make regular payments directly to the following:

_____

_____

_____

D. Debtor hereby surrenders the following personal or real property: _____

_____

_____

E. Miscellaneous provisions *(specify)*: _____

_____

_____

F. The trustee is authorized to disburse funds after the date of confirmation in open court.

This form is mandatory by Order of the United States Bankruptcy Court for the Central District of California.

Revised December 2003   F 3015-1.1

Individual Bankruptcy and Restructuring   175

CHAPTER 13 REPAYMENT PLAN

Case No.: _____

VIII.   REVESTMENT OF PROPERTY

Property of the estate shall not revest in the debtor until such time as a discharge is granted or the case is dismissed. Revestment shall be subject to all liens and encumbrances in existence when the case was filed, except those liens avoided by court order or extinguished by operation of law. In the event the case is converted to a case under chapter 7, 11, or 12 of the Bankruptcy Code, the property of the estate shall vest in accordance with applicable law. After confirmation of the plan, the chapter 13 trustee shall have no further authority or fiduciary duty regarding use, sale, or refinance of property of the estate, except to respond to any motion for proposed use, sale, or refinance as required by the Chapter 13 General Order of this court. Prior to any discharge or dismissal, the debtor must seek approval of the court to purchase, sell, or refinance real property.

Dated: _____   _____
                                                     Attorney for Debtor(s)

I declare under penalty of perjury that the foregoing is true and correct.

Executed at _____, California   _____
                                                     Debtor

Executed on: _____   _____
                                                     Joint Debtor

This form is mandatory by Order of the United States Bankruptcy Court for the Central District of California.

Revised December 2003

F 3015-1.1

176   Individual Bankruptcy and Restructuring

APPENDIX 27:
DEBTOR'S STATEMENT OF CURRENT MONTHLY INCOME AND CALCULATION OF COMMITMENT PERIOD AND DISPOSABLE INCOME IN A CHAPTER 13 CASE (FORM B22C)

Form B22C (Chapter 13) (10/05)

In re _____
                  Debtor(s)

Case Number: _____
                  (If known)

According to the calculations required by this statement:
☐ The applicable commitment period is 3 years.
☐ The applicable commitment period is 5 years.
☐ Disposable income is determined under § 1325(b)(3).
☐ Disposable income is not determined under § 1325(b)(3).
(Check the boxes as directed in Lines 17 and 23 of this statement.)

STATEMENT OF CURRENT MONTHLY INCOME AND CALCULATION OF COMMITMENT PERIOD AND DISPOSABLE INCOME
FOR USE IN CHAPTER 13

In addition to Schedules I and J, this statement must be completed by every individual Chapter 13 debtor, whether or not filing jointly. Joint debtors may complete one statement only.

Part I. REPORT OF INCOME

				Column A Debtor's Income	Column B Spouse's Income
1	**Marital/filing status.** Check the box that applies and complete the balance of this part of this statement as directed. a. ☐ Unmarried. **Complete only Column A ("Debtor's Income") for Lines 2-10.** b. ☐ Married. **Complete both Column A ("Debtor's Income") and Column B ("Spouse's Income") for Lines 2-10.** All figures must reflect average monthly income for the six calendar months prior to filing the bankruptcy case, ending on the last day of the month before the filing. If you received different amounts of income during these six months, you must total the amounts received during the six months, divide this total by six, and enter the result on the appropriate line.					
2	**Gross wages, salary, tips, bonuses, overtime, commissions.**			$	$
3	**Income from the operation of a business, profession, or farm.** Subtract Line b from Line a and enter the difference on Line 3. Do not enter a number less than zero. **Do not include any part of the business expenses entered on Line b as a deduction in Part IV.**				
	a.	Gross receipts	$		
	b.	Ordinary and necessary business expenses	$		
	c.	Business income	Subtract Line b from Line a	$	$
4	**Rent and other real property income.** Subtract Line b from Line a and enter the difference on Line 4. Do not enter a number less than zero. **Do not include any part of the operating expenses entered on Line b as a deduction in Part IV.**				
	a.	Gross receipts	$		
	b.	Ordinary and necessary operating expenses	$		
	c.	Rental income	Subtract Line b from Line a	$	$
5	**Interest, dividends, and royalties.**			$	$
6	**Pension and retirement income.**			$	$
7	**Regular contributions to the household expenses of the debtor or the debtor's dependents, including child or spousal support.** Do not include contributions from the debtor's spouse.			$	$
8	**Unemployment compensation.** Enter the amount in the appropriate column(s) of Line 8. However, if you contend that unemployment compensation received by you or your spouse was a benefit under the Social Security Act, do not list the amount of such compensation in Column A or B, but instead state the amount in the space below: Unemployment compensation claimed to be a benefit under the Social Security Act Debtor $ _____ Spouse $ _____			$	$
9	**Income from all other sources.** Specify source and amount. If necessary, list additional sources on a separate page. Total and enter on Line 9. **Do not include** any benefits received under the Social Security Act or payments received as a victim of a war crime, crime against humanity, or as a victim of international or domestic terrorism.				
	a.		$		
	b.		$		
				$	$
10	**Subtotal.** Add Lines 2 thru 9 in Column A, and, if Column B is completed, add Lines 2 through 9 in Column B. Enter the total(s).			$	$
11	**Total.** If Column B has been completed, add Line 10, Column A to Line 10, Column B, and enter the total. If Column B has not been completed, enter the amount from Line 10, Column A.			$	

DEBTOR'S STATEMENT OF CURRENT MONTHLY INCOME IN A CHAPTER 13 CASE

	Part II. CALCULATION OF § 1325(b)(4) COMMITMENT PERIOD	
12	Enter the amount from Line 11.	
13	**Marital adjustment.** If you are married, but are not filing jointly with your spouse, AND if you contend that calculation of the commitment period under § 1325(b)(4) does not require inclusion of the income of your spouse, enter the amount of the income listed in Line 10, Column B that was NOT regularly contributed to the household expenses of you or your dependents. Otherwise, enter zero.	
14	Subtract Line 13 from Line 12 and enter the result.	
15	**Annualized current monthly income for § 1325(b)(4).** Multiply the amount from Line 14 by the number 12 and enter the result.	$
16	**Applicable median family income.** Enter the median family income for applicable state and household size. (This information is available by family size at www.usdoj.gov/ust/ or from the clerk of the bankruptcy court.) a. Enter debtor's state of residence: _____ b. Enter debtor's household size: _____	$
17	**Application of § 1325(b)(4).** Check the applicable box and proceed as directed. ☐ **The amount on Line 15 is less than the amount on Line 16.** Check the box for "The applicable commitment period is 3 years" at the top of page 1 of this statement and complete Part VII of this statement. **Do not complete Parts III, IV, V or VI.** ☐ **The amount on Line 15 is not less than the amount on Line 16.** Check the box for "The applicable commitment period is 5 years" at the top of page 1 of this statement and continue with Part III of this statement.	

	Part III. APPLICATION OF § 1325(b)(3) FOR DETERMINING DISPOSABLE INCOME	
18	Enter the amount from Line 11.	$
19	**Marital adjustment.** If you are married, but are not filing jointly with your spouse, enter the amount of the income listed in Line 10, Column B that was NOT regularly contributed to the household expenses of you or your dependents. If you are unmarried or married and filing jointly with your spouse, enter zero.	$
20	**Current monthly income for § 1325(b)(3).** Subtract Line 19 from Line 18 and enter the result.	
21	**Annualized current monthly income for § 1325(b)(3).** Multiply the amount from Line 20 by the number 12 and enter the result.	$
22	**Applicable median family income.** Enter the amount from Line 16.	$
23	**Application of § 1325(b)(3).** Check the applicable box and proceed as directed. ☐ **The amount on Line 21 is more than the amount on Line 22.** Check the box for "Disposable income is determined under § 1325(b)(3)" at the top of page 1 of this statement and complete the remaining parts of this statement. ☐ **The amount on Line 21 is not more than the amount on Line 22.** Check the box for "Disposable income is not determined under § 1325(b)(3)" at the top of page 1 of this statement and complete Part VII of this statement. **Do not complete Parts IV, V, or VI.**	

	Part IV. CALCULATION OF DEDUCTIONS ALLOWED UNDER § 707(b)(2)	
	Subpart A: Deductions under Standards of the Internal Revenue Service (IRS)	
24	**National Standards: food, clothing, household supplies, personal care, and miscellaneous.** Enter the "Total" amount from IRS National Standards for Allowable Living Expenses for the applicable family size and income level. (This information is available at www.usdoj.gov/ust/ or from the clerk of the bankruptcy court.)	$
25A	**Local Standards: housing and utilities; non-mortgage expenses.** Enter the amount of the IRS Housing and Utilities Standards; non-mortgage expenses for the applicable county and family size. (This information is available at www.usdoj.gov/ust/ or from the clerk of the bankruptcy court).	$

Form B 22C (Chapter 13) (10/05) 3

25B	**Local Standards: housing and utilities; mortgage / rent expense.** Enter, in Line a below, the amount of the IRS Housing and Utilities Standards; mortgage/rent expense for your county and family size (this information is available at www.usdoj.gov/ust/ or from the clerk of the bankruptcy court); enter on Line b the total of the Average Monthly Payments for any debts secured by your home, as stated in Line 47; subtract Line b from Line a and enter the result in Line 25B. **Do not enter an amount less than zero.**	
	a. IRS Housing and Utilities Standards; mortgage/rent Expense	$
	b. Average Monthly Payment for any debts secured by your home, if any, as stated in Line 47	$
	c. Net mortgage/rental expense	Subtract Line b from Line a. $

| 26 | **Local Standards: housing and utilities; adjustment.** if you contend that the process set out in Lines 25A and 25B does not accurately compute the allowance to which you are entitled under the IRS Housing and Utilities Standards, enter any additional amount to which you contend you are entitled, and state the basis for your contention in the space below:
_____
_____
_____ | $ |

| 27 | **Local Standards: transportation; vehicle operation / public transportation expense.** You are entitled to an expense allowance in this category regardless of whether you pay the expenses of operating a vehicle and regardless of whether you use public transportation.
Check the number of vehicles for which you pay the operating expenses or for which the operating expenses are included as a contribution to your household expenses in Line 7. ☐ 0 ☐ 1 ☐ 2 or more.
Enter the amount from IRS Transportation Standards, Operating Costs & Public Transportation Costs for the applicable number of vehicles in the applicable Metropolitan Statistical Area or Census Region. (This information is available at www.usdoj.gov/ust/ or from the clerk of the bankruptcy court.) | $ |

28	**Local Standards: transportation ownership / lease expense; Vehicle 1.** Check the number of vehicles for which you claim an ownership/lease expense. (You may not claim an ownership/lease expense for more than two vehicles.) ☐ 1 ☐ 2 or more. Enter, in Line a below, the amount of the IRS Transportation Standards, Ownership Costs, First Car (available at www.usdoj.gov/ust/ or from the clerk of the bankruptcy court); enter in Line b the total of the Average Monthly Payments for any debts secured by Vehicle 1, as stated in Line 47; subtract Line b from Line a and enter the result in Line 28. **Do not enter an amount less than zero.**	
	a. IRS Transportation Standards, Ownership Costs, First Car	$
	b. Average Monthly Payment for any debts secured by Vehicle 1, as stated in Line 47	$
	c. Net ownership/lease expense for Vehicle 1	Subtract Line b from Line a. $

29	**Local Standards: transportation ownership / lease expense; Vehicle 2.** Complete this Line only if you checked the "2 or more" Box in Line 28. Enter, in Line a below, the amount of the IRS Transportation Standards, Ownership Costs, Second Car (available at www.usdoj.gov/ust/ or from the clerk of the bankruptcy court); enter in Line b the total of the Average Monthly Payments for any debts secured by Vehicle 2, as stated in Line 47; subtract Line b from Line a and enter the result in Line 29. **Do not enter an amount less than zero.**	
	a. IRS Transportation Standards, Ownership Costs, Second Car	$
	b. Average Monthly Payment for any debts secured by Vehicle 2, as stated in Line 47	$
	c. Net ownership/lease expense for Vehicle 2	Subtract Line b from Line a. $

| 30 | **Other Necessary Expenses: taxes.** Enter the total average monthly expense that you actually incur for all federal, state, and local taxes, other than real estate and sales taxes, such as income taxes, self employment taxes, social security taxes, and Medicare taxes. **Do not include real estate or sales taxes.** | $ |

| 31 | **Other Necessary Expenses: mandatory payroll deductions.** Enter the total average monthly payroll deductions that are required for your employment, such as mandatory retirement contributions, union dues, and uniform costs. **Do not include discretionary amounts, such as non-mandatory 401(k) contributions.** | $ |

DEBTOR'S STATEMENT OF CURRENT MONTHLY INCOME IN A CHAPTER 13 CASE

Form B 22C (Chapter 13) (10/05)   4

32	**Other Necessary Expenses: life insurance.** Enter average monthly premiums that you actually pay for term life insurance for yourself. **Do not include premiums for insurance on your dependents, for whole life or for any other form of insurance.**	$
33	**Other Necessary Expenses: court-ordered payments.** Enter the total monthly amount that you are required to pay pursuant to court order, such as spousal or child support payments. **Do not include payments on past due support obligations included in Line 49.**	$
34	**Other Necessary Expenses: education for employment or for a physically or mentally challenged child.** Enter the total monthly amount that you actually expend for education that is a condition of employment and for education that is required for a physically or mentally challenged dependent child for whom no public education providing similar services is available.	
35	**Other Necessary Expenses: childcare.** Enter the average monthly amount that you actually expend on childcare. **Do not include payments made for children's education.**	$
36	**Other Necessary Expenses: health care.** Enter the average monthly amount that you actually expend on health care expenses that are not reimbursed by insurance or paid by a health savings account. **Do not include payments for health insurance listed in Line 39.**	$
37	**Other Necessary Expenses: telecommunication services.** Enter the average monthly expenses that you actually pay for cell phones, pagers, call waiting, caller identification, special long distance, or internet services necessary for the health and welfare of you or your dependents. **Do not include any amount previously deducted.**	$
38	**Total Expenses Allowed under IRS Standards.** Enter the total of Lines 24 through 37.	$

Subpart B: Additional Expense Deductions under § 707(b)
Note: Do not include any expenses that you have listed in Lines 24-37

39	**Health Insurance, Disability Insurance, and Health Savings Account Expenses.** List the average monthly amounts that you actually expend in each of the following categories and enter the total.			
	a.	Health Insurance	$	
	b.	Disability Insurance	$	
	c.	Health Savings Account	$	
			Total: Add Lines a, b, and c	$

40	**Continued contributions to the care of household or family members.** Enter the actual monthly expenses that you will continue to pay for the reasonable and necessary care and support of an elderly, chronically ill, or disabled member of your household or member of your immediate family who is unable to pay for such expenses. **Do not include payments listed in Line 34.**	$
41	**Protection against family violence.** Enter any average monthly expenses that you actually incurred to maintain the safety of your family under the Family Violence Prevention and Services Act or other applicable federal law.	$
42	**Home energy costs in excess of the allowance specified by the IRS Local Standards.** Enter the average monthly amount by which your home energy costs exceed the allowance in the IRS Local Standards for Housing and Utilities. **You must provide your case trustee with documentation demonstrating that the additional amount claimed is reasonable and necessary.**	$
43	**Education expenses for dependent children under 18.** Enter the average monthly expenses that you actually incur, not to exceed $125 per child, in providing elementary and secondary education for your dependent children less than 18 years of age. **You must provide your case trustee with documentation demonstrating that the amount claimed is reasonable and necessary and not already accounted for in the IRS Standards.**	$
44	**Additional food and clothing expense.** Enter the average monthly amount by which your food and clothing expenses exceed the combined allowances for food and apparel in the IRS National Standards, not to exceed five percent of those combined allowances. (This information is available at www.usdoj.gov/ust/ or from the clerk of the bankruptcy court.) **You must provide your case trustee with documentation demonstrating that the additional amount claimed is reasonable and necessary.**	$
45	**Continued charitable contributions.** Enter the amount that you will continue to contribute in the form of cash or financial instruments to a charitable organization as defined in 26 U.S.C. § 170(c)(1)-(2).	$
46	**Total Additional Expense Deductions under § 707(b).** Enter the total of Lines 39 through 45.	$

Form B 22C (Chapter 13) (10/05)   5

Subpart C: Deductions for Debt Payment				
47	**Future payments on secured claims.** For each of your debts that is secured by an interest in property that you own, list the name of the creditor, identify the property securing the debt, and state the Average Monthly Payment. The Average Monthly Payment is the total of all amounts contractually due to each Secured Creditor in the 60 months following the filing of the bankruptcy case, divided by 60. Mortgage debts should include payments of taxes and insurance required by the mortgage. If necessary, list additional entries on a separate page.			
		Name of Creditor	Property Securing the Debt	60-month Average Payment
	a.			$
	b.			$
	c.			$
			Total: Add Lines a, b, and c	$

48	**Past due payments on secured claims.** If any of the debts listed in Line 47 are in default, and the property securing the debt is necessary for your support or the support of your dependents, you may include in your deductions 1/60th of the amount that you must pay the creditor as a result of the default (the "cure amount") in order to maintain possession of the property. List any such amounts in the following chart and enter the total. If necessary, list additional entries on a separate page.			
		Name of Creditor	Property Securing the Debt in Default	1/60th of the Cure Amount
	a.			$
	b.			$
	c.			$
			Total: Add Lines a, b, and c	$

49	**Payments on priority claims.** Enter the total amount of all priority claims (including priority child support and alimony claims), divided by 60.	$

50	**Chapter 13 administrative expenses.** Multiply the amount in Line a by the amount in Line b, and enter the resulting administrative expense.			
	a.	Projected average monthly Chapter 13 plan payment.	$	
	b.	Current multiplier for your district as determined under schedules issued by the Executive Office for United States Trustees. (This information is available at www.usdoj.gov/ust/ or from the clerk of the bankruptcy court.)	x	
	c.	Average monthly administrative expense of Chapter 13 case	Total: Multiply Lines a and b	$

51	**Total Deductions for Debt Payment.** Enter the total of Lines 47 through 50.	$

Subpart D: Total Deductions Allowed under § 707(b)(2)		
52	**Total of all deductions allowed under § 707(b)(2).** Enter the total of Lines 38, 46, and 51.	$

Part V. DETERMINATION OF DISPOSABLE INCOME UNDER § 1325(b)(2)

53	**Total current monthly income.** Enter the amount from Line 20.	$
54	**Support income.** Enter the monthly average of any child support payments, foster care payments, or disability payments for a dependent child, included in Line 7, that you received in accordance with applicable nonbankruptcy law, to the extent reasonably necessary to be expended for such child.	$
55	**Qualified retirement deductions.** Enter the monthly average of (a) all contributions or wage deductions made to qualified retirement plans, as specified in § 541(b)(7) and (b) all repayments of loans from retirement plans, as specified in § 362(b)(19).	$
56	**Total of all deductions allowed under § 707(b)(2).** Enter the amount from Line 52.	$
57	**Total adjustments to determine disposable income.** Add the amounts on Lines 54, 55, and 56 and enter the result.	$
58	**Monthly Disposable Income Under § 1325(b)(2).** Subtract Line 57 from Line 53 and enter the	$

DEBTOR'S STATEMENT OF CURRENT MONTHLY INCOME IN A CHAPTER 13 CASE

Form B 22C (Chapter 13) (10/05)   6

result.

Part VI: ADDITIONAL EXPENSE CLAIMS

59

Other Expenses. List and describe any monthly expenses, not otherwise stated in this form, that are required for the health and welfare of you and your family and that you contend should be an additional deduction from your current monthly income under § 707(b)(2)(A)(ii)(I). If necessary, list additional sources on a separate page. All figures should reflect your average monthly expense for each item. Total the expenses.

	Expense Description	Monthly Amount
a.		$
b.		$
c.		$
	Total: Add Lines a, b, and c	$

Part VII: VERIFICATION

60

I declare under penalty of perjury that the information provided in this statement is true and correct. *(If this a joint case, both debtors must sign.)*

Date: _____   Signature: _____
                                                         (Debtor)

Date: _____   Signature: _____
                                              (Joint Debtor, if any)

APPENDIX 28:
ORDER CONFIRMING CHAPTER 13 PLAN
(FORM B230B)

B 230B
(8/96)

United States Bankruptcy Court

_____ District Of _____

In re

Case No. _____

Debtor

Chapter 13

ORDER CONFIRMING CHAPTER 13 PLAN

The debtor's plan was filed on _____, and was modified on _____.
                                         (date)   (date)
The plan or a summary of the plan was transmitted to creditors pursuant to Bankruptcy Rule 3015. The court

finds that the plan meets the requirements of 11 U.S.C. § 1325.

IT IS ORDERED THAT:

The debtor's chapter 13 plan is confirmed, with the following provisions:

1. Payments:

    Amount of each payment: $_____

    Due date of each payment: ☐ the _____day of each month, or
                                            ☐ _____

    Period of payments: ☐ _____ months,
                                  ☐ until a _____% dividend is paid to creditors holding
    allowed unsecured claims, or
                                  ☐ _____

Payable to:

_____Standing Trustee

_____

_____

_____

2. Attorney's Fees:

    The debtor's attorney is awarded a fee in the amount of $_____, of which $_____ is
    due and payable from the estate.

3. [Other provisions as needed]

_____   _____
        Date   Bankruptcy Judge

APPENDIX 29:
ORDER GRANTING A DISCHARGE OF DEBTOR AFTER COMPLETION OF CHAPTER 13 PLAN (FORM B18W)

B 18W
(10/05)

United States Bankruptcy Court

_____ District Of _____

In re

Case No. _____

Debtor*

Address: Chapter 13

Last four digits of Social Security No(s).:
Employer's Tax I.D. No(s). [if any]:

DISCHARGE OF DEBTOR AFTER COMPLETION
OF CHAPTER 13 PLAN

It appearing that the debtor is entitled to a discharge,

IT IS ORDERED:

The debtor is granted a discharge under section 1328(a) of title 11, United States Code, (the Bankruptcy Code).

BY THE COURT

Dated: _____   _____
                                              United States Bankruptcy Judge

SEE THE BACK OF THIS ORDER FOR IMPORTANT INFORMATION.

_____
Set forth all names, including trade names, used by the debtor within the last 8 years. (Federal Rule of Bankruptcy Procedure 1005).

Form B 18W continued
(10/05)

EXPLANATION OF BANKRUPTCY DISCHARGE
IN A CHAPTER 13 CASE

This court order grants a discharge to the person named as the debtor after the debtor has completed all payments under the chapter 13 plan. It is not a dismissal of the case.

Collection of Discharged Debts Prohibited

The discharge prohibits any attempt to collect from the debtor a debt that has been discharged. For example, a creditor is not permitted to contact a debtor by mail, phone, or otherwise, to file or continue a lawsuit, to attach wages or other property, or to take any other action to collect a discharged debt from the debtor. *[In a case involving community property:* There are also special rules that protect certain community property owned by the debtor's spouse, even if that spouse did not file a bankruptcy case.]* A creditor who violates this order can be required to pay damages and attorney's fees to the debtor.

However, a creditor may have the right to enforce a valid lien, such as a mortgage or security interest, against the debtor's property after the bankruptcy, if that lien was not avoided or eliminated in the bankruptcy case. Also, a debtor may voluntarily pay any debt that has been discharged.

Debts That are Discharged

The chapter 13 discharge order eliminates a debtor's legal obligation to pay a debt that is discharged. Most, but not all, types of debts are discharged if the debt is provided for by the chapter 13 plan or is disallowed by the court pursuant to section 502 of the Bankruptcy Code.

Debts that are Not Discharged.

Some of the common types of debts which are not discharged in a chapter 13 bankruptcy case are:

a. Domestic support obligations;

b. Debts for most student loans;

c. Debts for most fines, penalties, forfeitures, or criminal restitution obligations;

d. Debts for personal injury or death caused by the debtor's operation of a motor vehicle, vessel, or aircraft while intoxicated;

e. Debts for restitution, or damages, awarded in a civil action against the debtor as a result of malicious or willful injury by the debtor that caused personal injury to an individual or the death of an individual (in a case filed on or after October 17, 2005);

f. Debts provided for under section 1322(b)(5) of the Bankruptcy Code and on which the last payment is due after the date on which the final payment under the plan was due;

g. Debts for certain consumer purchases made after the bankruptcy case was filed if prior approval by the trustee of the debtor's incurring the debt was practicable but was not obtained;

h. Debts for most taxes to the extent not paid in full under the plan (in a case filed on or after October 17, 2005); and

i. Some debts which were not properly listed by the debtor (in a case filed on or after October 17, 2005).

This information is only a general summary of the bankruptcy discharge. There are exceptions to these general rules. Because the law is complicated, you may want to consult an attorney to determine the exact effect of the discharge in this case.

APPENDIX 30:
NOTICE OF CHAPTER 11 BANKRUPTCY CASE, MEETING OF CREDITORS AND DEADLINES (FORM B9E)

FORM B9E (Chapter 11 Individual or Joint Debtor Case (10/05))

UNITED STATES BANKRUPTCY COURT_____District of_____

Notice of
Chapter 11 Bankruptcy Case, Meeting of Creditors, & Deadlines

[A chapter 11 bankruptcy case concerning the debtor(s) listed below was filed on _____ (date).]
or [A bankruptcy case concerning the debtor(s) listed below was originally filed under chapter_____on
_____ (date) and was converted to a case under chapter 11 on_____.]

You may be a creditor of the debtor. **This notice lists important deadlines.** You may want to consult an attorney to protect your rights. All documents filed in the case may be inspected at the bankruptcy clerk's office at the address listed below.
NOTE: The staff of the bankruptcy clerk's office cannot give legal advice.

See Reverse Side for Important Explanations

Debtor(s) (name(s) and address):	Case Number:
	Last four digits of Social Security No./Complete EIN or other Taxpayer ID No.:
Telephone number:	
All other names used by the Debtor(s) in the last 8 years (include married, maiden, and trade names):	Attorney for Debtor(s) (name and address):
	Telephone number:

Meeting of Creditors

Date: / /   Time: (   ) A. M.   Location:
                                    (   ) P. M.

Deadlines:
Papers must be *received* by the bankruptcy clerk's office by the following deadlines:

Deadline to File a Proof of Claim:
Notice of deadline will be sent at a later time.

Foreign Creditors
A creditor to whom this notice is sent at a foreign address should read the information under "Claims" on the reverse side.

Deadline to File a Complaint to Determine Dischargeability of Certain Debts:

Deadline to File a Complaint Objecting to Discharge of the Debtor:

First date set for hearing on confirmation of plan
Notice of that date will be sent at a later time.

Deadline to Object to Exemptions:
Thirty (30) days after the *conclusion* of the meeting of creditors.

Creditors May Not Take Certain Actions:

In most instances, the filing of the bankruptcy case automatically stays certain collection and other actions against the debtor and the debtor's property. Under certain circumstances, the stay may be limited to 30 days or not exist at all, although the debtor can request the court to extend or impose a stay. If you attempt to collect a debt or take other action in violation of the Bankruptcy Code, you may be penalized. Consult a lawyer to determine your rights in this case.

Address of the Bankruptcy Clerk's Office:	For the Court:
	Clerk of the Bankruptcy Court:
Telephone number:	
Hours Open:	Date:

NOTICE OF CHAPTER 11 BANKRUPTCY CASE, MEETING OF CREDITORS AND DEADLINES

EXPLANATIONS   Form B9E (10/05)

Filing of Chapter 11 Bankruptcy Case	A bankruptcy case under Chapter 11 of the Bankruptcy Code (title 11, United States Code) has been filed in this court by or against the debtor(s) listed on the front side, and an order for relief has been entered. Chapter 11 allows a debtor to reorganize or liquidate pursuant to a plan. A plan is not effective unless confirmed by the court. You may be sent a copy of the plan and a disclosure statement telling you about the plan, and you might have the opportunity to vote on the plan. You will be sent notice of the date of the confirmation hearing, and you may object to confirmation of the plan and attend the confirmation hearing. Unless a trustee is serving, the debtor will remain in possession of the debtor's property and may continue to operate any business.
Legal Advice	The staff of the bankruptcy clerk's office cannot give legal advice. Consult a lawyer to determine your rights in this case.
Creditors Generally May Not Take Certain Actions	Prohibited collection actions are listed in Bankruptcy Code § 362. Common examples of prohibited actions include contacting the debtor by telephone, mail, or otherwise to demand repayment; taking actions to collect money or obtain property from the debtor; repossessing the debtor's property; starting or continuing lawsuits or foreclosures; and garnishing or deducting from the debtor's wages. Under certain circumstances, the stay may be limited to 30 days or not exist at all, although the debtor can request the court to extend or impose a stay.
Meeting of Creditors	A meeting of creditors is scheduled for the date, time, and location listed on the front side. *The debtor (both spouses in a joint case) must be present at the meeting to be questioned under oath by the trustee and by creditors.* Creditors are welcome to attend, but are not required to do so. The meeting may be continued and concluded at a later date without further notice. The court, after notice and a hearing, may order that the United States trustee not convene the meeting if the debtor has filed a plan for which the debtor solicited acceptances before filing the case.
Claims	A Proof of Claim is a signed statement describing a creditor's claim. If a Proof of Claim form is not included with this notice, you can obtain one at any bankruptcy clerk's office. You may look at the schedules that have been or will be filed at the bankruptcy clerk's office. If your claim is scheduled and is *not* listed as disputed, contingent, or unliquidated, it will be allowed in the amount scheduled unless you filed a Proof of Claim or you are sent further notice about the claim. Whether or not your claim is scheduled, you are permitted to file a Proof of Claim. If your claim is not listed at all *or* if your claim is listed as disputed, contingent, or unliquidated, then you must file a Proof of Claim or you might not be paid any money on your claim and may be unable to vote on a plan. The court has not yet set a deadline to file a Proof of Claim. If a deadline is set, you will be sent another notice. A secured creditor retains rights in its collateral regardless of whether that creditor files a Proof of Claim. Filing a Proof of Claim submits the creditor to the jurisdiction of the bankruptcy court, with consequences a lawyer can explain. For example, a secured creditor who files a Proof of Claim may surrender important nonmonetary rights, including the right to a jury trial. **Filing Deadline for a Foreign Creditor:** The deadlines for filing claims set forth on the front of this notice apply to all creditors. If this notice has been mailed to a creditor at a foreign address, the creditor may file a motion requesting the court to extend the deadline.
Discharge of Debts	Confirmation of a chapter 11 plan may result in a discharge of debts, which may include all or part of your debt. *See* Bankruptcy Code § 1141 (d). Unless the court orders otherwise, however, the discharge will not be effective until completion of all payments under the plan. A discharge means that you may never try to collect the debt from the debtor except as provided in the plan. If you believe that a debt owed to you is not dischargeable under Bankruptcy Code § 523 (a) (2), (4), or (6), you must start a lawsuit by filing a complaint in the bankruptcy clerk's office by the "Deadline to File a Complaint to Determine Dischargeability of Certain Debts" listed on the front side. The bankruptcy clerk's office must receive the complaint and any required filing fee by that Deadline. If you believe that the debtor is not entitled to receive a discharge under Bankruptcy Code § 1141 (d) (3), you must file a complaint with the required filing fee in the bankruptcy clerk's office not later than the first date set for the hearing on confirmation of the plan. You will be sent another notice informing you of that date.
Exempt Property	The debtor is permitted by law to keep certain property as exempt. Exempt property will not be sold and distributed to creditors, even if the debtor's case is converted to chapter 7. The debtor must file a list of property claimed as exempt. You may inspect that list at the bankruptcy clerk's office. If you believe that an exemption claimed by the debtor is not authorized by law, you may file an objection to that exemption. The bankruptcy clerk's office must receive the objection by the "Deadline to Object to Exemptions" listed on the front side.
Bankruptcy Clerk's Office	Any paper that you file in this bankruptcy case should be filed at the bankruptcy clerk's office at the address listed on the front side. You may inspect all papers filed, including the list of the debtor's property and debts and the list of the property claimed as exempt, at the bankruptcy clerk's office.
Foreign Creditors	Consult a lawyer familiar with United States bankruptcy law if you have any questions regarding your rights in this case.

Refer To Other Side For Important Deadlines and Notices

APPENDIX 31:
ORDER APPROVING THE DISCLOSURE STATEMENT AND FIXING TIME FOR FILING ACCEPTANCES OR REJECTIONS OF THE PLAN (FORM B13)

Official Form 13
(12/03)

Form 13. ORDER APPROVING DISCLOSURE STATEMENT AND FIXING TIME
FOR FILING ACCEPTANCES OR REJECTIONS OF PLAN,
COMBINED WITH NOTICE THEREOF

[Caption as in Form 16A]

ORDER APPROVING DISCLOSURE STATEMENT AND FIXING TIME
FOR FILING ACCEPTANCES OR REJECTIONS OF PLAN,
COMBINED WITH NOTICE THEREOF

A disclosure statement under chapter 11 of the Bankruptcy Code having been filed by _____, on _____ [*if appropriate*, and by _____, on _____], referring to a plan under chapter 11 of the Code filed by _____, on _____ [*if appropriate*, and by _____, on _____ respectively] [*if appropriate*, as modified by a modification filed on _____]; and

It having been determined after hearing on notice that the disclosure statement [*or* statements] contain[s] adequate information:

IT IS ORDERED, and notice is hereby given, that:

A. The disclosure statement filed by _____ dated _____ [*if appropriate*, and by _____, dated _____ is [are] approved.

B. _____ is fixed as the last day for filing written acceptances or rejections of the plan [*or* plans] referred to above.

C. Within _____ days after the entry of this order, the plan [*or* plans] *or* a summary *or* summaries thereof approved by the court, [and [*if appropriate*] a summary approved by the court of its opinion, if any, dated _____, approving the disclosure statement [*or* statements]], the disclosure statement [*or* statements], and a ballot conforming to Official Form 14 shall be mailed to creditors, equity security holders, and other parties in interest, and shall be transmitted to the United States trustee, as provided in Fed. R. Bankr. P. 3017(d).

D. If acceptances are filed for more than one plan, preferences among the plans so accepted may be indicated.

E. *[If appropriate]* _____ is fixed for the hearing on confirmation of the plan [*or* plans].

F. *[If appropriate]* _____ is fixed as the last day for filing and serving pursuant to Fed. R. Bankr. P. 3020(b)(1) written objections to confirmation of the plan.

Dated: _____

BY THE COURT

_____
United States Bankruptcy Judge

[If the court directs that a copy of the opinion should be transmitted in lieu of or in addition to the summary thereof, the appropriate change should be made in paragraph C of this order.]

APPENDIX 32:
BALLOT FOR ACCEPTING OR REJECTING THE PLAN (FORM B14)

Official Form 14
(12/03)

Form 14. CLASS [ ] BALLOT FOR ACCEPTING OR REJECTING PLAN OF REORGANIZATION

[Caption as in Form 16A]

CLASS [ ] BALLOT FOR ACCEPTING OR REJECTING PLAN OF REORGANIZATION

[Proponent] filed a plan of reorganization dated *[Date]* (the "Plan") for the Debtor in this case. The Court has *[conditionally]* approved a disclosure statement with respect to the Plan (the "Disclosure Statement"). The Disclosure Statement provides information to assist you in deciding how to vote your ballot. If you do not have a Disclosure Statement, you may obtain a copy from *[name, address, telephone number and telecopy number of proponent/proponent's attorney.]* Court approval of the disclosure statement does not indicate approval of the Plan by the Court.

You should review the Disclosure Statement and the Plan before you vote. You may wish to seek legal advice concerning the Plan and your classification and treatment under the Plan. Your *[claim] [equity interest]* has been placed in class [ ] under the Plan. If you hold claims or equity interests in more than one class, you will receive a ballot for each class in which you are entitled to vote.

If your ballot is not received by *[name and address of proponent's attorney or other appropriate address]* on or before *[date]*, and such deadline is not extended, your vote will not count as either an acceptance or rejection of the Plan.

If the Plan is confirmed by the Bankruptcy Court it will be binding on you whether or not you vote.

ACCEPTANCE OR REJECTION OF THE PLAN

[At this point the ballot should provide for voting by the particular class of creditors or equity holders receiving the ballot using one of the following alternatives:]

[If the voter is the holder of a secured, priority, or unsecured nonpriority claim:]

The undersigned, the holder of a Class [ ] claim against the Debtor in the unpaid amount of Dollars ($)

[or, if the voter is the holder of a bond, debenture, or other debt security:]

The undersigned, the holder of a Class [ ] claim against the Debtor, consisting of Dollars ($) principal amount of *[describe bond, debenture, or other debt security]* of the Debtor (For purposes of this Ballot, it is not necessary and you should not adjust the principal amount for any accrued or unmatured interest.)

[or, if the voter is the holder of an equity interest:]

The undersigned, the holder of Class [ ] equity interest in the Debtor, consisting of _____ shares or other interests of *[describe equity interest]* in the Debtor

BALLOT FOR ACCEPTING OR REJECTING THE PLAN

Official Form 14 continued
(12/03)

[In each case, the following language should be included:]

(Check one box only)

[ ] ACCEPTS THE PLAN   [ ] REJECTS THE PLAN

Dated: _____

Print or type name: _____

Signature: _____

Title (if corporation or partnership) _____

Address: _____

                _____

RETURN THIS BALLOT TO:

[Name and address of proponent's attorney or other appropriate address]

APPENDIX 33:
ORDER CONFIRMING THE PLAN
(FORM B15)

Form B15
(Rev. 12/01)

Form 15. ORDER CONFIRMING PLAN

[Caption as in Form 16A]

ORDER CONFIRMING PLAN

The plan under chapter 11 of the Bankruptcy Code filed by _____, on _____ *[if applicable,* as modified by a modification filed on _____,] or a summary thereof, having been transmitted to creditors and equity security holders; and

It having been determined after hearing on notice that the requirements for confirmation set forth in 11 U.S.C. § 1129(a) *[or, if appropriate,* 11 U.S.C. § 1129(b)] have been satisfied;

IT IS ORDERED that:

The plan filed by _____, on _____, *[If appropriate, include dates and any other pertinent details of modifications to the plan]* is confirmed. *[If the plan provides for an injunction against conduct not otherwise enjoined under the Code, include the information required by Rule 3020.]*

A copy of the confirmed plan is attached.

Dated: _____

BY THE COURT

_____
United States Bankruptcy Judge.

APPENDIX 34:
NOTICE OF CHAPTER 12 BANKRUPTCY CASE, MEETING OF CREDITORS AND DEADLINES (FORM B9G)

FORM B9G (Chapter 12 Individual or Joint Debtor Family Farmer (10/05))

UNITED STATES BANKRUPTCY COURT_____District of_____

Notice of
Chapter 12 Bankruptcy Case, Meeting of Creditors, & Deadlines

[The debtor(s) listed below filed a chapter 12 bankruptcy case on _____(date).]
or [A bankruptcy case concerning the debtor(s) listed below was originally filed under chapter_____on
_____ (date) and was converted to a case under chapter 12 on_____.]

You may be a creditor of the debtor. **This notice lists important deadlines.** You may want to consult an attorney to protect your rights. All documents filed in the case may be inspected at the bankruptcy clerk's office at the address listed below.
NOTE: The staff of the bankruptcy clerk's office cannot give legal advice.

See Reverse Side for Important Explanations

Debtor(s) (name(s) and address):	Case Number:
	Last four digits of Social Security No./Complete EIN or other Taxpayer ID No.:
Telephone number:	
All other names used by the Debtor(s) in the last 8 years (include married, maiden, and trade names):	Bankruptcy Trustee (name and address):
Attorney for Debtor(s) (name and address):	
Telephone number:	Telephone number:

Meeting of Creditors

Date: / / Time: ( ) A. M. ( ) P. M.	Location:

Deadlines:
Papers must be *received* by the bankruptcy clerk's office by the following deadlines:

Deadline to File a Proof of Claim:

For all creditors(except a governmental unit):   For a governmental unit:

Foreign Creditors
A creditor to whom this notice is sent at a foreign address should read the information under "Claims" on the reverse side.

Deadline to File a Complaint to Determine Dischargeability of Certain Debts:

Deadline to Object to Exemptions:
Thirty (30) days after the *conclusion* of the meeting of creditors.

Filing of Plan, Hearing on Confirmation of Plan
[The debtor has filed a plan. The plan or a summary of the plan is enclosed. The hearing on confirmation will be held:
Date:_____Time:_____Location:_____]
or [The debtor has filed a plan. The plan or a summary of the plan and notice of confirmation hearing will be sent separately.]
or [The debtor has not filed a plan as of this date. You will be sent separate notice of the hearing on confirmation of the plan.]

Creditors May Not Take Certain Actions:
In most instances, the filing of the bankruptcy case automatically stays certain collection and other actions against the debtor, the debtor's property, and certain codebtors. Under certain circumstances, the stay may be limited to 30 days or not exist at all, although the debtor can request the court to extend or impose a stay. If you attempt to collect a debt or take other action in violation of the Bankruptcy Code, you may be penalized. Consult a lawyer to determine your rights in this case.

Address of the Bankruptcy Clerk's Office:	**For the Court:**
	Clerk of the Bankruptcy Court:
Telephone number:	
Hours Open:	Date:

	EXPLANATIONS　　　　　　　　　　　　　　　Form B9G (10/05)
Filing of Chapter 12 Bankruptcy Case	A bankruptcy case under Chapter 12 of the Bankruptcy Code (title 11, United States Code) has been filed in this court by the debtor(s) listed on the front side, and an order for relief has been entered. Chapter 12 allows family farmers to adjust their debts pursuant to a plan. A plan is not effective unless confirmed by the court. You may object to confirmation of the plan and appear at the confirmation hearing. A copy or summary of the plan [is included with this notice] *or* [will be sent to you later], and [the confirmation hearing will be held on the date indicated on the front of this notice] *or* [you will be sent notice of the confirmation hearing]. The debtor will remain in possession of the debtor's property and may continue to operate the debtor's business unless the court orders otherwise.
Legal Advice	The staff of the bankruptcy clerk's office cannot give legal advice. Consult a lawyer to determine your rights in this case.
Creditors Generally May Not Take Certain Actions	Prohibited collection actions against the debtor and certain codebtors are listed in Bankruptcy Code § 362 and § 1201. Common examples of prohibited actions include contacting the debtor by telephone, mail, or otherwise to demand repayment; taking actions to collect money or obtain property from the debtor; repossessing the debtor's property; starting or continuing lawsuits or foreclosures; and garnishing or deducting from the debtor's wages. Under certain circumstances, the stay may be limited in duration or not exist at all, although the debtor may have the right to request the court to extend or impose a stay.
Meeting of Creditors	A meeting of creditors is scheduled for the date, time, and location listed on the front side. *The debtor (both spouses in a joint case) must be present at the meeting to be questioned under oath by the trustee and by creditors.* Creditors are welcome to attend, but are not required to do so. The meeting may be continued and concluded at a later date without further notice.
Claims	A Proof of Claim is a signed statement describing a creditor's claim. If a Proof of Claim form is not included with this notice, you can obtain one at any bankruptcy clerk's office. A secured creditor retains rights in its collateral regardless of whether that creditor files a Proof of Claim. If you do not file a Proof of Claim by the "Deadline to File a Proof of Claim" listed on the front side, you might not be paid any money on your claim from other assets in the bankruptcy case. To be paid you must file a Proof of Claim even if your claim is listed in the schedules filed by the debtor. Filing a Proof of Claim submits the creditor to the jurisdiction of the bankruptcy court, with consequences a lawyer can explain. For example, a secured creditor who files a Proof of Claim may surrender important nonmonetary rights, including the right to a jury trial. **Filing Deadline for a Foreign Creditor:** The deadlines for filing claims set forth on the front of this notice apply to all creditors. If this notice has been mailed to a creditor at a foreign address, the creditor may file a motion requesting the court to extend the deadline.
Discharge of Debts	The debtor is seeking a discharge of most debts, which may include your debt. A discharge means that you may never try to collect the debt from the debtor. If you believe that a debt owed to you is not dischargeable under Bankruptcy Code § 523 (a) (2), (4), or (6), you must start a lawsuit by filing a complaint in the bankruptcy clerk's office by the "Deadline to File a Complaint to Determine Dischargeability of Certain Debts" listed on the front side. The bankruptcy clerk's office must receive the complaint and any required filing fee by that Deadline.
Exempt Property	The debtor is permitted by law to keep certain property as exempt. Exempt property will not be sold and distributed to creditors, even if the debtor's case is converted to chapter 7. The debtor must file a list of all property claimed as exempt. You may inspect that list at the bankruptcy clerk's office. If you believe that an exemption claimed by the debtor is not authorized by law, you may file an objection to that exemption. The bankruptcy clerk's office must receive the objection by the "Deadline to Object to Exemptions" listed on the front side.
Bankruptcy Clerk's Office	Any paper that you file in this bankruptcy case should be filed at the bankruptcy clerk's office at the address listed on the front side. You may inspect all papers filed, including the list of the debtor's property and debts and the list of the property claimed as exempt, at the bankruptcy clerk's office.
Foreign Creditors	Consult a lawyer familiar with United States bankruptcy law if you have any questions regarding your rights in this case.

Refer To Other Side For Important Deadlines and Notices

APPENDIX 35:
ORDER CONFIRMING CHAPTER 12 PLAN
(FORM B230A)

B 230A
(8/96)

United States Bankruptcy Court

_____ District Of _____

In re

Case No. _____

Chapter _____

Debtor

ORDER CONFIRMING CHAPTER 12 PLAN

The debtor's plan was filed on _____ (date), and was modified on
_____ (date). The plan or a summary of the plan was transmitted to creditors pursuant to Bankruptcy Rule 3015. The court finds that the plan meets the requirements of 11 U.S.C. § 1225.

IT IS ORDERED THAT:

The debtor's chapter 12 plan is confirmed, with the following provisions:

1. Payments:

   Amount of each payment: $_____

   Due date of each payment: ☐ the _____day of each month, or
   ☐ _____

   Period of payments: ☐ _____ months,
   ☐ until a _____% dividend is paid to creditors holding allowed unsecured claims, or
   ☐ _____

   Payable to:

   _____Standing Trustee

   _____

   _____

   _____

2. Attorney's Fees:

   The debtor's attorney is awarded a fee in the amount of $_____, of which $_____ is due and payable from the estate.

3. [Other provisions as needed]

_____   _____
Date   Bankruptcy Judge

APPENDIX 36:
ORDER GRANTING A DISCHARGE OF DEBTOR AFTER COMPLETION OF CHAPTER 12 PLAN (FORM B18F)

Form B 18F
(10/05)

United States Bankruptcy Court

_____ District Of _____

In Re   Case No. _____

Debtor*

Address: Chapter 12

Last four digits of Social Security No(s).:
Employers's Tax I.D. No(s). [if any]:

DISCHARGE OF DEBTOR AFTER COMPLETION
OF CHAPTER 12 PLAN

It appearing that the debtor is entitled to a discharge,

IT IS ORDERED:

The debtor is granted a discharge under section 1228(a) of title 11, United States Code, (the Bankruptcy Code

BY THE COURT

Dated: _____   _____
                                 United States Bankruptcy Judge

SEE THE BACK OF THIS ORDER FOR IMPORTANT INFORMATION.

*Set forth all names, including trade names, used by the debtor within the last 8 years. (Federal Rule of Bankruptcy Procedure 1005).

Form B 18F continued
(10/05)

EXPLANATION OF BANKRUPTCY DISCHARGE
IN A CHAPTER 12 CASE

This court order grants a discharge to the person named as the debtor after the debtor has fulfilled all requirements under the chapter 12 plan. It is not a dismissal of the case.

Collection of Discharged Debts Prohibited

The discharge prohibits any attempt to collect from the debtor a debt that has been discharged. For example, a creditor is not permitted to contact a debtor by mail, phone, or otherwise, to file or continue a lawsuit, to attach wages or other property, or to take any other action to collect a discharged debt from the debtor. *[In a case involving community property:* There are also special rules that protect certain community property owned by the debtor's spouse, even if that spouse did not file a bankruptcy case.] A creditor who violates this order can be required to pay damages and attorney's fees to the debtor.

However, a creditor may have the right to enforce a valid lien, such as a mortgage or security interest, against the debtor's property after the bankruptcy, if that lien was not avoided or eliminated in the bankruptcy case. Also, a debtor may voluntarily pay any debt that has been discharged.

Debts That are Discharged

The chapter 12 discharge order eliminates a debtor's legal obligation to pay a debt that is discharged. Most, but not all, types of debts are discharged if the debt is provided for by the chapter 12 plan or is disallowed by the court pursuant to section 502 of the Bankruptcy Code.

Debts that are Not Discharged.

Some of the common types of debts which are not discharged in a chapter 12 bankruptcy case are:

a. Debts for most taxes; and, in a case filed on or after October 17, 2005, debts incurred to pay nondischargeable taxes;

b. Debts that are domestic support obligations;

c. Debts for most student loans;

d. Debts provided for under sections 1222(b)(5)or (b)(9) of the Bankruptcy Code and on which the last payment or other transfer is due after the date on which the final payment under the plan was due;

e. Debts for most fines, penalties, forfeitures, or criminal restitution obligations;

f. Debts for personal injuries or death caused by the debtor's operation of a motor vehicle, vessel, or aircraft while intoxicated;

g. Some debts which were not properly listed by the debtor;

h. Debts that the bankruptcy court specifically has decided or will decide in this bankruptcy case are not discharged; and

i. Debts owed to certain pension, profit sharing, stock bonus, other retirement plans, or to the Thrift Savings Plan for federal employees for certain types of loans from these plans (in a case filed on or after October 17, 2005).

This information is only a general summary of the bankruptcy discharge. There are exceptions to these general rules. Because the law is complicated, you may want to consult an attorney to determine the exact effect of the discharge in this case.

GLOSSARY

Abandonment—refers to the trustee, subject to court approval, releasing the estate's interest in certain property.

Accord and Satisfaction—Accord and satisfaction refers to the payment of money, or other thing of value, which is usually less than the amount owed or demanded, in exchange for extinguishment of the debt.

Accrue—To occur or come into existence.

Administrative Claim—A claim which takes priority in payment over any pre-petition claims in a pending bankruptcy case.

Adversary—Opponent or litigant in a legal controversy or litigation.

Adversary Proceeding—A lawsuit related to the debtor's bankruptcy case that is commenced by filing a complaint with the bankruptcy court.

Appearance—To come into court, personally or through an attorney, after being summoned.

Appellate Court—A court having jurisdiction to review the law as applied to a prior determination of the same case.

Appraisal—An opinion concerning the value of a piece of property.

Arrears—Payments which are due but not yet paid.

Asset—The entirety of a person's property, either real or personal.

Assignee—An assignee is a person to whom an assignment is made, also known as a grantee.

Assignment—An assignment is the transfer of an interest in a right or property from one party to another.

Automatic Stay—An injunction that automatically stops lawsuits, foreclosures, garnishments, and all collection activity against the debtor the moment a bankruptcy petition is filed.

Bad Faith—A willful failure to comply with one's statutory or contractual obligations.

Bad Title—A title which is not legally sufficient to transfer property to the purchaser.

Bankrupt—The state or condition of one who is unable to pay his debts as they are, or become, due.

Bankruptcy—A legal procedure for resolving debt problems of individuals and businesses pursuant to Title 11 of the United States Code.

Bankruptcy Code—The informal name for Title 11 of the United States Code.

Bankruptcy Court—Refers to a division of the Federal District Court and/or the bankruptcy judges in regular active service in each District.

Bankruptcy Estate—All of the legal and equitable interests in property held by the debtor at the time he or she files the bankruptcy petition.

Bankruptcy Judge—A judicial officer of the United States district court who is the court official with decision-making power over federal bankruptcy cases.

Bankruptcy Mill—A business not authorized to practice law that provides bankruptcy counseling and prepares bankruptcy petitions.

Bankruptcy Petition—A formal request for the protection of the federal bankruptcy laws.

Bankruptcy Trustee—A private individual or corporation appointed in all Chapter 7, Chapter 12, and Chapter 13 cases to represent the interests of the bankruptcy estate and the debtor's creditors.

Bench—The court and the judges composing the court collectively.

Bona Fide Purchaser—One who pays valuable consideration for a purchase.

Breach of Duty—In a general sense, any violation or omission of a legal or moral duty.

Burden of Proof—The duty of a party to substantiate an allegation or issue to convince the trier of fact as to the truth of their claim.

Business Bankruptcy—A bankruptcy in which the debtor is a business or an individual involved in business and the debts are for business purposes.

Chapter 7—The chapter of the Bankruptcy Code providing for the liquidation—i.e., the sale—of a debtor's nonexempt property and the distribution of the proceeds to creditors.

Chapter 9—The chapter of the Bankruptcy Code providing for reorganization of municipalities, including cities, towns, villages, counties, taxing districts, municipal utilities, and school districts.

Chapter 11—The chapter of the Bankruptcy Code providing for reorganization whereby the debtor usually proposes a plan of reorganization to keep its business alive and pay creditors over time.

Chapter 12—The chapter of the Bankruptcy Code providing for adjustment of debts of a "family farmer," or a "family fisherman" as those terms are defined in the Bankruptcy Code.

Chapter 13—The chapter of the Bankruptcy Code providing for adjustment of debts of an individual with regular income.

Chattel—Any tangible, movable piece of personal property as opposed to real property.

Claim—A creditor's assertion of a right to payment from a debtor or the debtor's property.

Collateral—Property which is pledged as additional security for a debt, such as a loan.

Complaint—The first document in a lawsuit that notifies the court and the defendant of a claim against the defendant by the plaintiff which contains a request for relief.

Commingle—To combine funds or property into a common fund.

Commingling of Funds—The act of mixing a client's funds with that of a fiduciary, trustee or lawyer's own funds.

Community Property—A form of ownership in a minority of states where a husband and wife are deemed to own property in common, including earnings, each owning an undivided one-half interest in the property.

Compromise and Settlement—An arrangement arrived at, either in court or out of court, for settling a dispute upon what appears to the parties to be equitable terms.

Confession of Judgment—An admission of a debt by the debtor which may be entered as a judgment without the necessity of a formal legal proceeding.

Confirmation—Approval of a plan of reorganization by a bankruptcy judge.

Consent Judgment—An agreement reached by the parties and entered on the record with judicial approval with the same effect as a judgment.

Consumer Debtor—A debtor whose debts are primarily consumer debts.

Consumer Debts—Debts incurred for personal, as opposed to business, needs.

Contested Matter—Matters that are disputed but are not within the definition of an adversary proceeding under the bankruptcy rules.

Contingent Claim—A claim that may be owed by the debtor under certain circumstances, such as a co-signer.

Conversion—The process by which the court, the debtor, or a creditor in a bankruptcy case pending under one chapter transfers the case to another chapter.

Court—The branch of government responsible for the resolution of disputes arising under the laws of the government.

Credit—Credit is that which is extended to the buyer or borrower on the seller or lender's belief that that which is given will be repaid.

Credit Counseling—Generally refers to two events in individual bankruptcy cases: (1) the "individual or group briefing" from a nonprofit budget and credit counseling agency that individual debtors must attend prior to filing under any chapter of the Bankruptcy Code; and (2) the "instructional course in personal financial management" in chapters 7 and 13 that an individual debtor must complete before a discharge is entered.

Creditor—One to whom the debtor owes money or who claims to be owed money by the debtor.

Creditors' Meeting—The meeting of creditors required by section 341 of the Bankruptcy Code at which the debtor is questioned under oath by creditors, a trustee, examiner, or the U.S. trustee about the debtor's financial affairs.

Debtor—A person who has filed a petition for relief under the bankruptcy laws.

Deed—A legal instrument conveying title to real property.

Default—Default is a failure to discharge a duty or do that which ought to be done.

Defendant—One against whom a lawsuit is filed.

Discharge—A court order which eliminates certain debts owed by the debtor for which the creditor may no longer seek payment.

Dischargeable Debt—A debt for which the Bankruptcy Code allows the debtor's personal liability to be eliminated.

Disclosure Statement—A written document prepared by the Chapter 11 debtor or other plan proponent that is designed to provide "adequate information" to creditors to enable them to evaluate the chapter 11 plan or reorganization.

Dismissal—The termination of a pending bankruptcy case.

Docket—A list of cases on the court's calendar.

Earned Income—Income which is gained through one's labor and services, as opposed to investment income.

Equity—The value of a debtor's interest in property that remains after liens and other creditors' interests are considered.

Escrow—The arrangement for holding instruments or money which is not to be released until certain specified conditions are met.

Estate—The entirety of the debtor's property, real or personal.

Executory Contract—An executory contract is one which has not yet been fully completed or performed at the time the debtor files a bankruptcy petition.

Executory Lease – Leases under which both parties to the lease have duties remaining to be performed.

Exempt—A description of any property that a debtor may prevent creditors from recovering.

Exempt Property—Certain property owned by an individual debtor that the Bankruptcy Code or applicable state law permits the debtor to keep from unsecured creditors.

Face Sheet Filing—A bankruptcy case filed either without schedules or with incomplete schedules listing few creditors and debts.

Fact Finder—In a judicial or administrative proceeding, the person, or group of persons, that has the responsibility of determining the acts relevant to decide a controversy.

Fact Finding—A process by which parties present their evidence and make their arguments to a neutral person, who issues a nonbinding report based on the findings, which usually contains a recommendation for settlement.

Family Farmer or Fisherman—An individual, individual and spouse, corporation, or partnership engaged in a farming or fishing operation that meets certain debt limits and other statutory criteria for filing a petition under chapter 12.

Fiduciary—A fiduciary is a person having a legal duty, created by an undertaking, to act primarily for the benefit of another in matters connected with the undertaking.

Filing Fee—The amount charged by the bankruptcy court for filing a bankruptcy petition.

Finance Charge—Any charge for an extension of credit, such as interest.

Finding—Decisions made by the court on issues of fact or law.

Fixed Income—Income which is unchangeable.

Fixture—Chattel which has become permanently and physically attached to real property, and which would not be easily removed.

Fraud—A false representation of a matter of fact, whether by words or by conduct, by false or misleading allegations, or by concealment of that which should have been disclosed, which deceives and is intended to deceive another, and thereby causes injury to that person.

Fraudulent Transfer—A transfer of a debtor's property made with the intent to defraud or for which the debtor receives less than the transferred property's value.

Fresh Start—The characterization of a debtor's status after bankruptcy, i.e., free of most debts.

Garnish—To attach the wages or property of an individual.

Garnishee—A person who receives notice to hold the assets of another, which are in his or her possession, until such time as a court orders the disposition of the property.

Hearing—A proceeding to determine an issue of fact based on the evidence presented.

Homestead—The house, outbuilding, and land owned and used as a dwelling by the head of the family.

In Formal Pauperis—Latin for "in the manner of a pauper." It refers to the right of a party to proceed with a lawsuit without costs or certain formalities.

Insider—Any relative of the debtor.

Insolvent—The status of having debts which exceed one's assets.

Installment Contract—An installment contract is one in which the obligation, such as the payment of money, is divided into a series of successive performances over a period of time.

Interest—An amount of money paid by a borrower to a lender for the use of the lender's money.

Involuntary Petition—A petition filed by an individual's creditors attempting to force him or her into bankruptcy.

Joint Administration—A court-approved mechanism under which two or more cases can be administered together.

Joint Petition—One bankruptcy petition filed by a husband and wife together.

Joint Tenancy—The ownership of property by two or more persons who each have an undivided interest in the whole property, with the right of survivorship, whereby upon the death of one joint tenant, the remaining joint tenants assume ownership.

Judgment—A judgment is a final determination by a court that an obligation, e.g., a sum of money, is owed by one party to another party.

Judgment Creditor—A creditor who has obtained a judgment against a debtor, which judgment may be enforced to obtain payment of the amount due.

Judgment Debtor—An individual who owes a sum of money, and against whom a judgment has been awarded for that debt.

Judgment Proof—Refers to the status of an individual who does not have the financial resources or assets necessary to satisfy a judgment.

Jurisdiction—The power to hear and determine a case.

Levy—To seize property in order to satisfy a judgment.

Lien—A claim upon specific property designed to secure payment of a debt or performance of an obligation.

Liquidated Claim—A creditor's claim for a fixed amount of money.

Liquidation—A sale of a debtor's property with the proceeds to be used for the benefit of creditors.

Loan Principal—The loan principal is the amount of the debt not including interest or any other additions.

Marital Property—Property purchased by persons while married to each other.

Maturity Date—The date upon which a creditor is designated to receive payment of a debt, such as payment of the principal value of a bond to a bondholder by the issuing company or governmental entity.

Means Test—Test applied to determine whether an individual debtor's chapter 7 filing is presumed to be an abuse of the Bankruptcy Code requiring dismissal, or conversion of the case to a chapter 13 case.

Monthly Income—The average monthly income received by the debtor over the six calendar months before commencement of the bankruptcy case.

Mortgage—A written instrument, duly executed and delivered, that creates a lien upon real estate as security for the payment of a specific debt.

Motion—An application to the court requesting an order or ruling in favor of the applicant.

Motion to Lift the Automatic Stay—A request by a creditor to allow the creditor to take action against the debtor or the debtor's property that would otherwise be prohibited by the automatic stay.

Natural Person—A human being as opposed to an artificial "person" such as a corporation.

Negotiable Instrument—A signed writing which contains an unconditional promise to pay a sum of money, either on demand or at a specified time, payable to the order of the bearer.

Net Worth—The difference between one's assets and liabilities.

No-Asset Case—A chapter 7 case where there are no assets available to satisfy any portion of the creditors unsecured claims.

Nondischargeable Debt—A debt that cannot be eliminated in bankruptcy.

Note—A writing which promises payment of a debt.

Objection to Discharge—A trustee's or creditor's objection to the debtor being released from personal liability for certain dischargeable debts.

Objection to Exemption—A trustee's or creditor's objection to the debtor's attempt to claim certain property as exempt from liquidation by the trustee to creditors.

Obligee—An obligee is one who is entitled to receive a sum of money or performance from the obligor.

Obligor—An obligor is one who promises to perform or pay a sum of money under a contract.

Paramount Title—Refers to title which is superior over any other claim of title.

Parties—The disputants.

Partition—A division of real property among co-owners.

Party in Interest—A party who has standing to be heard by the court in a matter to be decided in the bankruptcy case.

Pecuniary—A term relating to monetary matters.

Personal Property—All property that is not real property.

Petition—The document filed with the bankruptcy court which begins the bankruptcy case.

Petitioner—One who files a petition with the bankruptcy court.

Petition Preparer—A business not authorized to practice law that prepares bankruptcy petitions.

Plan—A debtor's detailed description of how the debtor proposes to pay creditors' claims over a fixed period of time.

Plaintiff—One that files a formal complaint with the court.

Post-Petition Transfer—A transfer of the debtor's property made after the commencement of the case.

Pre-Bankruptcy Planning—The arrangement of a debtor's property to allow the debtor to take maximum advantage of exemptions.

Preferential Debt Payment—A debt payment made to a creditor in the 90-day period before a debtor files bankruptcy that gives the creditor more than the creditor would receive in the debtor's chapter 7 case.

Pre-Petition—Occurrences which take place before a petition is filed in bankruptcy court.

Priority—The Bankruptcy Code's statutory ranking of unsecured claims that determines the order in which unsecured claims will be paid if there is not enough money to pay all unsecured claims in full.

Priority Claim—An unsecured claim that is entitled to be paid ahead of other unsecured claims that are not entitled to priority status.

Proof of Claim—A written statement and verifying documentation filed by a creditor that describes the reason the debtor owes the creditor

Property of the Estate—All legal or equitable interests of the debtor in property as of the commencement of the case.

Reaffirmation Agreement—An agreement by a chapter 7 debtor to continue paying a dischargeable debt after the bankruptcy, usually for the purpose of keeping the collateral that would otherwise be subject to repossession.

Real Property—Land, and generally whatever is erected or growing upon or affixed to the land.

Referee—An individual who is appointed by the court for a specific issue and empowered to determine issues of fact for the purpose of reporting to the court concerning the particular issue so that the court can render a judgment.

Referee's Deed—A deed given by a referee or other public officer pursuant to a court order for the sale of property.

Relief—The remedies afforded a complainant by the court.

Remedy—Refers to the means by which a right is enforced or a violation of a right is compensated.

Rescission—The cancellation of a contract which returns the parties to the positions they were in before the contract was made.

Satisfaction—The discharge and release of an obligation.

Schedules—List submitted by the debtor along with the petition showing the debtor's assets, liabilities, and other financial information.

Secured Creditor—An individual or business holding a claim against the debtor that is secured by a lien on property of the estate or that is subject to a right of setoff.

Secured Debt—Debt backed by a mortgage, pledge of collateral, or other lien.

Seised—The status of lawfully owning and possessing real property.

Separate Property—Property owned by a married person in his or her own right during marriage.

Settlement—An agreement by the parties to a dispute on a resolution of the claims, usually requiring some mutual action, such as payment of money in consideration of a release of claims.

Statement of Financial Affairs—A series of questions the debtor must answer in writing concerning such items as sources of income, transfers of property, and lawsuits by creditors.

Statement of Intention—A declaration made by a chapter 7 debtor concerning plans for dealing with consumer debts that are secured by property of the estate.

Statute of Limitations—Any law which fixes the time within which parties must take judicial action to enforce rights or thereafter be barred from enforcing them.

Stipulation—An admission or agreement made by parties to a lawsuit concerning the pending matter.

Substantial Abuse—The characterization of a bankruptcy case filed by an individual whose debts are primarily consumer debts where the court finds that the granting of relief would be an abuse of chapter 7 because, for example, the debtor can pay its debts.

Substantive Consolidation—Putting the assets and liabilities of two or more related debtors into a single pool to pay creditors.

Tangible Property—Property which is capable of being possessed, whether real or personal.

Tax—A sum of money assessed upon one's income, property and purchases, for the purpose of supporting the government.

Transfer—Any mode or means by which a debtor disposes of or parts with his or her property.

Trial—The judicial procedure whereby disputes are determined based on the presentation of issues of law and fact. Issues of fact are decided by the trier of fact, either the judge or jury, and issues of law are decided by the judge.

Trustee—The representative of the bankruptcy court who exercises statutory powers, principally for the benefit of the unsecured creditors, under the general supervision of the court and the direct supervision of the United States Trustee.

Undersecured Claim—A debt secured by property that is worth less than the full amount of the debt.

United States Trustee—The representative of the U.S. Department of Justice who oversees bankruptcy cases and appoints trustees to administer the property of the bankruptcy estate.

Unlawful Detainer Action—A lawsuit brought by a landlord against a tenant to evict the tenant from rental property.

Unliquidated Claim—A claim for which a specific value has not been determined.

Unscheduled Debt—A debt that should have been listed by the debtor in the schedules filed with the court but was not.

Unsecured Claim—A claim or debt for which a creditor holds no special assurance of payment.

Voluntary Transfer—The transfer of a debtor's property with the debtor's consent.

Voidable—Capable of being rendered void and unenforceable.

BIBLIOGRAPHY AND ADDITIONAL READING

The American Bankruptcy Institute (Date Visited: March 2006) <http:www.abiworld.org>.

Black's Law Dictionary, Fifth Edition. St. Paul, MN: West Publishing Company, 1979.

The United States Court System (Date Visited: March 2006) <http://www.uscourts.gov>.

The United States Department of Justice (Date Visited: March 2006) <http://www.usdoj.gov>.